W9-BLF-148

WITHDRAWN

No-20

BEYOND CONTAINMENT

Other Potomac Associates Books

HOPES AND FEARS OF THE AMERICAN PEOPLE

THE LIMITS TO GROWTH*

A NEW ISOLATIONISM: THREAT OR PROMISE?

U.S. HEALTH CARE: WHAT'S WRONG AND WHAT'S RIGHT

STATE OF THE NATION

A REORDERED WORLD: EMERGING
INTERNATIONAL ECONOMIC PROBLEMS

POTOMAC ASSOCIATES is a nonpartisan research and analysis organization which seeks to encourage lively inquiry into critical issues of public policy. Its purpose is to heighten public understanding and improve public discourse on significant contemporary problems, national and international.

POTOMAC ASSOCIATES provides a forum for distinctive points of view through publication of timely studies and occasional papers by outstanding authorities in the United States and abroad. Although publication implies belief by Potomac Associates in the basic importance and validity of each study, views expressed are those of the author.

POTOMAC ASSOCIATES is a non-tax-exempt firm located at 1707 L Street, NW, Washington, D.C. 20036.

POTOMAC ASSOCIATES books are distributed by Basic Books, 10 East 53 Street, New York, New York 10022.

*THE LIMITS TO GROWTH is published by Universe Books, 381 Park Avenue South, New York, New York 10016.

BEYOND CONTAINMENT
U.S. FOREIGN POLICY IN TRANSITION

EDITED BY ROBERT W. TUCKER
AND WILLIAM WATTS

POTOMAC ASSOCIATES
WASHINGTON, D.C.

50725

Published in the United States of America in 1973 by Potomac Associates, 1707 L Street NW, Washington, D.C. 20036

Copyright © 1973 by Potomac Associates with acknowledgments

First Printing: November 1973

All rights reserved. No part of this publication may be reproduced, stored in a retrieval system, or transmitted in any form or by any means, electronic, mechanical, photocopying, recording, or otherwise, without prior permission. For information, contact: Potomac Associates, 1707 L Street NW, Washington, D.C. 20036

Library of Congress Catalog Card Number: 73-82987
Cloth edition: ISBN 0-913998-00-1
Paperback edition: ISBN 0-913998-01-X

Typographical design by Ronald Clyne

Foreign Policy is published by National Affairs, Inc., in association with the Carnegie Endowment for International Peace, which bears no responsibility for the editorial content. Editorial Office: 345 East 46 Street, New York, New York 10017. Business Office: P.O. Box 379, Old Chelsea Station, New York, New York 10011.

This book is distributed by Basic Books, 10 East 53 Street, New York, New York 10022

Printed in the United States of America

CONTENTS

FOREIGN POLICY APPARATUS _____

FOREWORD

Potomac Associates was formed just over three years ago as a nonpartisan organization dedicated to encouraging independent and lively inquiry into critical issues of public policy. Our goal has been to heighten public understanding and improve public discourse on significant contemporary problems. With each of our publications we have tried to contribute to the positive interaction between citizens and policy-makers that is at the heart of a representative democratic system.

The present volume, *Beyond Containment: U.S. Foreign Policy in Transition,* and its companion, *A Reordered World: Emerging International Economic Problems,* are the products of Potomac Associates' cooperation with another relative newcomer to the forums of policy analysis, *Foreign Policy.* In bringing together some of the best articles from their first three years of publication with an original commentary and interpretation, we are guided by our belief that constructive change in our policies—both foreign and domestic—can only come from wider understanding and debate of the issues.

We hope that these books will serve that end.

William Watts
President
Potomac Associates

FOREIGN POLICY

We founded *Foreign Policy* in late 1970. It seemed to us then that the time was right for such a venture. As we wrote in the first issue,

the two editors of this magazine are old friends who have, during the past six years, disagreed sharply over Vietnam. Now, however, that there is broad agreement that the United States must withdraw militarily from Vietnam—although the how and the when may remain in dispute—we have decided to join together in an effort to stimulate rational discussion of the new directions required in American foreign policy. . . . The basic purposes of American foreign policy demand re-examination and redefinition. . . . A new magazine, having no institutional memory, can commence this task with a keener awareness that an era in American foreign policy which began in the late 1940s has ended.

Today, three years later, we think we can truthfully say that *Foreign Policy* has made a start on this task. Our pages have been open to contributors expressing the most divergent viewpoints, and their exchanges have demonstrated that rational foreign policy debate is again possible after the schisms over Vietnam. Our Editorial Board, whose advice and contributions have been invaluable to the magazine, reflects our broad political spectrum: Thomas L. Hughes (Chairman), W. Michael Blumenthal, Zbigniew Brzezinski, Richard N. Cooper, Richard A. Falk, David Halberstam, Morton H. Halperin, Stanley Hoffmann, Joseph S. Nye, Jr., John E. Rielly, James C. Thomson, Jr., and Richard H. Ullman. We have focused on the new issues confronting American foreign policy in the 1970s, such as international finance and trade, energy and resources, the shifts in the balance of power, the defects in our policy-making processes. And we have tried to deal with these issues in a fresh, constructive, and at times iconoclastic manner, reflecting our initial editorial commitment that *Foreign Policy* should be *"serious but not scholarly, lively but not glib, and critical without being negative."*

Foreign Policy owes much of its character and style to the late John Franklin Campbell, who did such a brilliant job as Managing Editor for the first five issues, and whose work has been carried on so successfully by the current Managing Editor, Richard Holbrooke, and the Associate Managing Editor, Pamela Gilfond. Beginning with Issue No. 7 the Carnegie Endowment for International Peace has shared in our operating costs, while bearing no responsibility for editorial content, and we are grateful for their help.

We are pleased that many of the articles on foreign policy we have published in the past three years have now been collected in this volume. Many of them received wide attention when they appeared, but all of them deserve this second reading. A companion volume of articles on international economic policy is being published simultaneously, and other volumes in this series will be issued from time to time.

Samuel P. Huntington
Warren Demian Manshel

BEYOND CONTAINMENT

INTRODUCTION

by Robert W. Tucker and William Watts

Are we witnessing the demise of the policy of containment? A growing number of observers apparently assume that we are. The age of containment, the now familiar argument runs, was the age of the cold war; with the passing of the cold war—and, of course, of the circumstances that conditioned it—containment has become obsolete. The Nixon Doctrine and policies have been interpreted as striking departures from the foundation of post-World War II policy. Indeed, many have found something akin to a formal death certificate of containment in *U.S. Foreign Policy for the 1970s (III)*, the 1972 presidential State of the World report to Congress. "Our alliances," the report declares, "are no longer addressed primarily to the containment of the Soviet Union and China behind an American shield. They are, instead, addressed to the creation with those powers of a stable world peace."*

There remain dissenters, however, to the view that containment, if not already dead, leads no more than a very truncated existence. Nor are they to be found only among more radical critics. Thus, among the contributors to this volume, Pierre Hassner finds containment as still the key, in 1971, to American policy toward the Soviet Union ("Pragmatic Conservatism in the White House," pp. 89-105). In his view the Nixon Doctrine has abandoned the missionary spirit of the Dulles and Kennedy eras; it has done so by returning to a still earlier and presumably more modest concept of containment, "the concept of holding the line until evolution makes allies more self-reliant and negotiations from strength more likely to influence the Soviet Union toward moderation."** Hassner's view must be seen in light of the developments in which it was formed: before the historic rapprochement with China, before the Peking and Moscow summits of 1972, the Washington summit of 1973, and the emergence of

*Richard M. Nixon, *U.S. Foreign Policy for the 1970s (III): The Emerging Structure of Peace* (Washington, D.C.: Government Printing Office, 1972), p. 6.

**It is indicative of the diversity of views held toward containment that Hassner can find in the "modesty" of the Nixon Doctrine "a return to the original Truman Doctrine." Others find in the Nixon Doctrine precisely the rejection of the original Truman Doctrine.

the triangular relationship, and before the conflicts of interest with allies—in part the result of the new approach to
adversaries—began to surface and command attention.
Nonetheless, another contributor, writing in the midst of
these developments, shares Hassner's assessment of the
continued relevance of containment. To Chalmers Roberts,
"the Nixon-Kissinger policy . . . is essentially a new form
of the old containment policy, a new method of attaining the
same end . . . " ("How Containment Worked," pp. 20-28).
Describing what he considers the fundamentals of containment policy, Roberts argues that phases and evolution apart
"containment remains to this day the principal basis of
American foreign policy."

If containment has died, then, its death appears only slightly
less controversial than its birth. Containment made its
appearance in the immediate postwar years as a term in the
celebrated "X" article by George F. Kennan. Under the title
"The Sources of Soviet Conduct" the "X" article appeared at a
time (July 1947) when Kennan had become head of the State
Department's newly formed Policy Planning Staff.* He
concluded that in the growing postwar confrontation with the
Soviet Union the "main element" of American policy should
be "a long-term, patient but firm and vigilant containment of
Russian expansive tendencies."**

In his *Memoirs: 1925-1950*, which appeared twenty years
later, Kennan has written of his dismay at the time over the
elevation of containment to the status of a doctrine, of his
consternation over the linking of his analysis and
prescriptions with the Truman Doctrine (March 1947), and of
his regret over those deficiencies of the "X" article that
obscured his true views and misled readers as sophisticated
as Walter Lippmann.† The Truman Doctrine was cast in
grandiose and sweeping terms. Its declaration that "it must
be the policy of the United States to support free peoples

---

*"The Sources of Soviet Conduct" was originally published in the July 1947
issue of *Foreign Affairs*. It has recently been republished, together with
Walter Lippmann's well-known response to Kennan, which first appeared in
the *New York Herald Tribune*, in Walter Lippman, *The Cold War: A Study in
U.S. Foreign Policy*, introduction by Ronald Steel (New York: Harper Torch-
books, 1972). The quotations of the Lippmann and Kennan essays are taken
from the Torchbook edition.
**Ibid., p. 66.
†George F. Kennan, *Memoirs: 1925-1950* (Boston: Atlantic Monthly Press,
Little, Brown and Company, 1967), pp. 313ff.

who are resisting subjugation by armed minorities or by outside pressures" held out the prospect of an overextended America committed by an indiscriminate anticommunism to intervene anywhere and everywhere to maintain the status quo. It also foreshadowed the later propensity to find in Soviet power a military threat, to be contained by military means. Kennan, however, insists that he had seen in Soviet power a political threat, to be contained primarily by political means. Moreover, in contrast to the indiscriminate character of the Truman Doctrine, he had intended to distinguish between areas vital to our security—above all, Western Europe—and areas that did not fall into this category. It was particularly on the latter point that Walter Lippmann in his essay *The Cold War* had concentrated his critique of the policy set forth in the "X" article—and in the Truman Doctrine. This resulted, in Kennan's view, in a "misunderstanding almost tragic in its dimensions."

Whatever Kennan's intent in writing the "X" article, however, the substance of the article was not markedly different from the substance of President Truman's historic statement. The "X" article was a model of stylistic grace and addressed to a select audience, whereas the Truman speech was cast in simple—and often strident—terms and addressed to the public at large. Even so, a careful reading of the two did not then, and does not now, reveal significant differences in policy implications for the means of containment or the areas to which containment was to apply. Nor does a comparison of the two suggest significant differences in analysis of the sources of Soviet conduct. Both viewed the growing conflict with the Soviet Union as rooted largely in intractable ideological differences. For this reason alone neither seriously entertained the prospect of reaching a settlement of the principal issues raised by the war and of achieving a more normal relationship with the Soviet Union—certainly not with the Soviet Union of Stalin. Although both sought to emphasize that the new policy was designed to avoid another great war, the avoidance of war was explicitly based on the premise of resolute opposition to Soviet expansion, whatever form that expansion might take, rather than on the possibility of negotiating differences arising from the war.

If, then, there is little reason to distinguish sharply between the containment of the "X" article and that of the Truman Doctrine, is there a better case for distinguishing between

the Truman Doctrine and the early policy of containment—
from 1946-47 to the early 1950s? Many nonrevisionist critics
believe that there is. In their view the course of American
foreign policy from the late 1940s to the late 1960s is nothing
so much as the triumph of the Truman Doctrine over a policy
that, in its origins, was modest and limited in its geographical scope and in its objectives. What began as a policy that
was Eurocentric, directed primarily against the expansion of
Soviet power, and designed to restore a balance of power,
ended as a policy unlimited in geographic scope, directed
against communism itself (or, more generally still, against
any radical revolution), and designed to preserve a global
status quo bearing little, if any, relation to the balance of
power.

It is quite true that in the early years of containment a nar-
rower and more traditional concept of interest, particularly
security interest, received the greater emphasis. In retrospect
a case can be made—and not only revisionists have made
it—that given the changed structure of American security and
the preponderant power we enjoyed at the end of the war, this
preoccupation with security was exaggerated. At the time,
however, it did not seem unreasonable. Even those who
discounted the prospect of a Soviet attack against Western
Europe did not and could not discount the prospect of communist governments' coming to power in one or more of the
major Western European states. Given the subservience of
communist parties to Moscow, it was taken for granted that
the accession to power of a local communist party would be
indistinguishable in its effects from the direct extension of
the Kremlin's power. Of equal importance was the widely
shared belief that the economic recovery, political stability,
and consequently the peace and security of Western Europe
depended upon a continent that was not divided. Opposed
though he was to the Truman Doctrine, Walter Lippmann did
not dissent from this view. The continued division of the
continent, he warned, held out the grave danger that "all
Western Europe might fall within the Russian sphere of influence and be dominated by the Soviet Union."* If anything,
Lippmann went further than most, in his insistence that
without the withdrawal of the Red Army from the center of
Europe there was no "possibility of a tolerable peace."**

*Lippmann, p. 29.
**Ibid., p. 27.

In this, we now know, Lippmann and others who shared his view of the consequences of a divided Europe have been proved wrong. Europe has remained divided and a tolerable peace has been achieved. Indeed, it may even be that this division, which more than anything else occasioned the cold war, has also been the only feasible way of dealing with the otherwise intractable situation resulting from the destruction of the pre-World War II balance of power and the creation of a vacuum in what had once been the center of the international system. However this may be, the point remains that a conventional security interest—security interpreted as depending on a balance of power centered in Europe—was a principal motive of American policy in the period in which the cold war was joined.

It was not the only interest though. For American policy was also expansionist.* Revisionist historians have exaggerated the deliberate quality of this expansionist interest and have overdrawn the consistency with which it was presumably translated into policy. In part, America's postwar expansion must be explained as the unforeseen and unintended results of the search for security. Once the cold war was fully joined, this expansion followed the seemingly inescapable dynamic of hegemonial conflict. Even so, these considerations cannot adequately account for the speed with which America's postwar expansion occurred, the means by which it was carried out, and the rather remarkable complacency with which we viewed it.

The tendency to expand must also be traced to our inordinate power and to our determination to use this power to ensure our particular version of a congenial international order. During World War II abundant evidence of this determination antedated serious conflict with the Soviet Union. To be sure, once that conflict arose security conventionally defined could no longer be readily separated from the larger purpose of employing our power to sustain a world favorable to American institutions and interests. Such separation would have proved difficult in any event, given the generous manner in which that larger purpose was defined—for it was practically indistinguishable from a world stabilized under American leadership.

*Here and throughout we do not, of course, imply territorial expansion, but the expansion of American influence.

Thus, the contrast commonly drawn between early containment policy and the Truman Doctrine, like the contrast commonly drawn between American policy in the late 1940s and the 1960s, must be treated with considerable caution. What is often seen as a change in outlook is instead a change in circumstances. The circumstances of the late 1940s limited the application of containment principally to Europe and made that application, whatever its larger interest, roughly identical with a balance-of-power policy. The later triumph of an expansionist and imperial policy over a policy initially characterized by limited and modest goals reflected a change in circumstances rather than, or as much as, a change in essential outlook. Without doubt, this later policy also reflected the relative success of the early policy of containment and the growth of interests concommitant with that very success. But if the appetite grew with the eating, it was still there at the start.

Containment thus initially expressed not only a conventional security interest but also an interest that went well beyond this. The Truman Doctrine only formed the most striking statement of the underlying ambiguity. By interpreting security as a function not only of a balance of power between states but of the internal order maintained by states, and not only by some states but by all states, the Truman Doctrine equated security with the maintenance of a world order that, under American leadership, would ensure the triumph of liberal-capitalist values. The equation cannot be dismissed as mere rhetoric, designed at the time to mobilize public opinion in support of limited policy actions—though taken seriously by succeeding administrations. Instead, it accurately expressed the magnitude of America's role and interests in the world as conceived at the inception of the cold war and of containment. American policy in the fifties and, even more, in the sixties is less a perversion of than a logical progression from this conception of role and interests.

2

Unless this continuity in postwar outlook and policy is acknowledged, the deeper lessons of Vietnam may well be lost. That containment, in Chalmers Roberts' words, finally "did get out of hand" is clear enough from our experience in Vietnam. The question nevertheless persists: why did it get out of hand? Why did it result in a Vietnam? Is the excess to which containment was carried in the 1960s to be attributed primarily to intellectual error, as the prevailing orthodoxy would have it? Did it stem from our inability, as Roberts believes, "to soon enough understand the reality of post-Stalin developments within the Communist orbit"? Are the "plain lessons of a bad decade" to be found, as John Kenneth Galbraith writes, in a mistaken obsession with the Third World, an overestimation of what American power could—and need—accomplish there, and in the inertial dynamics of a bureaucracy that has operated—above all in Vietnam—in response to its own needs rather than to national need ("The Plain Lessons of a Bad Decade," pp. 53-66)? Or is the story of United States policy toward Vietnam to be explained, as Leslie H. Gelb insists, not in inadvertence and a failure to foresee the consequences of our involvement but in misconceptions about the nature of civil conflict, in unexamined assumptions about what is vital to American security, and in the domestic constraints of anticommunism ("Vietnam: The System Worked," pp. 29-52)?

Each of these views has merit. Yet each leaves something to be desired. The excess to which containment finally led was, in some sense, the result of intellectual error, if only because American leaders very probably would have refrained from intervening in Vietnam (at any rate, on such a massive scale) had they known all the consequences of their actions. If intellectual error—a failure of political intelligence—is understood to mean no more than an inability to calculate the consequences of action, however roughly, then Vietnam must qualify as just that. Leslie Gelb apparently rejects even this meaning of intellectual error by his insistence that American involvement in Vietnam "did not stem from a failure to foresee consequences." Yet his rejection is not consistently carried through, since he acknowledges that American leaders hoped and believed that a strategy of escalation would eventually cause the communists to relent. Many of Gelb's objections to the quagmire thesis—which was initially propounded by Arthur Schlesinger, Jr., among others—are well taken. There is a point, however, at which the quagmire thesis is difficult, if not impossible, to refute.

The importance of the theme of intellectual error is instead to be found in the view that in the mid-1960s American leaders badly misread world developments in general and Vietnam in particular. But did they? Surely they did not misunderstand that the once-vaunted Sino-Soviet bloc had fallen apart, since their own testimony provides abundant evidence to the contrary. They did not misunderstand, as liberal critics have so often insisted, that the world, both communist and noncommunist, was becoming increasingly pluralistic. There is even reason to doubt that they were so dreadfully ignorant about elementary Vietnam realities, for if the Pentagon Papers do show a substantial ignorance about some of these realities, they also show an unwillingness to bow to others that were recognized.

If the circumstances of the mid-1960s had changed markedly from the preceding years, the record does not suggest that American leaders were unaware of changes that had occurred. Although the mood at the turn of the decade had been markedly pessimistic, it had clearly altered by 1965. The events of the early 1960s, and above all the Cuban missile crisis, had dissipated earlier fears that the tide was turning against the United States. Whereas in the late 1950s the conditions of competition between America and the communist nations were widely seen as increasingly to favor a communism still regarded as monolithic, by the mid-1960s these conditions were seen as having been dramatically reversed. In the period following the Cuban missile crisis, not only did the United States emerge in a position of marked economic and military preponderance, it did so at a time when the last semblance of any pretense to unity between the major communist powers was dropped and intense rivalry was openly acknowledged. Even the prospects in the underdeveloped world appeared to have suddenly changed. A few years before, the Soviets and Chinese were considered to enjoy most of the advantages in the competition for influence in the Third World; now the judgment was reversed and conditions marking the "crucial transitional process" were considered to favor an outcome congenial to American interests.

It was in these circumstances that the classic cold war abated and the détente with the Soviet Union began. Yet it was also in these circumstances that an expansionist and interventionary American policy in the Third World not only persisted but, if anything, intensified. This did not occur under the despairing expectation of a world balance of power that was turning against us, but under the exuberant expectation of "America preponderant." The fateful escalation of American involvement in Vietnam certainly was not undertaken on a note of joy. But neither was it undertaken with the apprehension and sense of foreboding that, in retrospect, is only too easy to read into it.

Given the general circumstances attending the 1965 escalation—circumstances it is only reasonable to assume policymakers appreciated— the question remains: why did we do it? May we explain Vietnam as a legacy of the cold war (particularly as the Asian legacy), of the momentum generated by the cold war, and of the habits of thought and action the cold war encouraged? No doubt, we may do so; but rather than resolving the issue this explanation only manages to restate it. What *was* the legacy of the cold war?

One legacy clearly was, as Galbraith has argued, the creation of a very large civilian and military bureaucracy for conducting foreign affairs. And this bureaucracy, as Morton H. Halperin has written, developed a life and purpose of its own with which succeeding presidents were forced to contend ("Why Bureaucrats Play Games," pp. 191-204). But does this warrant Galbraith's conclusion "that the inertial dynamics of the bureaucracy is the major explanation of the disasters of the decade"? A positive response must hold that bureaucratic power and authority have been supreme in foreign affairs and that presidents have been in large measure the prisoners of a bureaucratic machine that responds to its own needs rather than to national need. Yet as Stephen D. Krasner points out ("Are Bureaucracies Important?" pp. 205-12), the president selects the men who head the large bureaucracies and these individuals must, and commonly do, share his values. It is not apparent that there was a distinct bureaucratic view of the world, a view that in turn explains the disasters of the 1960s. Instead, as one observer has noted, the outlook of the bureaucracy was very much "the standard anticommunist posture that had long been a staple commodity of American politics, shared and disseminated by all the principal agencies of opinion in the country."* Nor is it apparent that the war in Vietnam dragged on after 1968—despite the ostensible invalidation of the reasons once given for intervening—because of "pure organizational momentum" and the inability of a bureaucracy, on its own, to undertake a drastic change of

*Francis Rourke, *Bureaucracy and Foreign Policy* (Baltimore: School of Advanced International Studies, Johns Hopkins University Press, 1972), p. 6.

course. Whatever else may be said of the Nixon administration's conduct of foreign policy, it can scarcely be charged with permitting high policy to be subject to bureaucratic control. The "disestablishment of the bureaucracy" that Galbraith called for in 1970 has generally been regarded as a distinctive achievement of the Nixon administration. The style and method of this achievement are described by John P. Leacacos ("Kissinger's Apparat," pp. 176-90) and I. M. Destler ("Can One Man Do?" pp. 165-75).

It is perhaps worth noting at this point that critics have increasingly found organizational shortcomings in the Nixon-Kissinger mode of operation.

The concentration of power in the White House has been criticized for the resultant slighting of key areas—international economics is one, Latin America is another. A limited staff, no matter how hard it works, no matter how imaginative its product and performance, simply cannot cope with all the major problems. And those areas neglected now may well prove to be even more troublesome later.

Again, what happens to continuity in such an imbalanced relationship? When the current White House principals depart from the scene, who picks up the pieces? What about all the background information, the implicit understandings, the unstated assumptions that will move to California or Cambridge? Far more than in the past, special knowledge is held by a few. For smoothness in future performance, critics contend, this knowledge needs to be diffused through the permanent foreign policy machinery.

The passion for secrecy is faulted as having been carried too far. It results in unnecessary insult to friends, as in the case of Japan, which in 1971 was left uninformed about U.S. economic restrictions and the new moves toward China. It has frequently kept in the dark the foreign policy bureaucracy, especially in the Department of State (at least until Kissinger added that Cabinet post to his portfolio), which stands increasingly demoralized and, after years of neglect and even humiliation, finds it ever harder to know what to do when called upon by the White House. Moreover, the administration is questioned about its concern for secrecy on the still broader grounds that it has contributed to the entrenchment of secrecy overall. As the conduct of foreign affairs has become more elitist, more concentrated in the hands of the few, it has led, some argue, to the further divorce of government from the people. What was promised as a more open administration has become even more closed than its predecessors. (Ironically, it is many of those same voices in academe and elsewhere who earlier wanted this kind of concentration—particularly in foreign matters, where, it was assumed, special training and background were required—who now worry over its consequences.)

Yet, despite the particular White House independence in the Nixonian way of doing things, the war continued and the determination to avoid defeat in Vietnam apparently remained unimpaired. If presidents have not been prisoners of the bureaucracy, have they been prisoners of public opinion and of the constraints imposed by domestic politics? Can fear of the domestic repercussions of "losing" another country to communism account for the determination of presidents to persist in Vietnam despite the difficulties attending the enterprise? In part, no doubt, it can and does. Certainly this fear was a very important consideration for President Kennedy. But then Kennedy was not only vulnerable to a charge he had liberally employed with respect to Cuba against the opposition in the 1960 election, he also did not have to make the kind of choices on Vietnam his successor had to make. Vietnam had Rubicons and Rubicons, and those crossed by Kennedy were by no means of the same magnitude as those crossed by President Johnson. Yet it is precisely in the case of President Johnson that the attempt to explain Vietnam largely as the result of domestic constraints seems least persuasive. The impressive mandate Johnson had received in the 1964 election had not been given on condition that South Vietnam would be preserved at almost any cost. It is obvious enough that the "loss" of South Vietnam through a refusal to escalate would have left Johnson vulnerable to the charge of appeasing communism. It is equally clear, however, that the decision to escalate, given the difficulties of escalation that were recognized at the time, carried its own domestic liabilities, and formidable ones at that. And no one has shown that Johnson believed these liabilities were out-weighed by the political hazards of allowing Saigon to go down.

It is easy to appear wise after the event. We know the domestic price that President Johnson finally had to pay for Vietnam, whereas we do not know the price he would have paid for refusing to escalate in 1965. But the argument that in foreign affairs presidents have been prisoners of the domestic political process has all too often been self-serving. It has been used to justify or excuse actions that would have been taken in any event. Moreover, the public's attitude toward presidential conduct of foreign policy since World War II has surely been more permissive than restrictive, and it seems doubtful that this permissiveness was obscured to so keen a political observer as Lyndon Johnson. While Johnson was clearly aware that he had to make a choice between refusing to escalate the American involvement in Vietnam and permitting communist expansion in Southeast Asia, the evidence does not show that the former alternative would have been politically suicidal or that Johnson believed it to be. A case for Vietnam that places domestic political compulsion on the same level as the presumed compulsions inherent in America's global role and interests remains undemonstrated.

It can, on the other hand, be amply demonstrated that the president and almost all of his principal advisors believed in the compulsions of this global role and in its applicability to Vietnam. The "vitalness" of Vietnam, as Leslie Gelb points out, was seldom, if ever, seriously questioned. To Gelb, as to many others, a major lesson to be drawn from Vietnam is that "the system worked" and worked so tragically well because it made little, if any, provision for determining what was and what was not vital to American security. Domestic compulsions apart, our commitment to Vietnam and our persistence in so dubious a venture resulted from unexamined and mistaken notions of security—above all, from an unquestioned faith in the domino theory, which rested in turn upon the equally unquestioned assumption that security, like peace, was indivisible.

We are back to the central theme of intellectual error: to error by default, perhaps, to error because of the rigid patterns of thought and action encouraged by years of cold war, but to error nonetheless. Moreover, the explanation of Vietnam as a failure of political intelligence seems even more persuasive the further we move from the events in question. In retrospect, it is the apparent excessiveness of concern with security that impresses many critics of the war. Yet an emphasis on security that now appears to many as having been almost inversely proportional to the actual security interests at stake need not be taken to mean that Vietnam resulted from mistaken notions of vital interest that went unexamined. It may be argued that the appeal to security in its more conventional and limited sense was misleading as applied to Vietnam and arose from the need of the Johnson administration to justify an imperial policy in terms of conventional security interests that no longer accurately defined this policy. But for the president and his principal advisers, the emphasis on Vietnam's "vitalness," though it may have been misleading, was certainly not the result of intellectual default. To say, as have Gelb and others, that the issue of interest went unexamined is to apply a standard of interest—namely, a conventional security interest—that was evidently not the standard applied by those who deemed the intervention necessary. To argue that the Johnson administration's emphasis on Vietnam's significance was mistaken is only to say that the war eventually threatened the larger interest it was intended to serve: the maintenance under American leadership of a stable world order that would ensure the triumph of liberal-capitalist values and institutions.

It was this larger interest—an imperial interest—that must ultimately explain Vietnam. In the purpose of maintaining a particular version of world order, in the equation of this order with American security, in the hubris of those who led the nation into war, and in the reluctance to withdraw from a conflict that could not be "won" without resort to odious measures, Vietnam affords a classic case of an imperial war. As such, it cannot be adequately explained as an ideological obsession pursued for its own sake or, more generally, as intellectual error (above all, in unexamined notions of national security). These and similar explanations of the policy and outlook that led to Vietnam—and that were bound to lead to a Vietnam—give to this policy and attendant outlook a quality of disinterestedness they did not possess and a quality of innocence they did not have. Such views imply that America's opposition to revolutionary movements is to be found in the apprehension, however misguided, that these movements threatened national security rather than in the apprehension that they would prove resistant to American influence and control. In so doing, they obscure the point that opposition to radical revolution is to be explained as much by the expectation that such revolution, if successful, would prove resistant to American control as by the fact that the revolution is radical. The policy that led to Vietnam was not the work of incompetent ideologues who were blind to political realities and oblivious to age-old considerations of interest. It was the work of men who, though they obviously made mistakes, wished to preserve America's global preponderance, and who not unreasonably saw in Vietnam a threat to the nation's preeminent position.

In the manner of all imperial visions, the vision of a preponderant America was solidly rooted in the will to exercise dominion over others. That this will was commonly cloaked in such disarming terms as "liberal internationalism" does not alter the reality. As Godfrey Hodgson points out in his analysis of the outlook of the men who comprised the core of the foreign policy establishment since World War II, "the Bay of Pigs was the sort of thing they meant by internationalism, and so was Vietnam" ("The Establishment," pp. 130-61). The policy of intervention that culminated in Vietnam was the expected response of an imperial power with a vital interest in maintaining an order that, apart from its material benefits, had become synonymous with the nation's vision of its role in history. It was the expected response of men who saw America, in Hodgson's words, "as the military and economic guarantor and moral leader of an enlightened, liberal, democratic, and capitalist world order."

3

"American foreign policy, after this trauma, will never again be the same," Irving Kristol observed in the spring of 1968.* That the war in Vietnam was a climactic event in the history of American foreign policy has since become a truism. That the war led to a breakdown in the foreign policy consensus of a generation is generally accepted. At the same time, it is apparent that the expectations of yesterday (the hopes of some and the fears of others) have not—or not yet—materialized: despite countless prophecies to the contrary, the essential structure of the nation's interests and commitments has been preserved. After an absence of five years, an observer returning from the moon would surely find change in America's world role. It remains an open question whether he would not be more impressed by the elements of continuity.

*Irving Kristol, "We Can't Resign as 'Policeman of the World,'" *The New York Times Magazine* (May 12, 1968), p. 25.

Nor is this all. Equally impressive is the domestic support—or acquiescence—foreign policy still enjoys. This support is admittedly a far cry from that given during the period of the cold war. Even so, it is a distinct improvement upon the low estate to which foreign policy had sunk as a result of Vietnam. When Richard Nixon came to office in 1969, it was commonly assumed that the war, by depriving foreign policy of essential domestic support, would place in serious jeopardy the prospect of maintaining America's global role and interests. Even more, given the controversy, frustration, and disillusion attending Vietnam, and given a growing emphasis on the importance of concentrating more of the nation's energies on domestic problems, it did not seem unreasonable to assume that foreign policy itself would increasingly become a political liability for future administrations.*

The reality has proved very different from these expectations. If Vietnam led to a breakdown in the post-World War II foreign policy consensus, the breakdown has scarcely been apparent in the intensity of opposition to the Nixon administration's foreign policy. By 1972, even Vietnam, the great issue that ostensibly resulted in the destruction of the old consensus, no longer provoked the kind of disaffection it once had. In retrospect, the response to the decision to send American and South Vietnamese forces into Cambodia in the spring of 1970 appears as the climax of opposition to the war. Two years later the intense aerial and naval measures taken against North Vietnam not only failed to elicit anything near a comparable reaction, they may well have been an asset in Mr. Nixon's reelection.

What is true of Vietnam is even truer of other and far less controversial features of the Nixon foreign policy. Whereas in the first two years of Mr. Nixon's first term public support of American foreign policy had reached a markedly low ebb, by 1972 and 1973 this earlier disaffection had clearly receded as a result of the president's rapprochement with China, the Peking and Moscow summits, and the apparent achievement—at least in the public's view—of a "peace with honor" in Vietnam. The remarkable fact is that in a period of four

---

*For a fuller discussion on shifts in public attitude see William Watts and Lloyd A. Free, editors, *State of the Nation* (Washington, D.C.: Potomac Associates, 1973), particularly pp. 34-9 and 203-4.

years President Nixon has gone a long way toward rehabili-
tating the nation's foreign policy in the eyes of the public. In
doing so, he consolidated his own position with the electorate. It is scarcely an exaggeration to say that if the
conduct of foreign policy retired one president in 1968, it was
a critical factor in reelecting his successor in 1972. Mr.
Nixon's achievement was even more remarkable in that his
successes in foreign policy were in no small measure facilitated by the expansion and refinement of the very methods
that helped drive his predecessor from office. For President
Nixon not only managed to add to the already impressive
powers in foreign policy passed on to him by previous presidents, he did so by carrying secrecy—and, when circumstances required, deceptiveness—to new heights, while in
some measure endowing it with a new kind of legitimacy.
And if this *tour de force* was placed in jeopardy, it was not so
placed because of a Congress or a public aroused over the
methods Mr. Nixon has employed in the conduct of foreign
policy. Whatever the future of the Nixon administration in the
aftermath of Watergate, that future would not be prejudiced
by its conduct in foreign affairs.

In part the Nixon success must be attributed to the skillful
manner with which the president gradually defused Vietnam,
the explosive issue that had helped carry him to office. During almost the entire period of his first term, Southeast Asia
remained the salient issue of foreign policy. Critics often accused Mr. Nixon of subverting the will of a majority that
clearly wanted an immediate end to the nation's involvement.
It would seem, however, that the president accurately dis-
cerned a public mood torn by contradictory desires. Although
wanting to end the nation's involvement in the war as quickly
as possible, the public was also reluctant to face up to the
possible, and even likely, consequences of immediate and
unilateral withdrawal. In this situation of public uncertainty
and indecision, Mr. Nixon did not so much subvert or defy
the public's will as take advantage of what he rightly perceived as ambivalence in that will. It is this ambivalence that
largely explains the public support of the measures taken in
the last six months of the war. By dramatically lowering the
costs of the war to the American people, while effectively exploiting public unwillingness to accept defeat (which was

equated with dishonor), the president was able to marshal majority support for measures that carried the war as never before to North Vietnam.

The last chapter of the Vietnam agony only underscored what had been apparent throughout the course of the conflict. In the absence of definitive results, public disaffection with the war was largely a function of costs. To the extent, therefore, that yesterday's expectations of far-reaching change in American foreign policy were based on the shift that eventually occurred in public attitudes toward war, the meaning of the shift was given a broader significance than it merited. In itself the shift was not necessarily indicative of a deeper change in outlook toward the nation's proper role and interests in the world. Instead, the evidence points to the conclusion that a majority of those who finally came to view the intervention as a mistake and to favor withdrawal did so on the grounds that we had not won the war and showed little prospect of doing so.

This is not to deny that Vietnam affected the public's attitude toward foreign policy as perhaps no other event since the early years of the cold war. But the deeper and more lasting effects of the war on the public remain uncertain. The only indisputable lesson that may be learned from Vietnam is that success in a relatively brief period is the great solvent of serious public disaffection over a foreign policy that entails dramatic costs in blood and treasure. But this lesson apart, and it is scarcely a novel one, the experience of Vietnam is less than revealing about the nature of the constraints policymakers will henceforth ignore at their peril. Certainly this experience affords little ground for the belief that, in the arena of foreign affairs, the public has broken its deeply ingrained habit of deferring to presidential judgment and initiative.

It was not only the public that responded to pragmatic considerations of cost and effectiveness in changing its attitude toward the war. So did the greater part of the disaffected among the foreign policy elites: some of them initially supported the intervention or, though entertaining doubts about its wisdom, fell short of clear opposition; others, though opposed to the war from the start, saw in it primarily a misapplication of American power because of the unfavorable circumstances in which that power was applied. Given these early positions toward the war, George Armstrong Kelly concludes that much of the liberal opposition to Vietnam after 1967, and particularly after 1968, "rings a little tinny" and that while "engaged in sincere repentance over Vietnam, our liberals are also engaged in a deeper hypocrisy than their doctrine permits them to fathom" ("A Strange Death for Liberal America," pp. 67-85). Whatever the merits of Kelly's judgment, it is clear that the character of much elite opposition to the war did not in and of itself suggest an essential break from the outlook and interests that had led to Vietnam. However sharp and even bitter the disagreement over the Nixon administration's handling of the war, that disagreement was not as such indicative of a broader disagreement over interests considered vital to the nation. Instead, it was indicative of a difference over how a disastrous war should be ended so as to prove least injurious to those greater interests.

It is true that liberal and moderate criticism of American foreign policy, though largely provoked by the war, went well beyond Vietnam. But the principal thrust of this larger criticism was directed less to the basic conceptions of role and interest that have defined post-World War II policy than to the nature of the world in which the nation's role and interests were to be preserved. Here again, however, the prevailing liberal critique did not so much signal a basic break from the foreign policy consensus as it did an insistence upon readjusting that consensus to changing circumstances abroad and at home. The Nixon administration responded to the larger debate occasioned by Vietnam by assimilating—indeed, by claiming as its own discovery—most of the major points that by 1968 had come to represent conventional criticism. And in doing so, however cautiously, it took much of the ground from under the larger debate.

Thus, it became the settled orthodoxy of the new administration that the conditions marking the period of the cold war had been profoundly altered and that American policy must adjust to a new world. A bipolar world had evolved into a multipolar world, at least politically and economically. The change required a new approach to both allies and adversaries. Toward the former a more balanced and equal relationship was called for that would evoke energies so far unused; toward the latter more creative connections, reflecting slow but growing accommodation, were deemed possible and desirable; toward the developing states a more relaxed position was promised. The liberal critique had insisted that an increasingly pluralistic world, though far more complicated than the world of the cold war, was nevertheless a safer world. For pluralism not only meant that communist expansion no longer carried the threat to American interests it once carried, but that the prospects of communist expansion in the developing nations had markedly declined. The Nixon administration cautiously endorsed this assessment and its emphasis on the "new capacities" of the developing nations to provide for their own security. Even in Asia the administration took a more relaxed view of the threat posed to American interests by acknowledging, if only indirectly, that Chinese power had been exaggerated, as had the ability and will to project this power, while the constraints on China's freedom of action had been largely ignored.

In these and other respects the Nixon administration responded to the common denominator of conventional criticism: the overextension of American power. It did so very cautiously, though, balancing bold assertion with careful qualification. Change was affirmed, but it should not be unsettling. Interests would henceforth determine commitments, but even where commitments no longer reflected interests, change must come slowly lest instability result and credibility be placed in question. Applied to Vietnam, these qualifications were themselves sufficient to justify continued American involvement in the war, whatever the wisdom of the initial intervention.

Despite its cautious and elaborately qualified character, as a statement of basic intent the Nixon Doctrine has been widely interpreted as a historic turning point in American foreign policy. Certainly, in its various formulations, it appeared to strike almost exactly the right note in responding to the prevailing criticism of American policy. It decried an outlook and style marked by unlimited aspirations and unmindful of what American power could reasonably accomplish. It called for a new modesty in thought and action by emphasizing the inherent limits to any nation's wisdom, understanding, and energy. It abandoned anticommunism as a guiding principle. Instead, its cool tone suggested that crusades of any kind were the very antithesis of the new style and outlook. Nor did it preclude change in the substance of American interests.

While refusing to concede to its critics on Vietnam, the administration did concede that a changed world not only required change in the methods of policy but in interests as well. Thus, in a pluralistic world the domino theory must at least be modified, but so also must the interest one has in each and every domino. Since pluralism implies that there is no "test case" for wars of national liberation, the interest in intervening in any particular war of national liberation is subject to change. Then, too, the manifest difficulties in maintaining durable influence in most of the Third World permit the downgrading of an interest that was once considered vital.

The question remains whether a change in tone and style, and a modest redefinition of interests contingent upon a cautiously optimistic view of the world, adds up to a historic turning point in American foreign policy. It would not appear so. Innovations in diplomatic method aside, and they have been considerable, the changes in role and interests foreshadowed by the Nixon Doctrine—and realized to date in policy—have been of modest proportion. The leitmotiv of this administration has been to change while conserving or to change in order to conserve. But in the substance of policy, conservation has clearly dominated over change. In the new world, America would still play a predominant role and Amercan power would still remain the indispensable element in fashioning a "stable and lasting structure of peace." Although this order would no longer be defined in ideological terms, the return to a more conventional idiom would not signal the abandonment of the nation's global interests and responsibilities. The detailed requirements of order would be relaxed somewhat, but not to the point of encouraging instability. America's position in the international hierarchy would be preserved. Change could be effected only in certain ways, while other types of changes would still be resisted.

It is this essential continuity of role and interests that explains the determination of the Nixon administration to vindicate the American commitment in Vietnam. Defeat in Vietnam, Mr. Nixon has insisted, would set off a deep and sustained public reaction against further involvement abroad, thus undermining the necessary support for maintaining America's global role. That role requires the public's continued confidence in American power and the ability and willingness of a president to use that power effectively when challenged. The same imperatives of prestige and credibility, the argument has run, hold true for adversaries and allies, especially in a period of retrenchment. That the circumstances in which the commitment to Vietnam was made have changed does not invalidate those imperatives. If the integrity of the larger structure of American interests is to be preserved, it is essential that there not be a modest retreat of American power, and not to appear to be one, as a response to defeat in Vietnam. Indeed, concern over the credibility and integrity of the American commitment has been particularly marked to an administration whose outlook has taken on the air of a settled imperial power shorn of much of its former exuberance over and confidence in what it can accomplish, yet determined to preserve the substance of its interests.*

Vietnam apart, the issue of change and continuity in American policy today may be found to turn on the question raised at the outset: are we witnessing the demise of the historic policy of containment? The rhetoric of the Nixon Doctrine notwithstanding, a positive response to this question must show that we are no longer primarily concerned with the expansion, however peripheral and indirect, of the Soviet Union (or China) and that in an age of pluralism we no longer oppose the emergence of communist regimes in the developing states.

What is the evidence that the Nixon policy reformulation has abandoned a former opposition to the prospect of communist regimes in the Third World? There is, of course, the de-emphasis of ideology and the fetish for explaining policy in the idiom of a traditional diplomacy. But the case for abandonment of an interest once deemed vital surely cannot rest on these features alone, unless it is assumed that the former policy of opposing the spread of communism in the developing states had only an ideological motivation (at any

*It is in the same light that Mr. Nixon's insistence upon "peace with honor" must be understood. While liberal critics of Vietnam have scoffed at and deplored the president's characterization of the settlement reached with Hanoi in early 1973, few have urged acceptance of the rather obvious alternative characterization. The suspicion arises that one reason most critics have not done so is because they, too, realize that in terms of domestic support for foreign policy the public must entertain the image—or illusion—of a peace with honor. Any other image would raise the serious prospect of public withdrawal of support for that larger policy of international involvement that continues to enjoy the support of a majority of those who have persistently attacked the president's course in Vietnam.

rate, after the early 1960s). If that assumption cannot bear critical examination, it evidently will not do to take the Nixon Doctrine at face value—indeed, to read into the new rhetoric more than what it plainly says. Clearly, the Third World has been demoted in the scale of concerns of the Nixon administration, so much so that this is one of the major indictments Pierre Hassner brings against the Nixon Doctrine, its indifference to social revolution and the conditions leading to social revolution, its vision of a tidy world in which the status quo is sanctified, and its conservative overvaluation, in a world ridden with social conflict, of diplomacy and strategy. Yet the significance of this demotion has never been put to a clear test. For this reason alone, what appears as a demotion in the scale of concerns may reflect less a redefinition of interests than a redefinition of the threat to interests that remain largely unchanged. In the absence of a meaningful test, a policy of restraint that appears almost to border on indifference toward the Third World may indicate little more than a guarded optimism over the unlikelihood of marked instability and a substantial reduction of American influence. While both the aspirations and fears of yesterday have receded, they have by no means disappeared.

In regard to the major communist powers, above all the Soviet Union, the view that containment has been abandoned rests upon a confusion of words with acts and, still more importantly, of diplomatic methods with strategic goals. To the extent that we have been told full details of the continuing Moscow-Washington exchanges, the new "era of negotiations" does not appear to have conceded any substantial interest to the Soviet Union that had not, in effect, been conceded by 1969. Nor has the Nixon administration weakened a credibility to employ force, if necessary, where vital interests are threatened. If anything, it created a rather different impression by its persistence in Vietnam and by the marked sensitivity with which it initially reacted to Soviet challenges to established American positions. That the result has not been to impair the effort to broaden détente with the Soviet Union and to initiate a new relationship with China may be attributed in part to novel and fortunate circumstances that, once perceived, were effectively exploited. Moreover, the improvement that has occurred in relations with the major communist powers must be attributed to the awareness that in meliorating these relations the proffered carrot may prove as important as the threatening stick. It is in the methods employed to develop the triangular relationship with the Soviet Union and China that the policy of containment has been changed.

The significance of these innovations in the methods of containment is not diminished by observing that they have been the product of necessity and that, in the perspective of time-honored conventions of diplomacy, they are scarcely new. For all this, they remain no less striking when juxtaposed with the methods of past administrations. Despite the changes in the means of containment in the period from Truman to Nixon, there remained an inner core of consistency in method that, as much as anything else, gave containment its distinctive cast. In essence a strategy of indirection, containment concentrated on alliance relationships and waited for a basic change in the external behavior of adversaries. Men might and did differ over whether the ultimate promise of containment would result primarily from internal change in the regimes of the principal communist powers (the position of George Kennan) or whether it would result simply from the eventual adjustment of these powers to an external environment they could no longer effectively exploit (the position of Dean Acheson). But this and other differences did not affect a more general agreement that change in the external behavior of adversaries would come, when it did come, as a result of what we did elsewhere. In his interview on the "X" article after twenty-five years (pp. 3-16), George Kennan expresses this essential agreement in declaring that "it has always been true that the secret of successful dealings with Russia itself—and the same now goes for China—is the proper handling of our relations with the remainder of the world that lies between us."

The Nixon reformulation of containment is novel to the degree that it is no longer content with a strategy of indirection which had as its principal corollary an emphasis on allied solidarity. While alliances remain important, there is no longer the same disposition to pay the price for them that previous administrations were once willing to pay. Allied relationships are henceforth to be balanced against the need to hold out positive inducements to adversaries in the hope that these inducements will progressively moderate their behavior and, eventually, promote a common interest in maintaining an order that has a broader and more durable base than the fear of mutual destruction.

It is apparent that the Nixon reformulation of containment reflects a more modest estimate of what American power can accomplish. It is equally apparent that it reflects domestic pressures for retrenchment and détente.* It is not apparent, however, that the Nixon policy reformulation was intended to foreshadow a substantially transformed and reduced position for the nation. On the contrary, the guiding assumption of this administration has been that the nation can maintain its predominant position in the world but at a lower and domestically tolerable price. On the theory that major allies have nowhere else to go—and, even more importantly perhaps, no will to go anywhere—they can be pressured to compromise on a range of economic and security issues. While our allies are deterred from challenging America's military hegemony over them, a hegemony the Nixon administration has shown no desire to relinquish in its quest for "more balanced and equal partnerships," the U.S. will presumably enjoy the freedom of maneuver and independence of action necessary to broaden a détente with its adversaries. Thus, while maintaining what amounts to a holding operation with respect to allies, a triangular relationship will be developed in which America holds the initiative, if only by virtue of its role as "balancer" between the great communist powers. And if the more grandiose aspirations of yesterday must be set aside, and equilibrium and stability acknowledged as the central goals of policy, there remains the satisfaction that America is still the principal guarantor of a global order now openly and without equivocation identified with the status quo.

*Many critics of the Nixon administration's alliance policy frequently neglect these pressures. Yet is it plausible to assume that America's major alliances could have been strengthened while the triangular game with Moscow and Peking was meaningfully pursued? Moreover, the alternative strategy of concentrating on alliance policy (in fact, the old strategy), though probably at the expense of détente, held out no assurance that the conflicts of interest that have arisen with major allies would have been resolved. Of course, these conflicts could be resolved if, apart from concessions on trade and monetary issues, America were generally to accept a position with respect to allies of an equal among equals. But there has been no more disposition among critics to accept such a status than there has been in the Nixon administration. Opposition to the military autonomy of Western Europe and Japan remains common ground to both parties.

In a period of supposed retrenchment, coming at the end of a deeply divisive war, the Nixon foreign policy is not only ambitious but audacious. Will it work? Even if allies should prove reasonably passive, adversaries reasonably restrained, and the Third World reasonably stable, can the administration's policy be expected to enjoy the domestic support it needs? Impressive arguments have been put forth that question whether, in Stanley Hoffmann's words, the balance will balance at home ("Will the Balance Balance at Home?" pp. 107-29). Whereas the Nixon strategy is one of continuing involvement (though, hopefully, at a lower cost), the public is more inward oriented than it has been since the years before World War II. To be successful the new policy requires an isolation from domestic currents. Will the public mood in the aftermath of Vietnam permit such isolation? And to the extent the public has already supported the Nixon administration's policies, has it understood their real meaning? Once that meaning becomes apparent, and the high costs of these policies become equally apparent, is it not reasonable to expect public support to decline? When it does, what will this or succeeding administrations have to fall back on? The bulwark of anticommunism no longer can be expected to provide the support for policy it once did. Vietnam broke this all-important element, this binding cement, of the postwar consensus. The Nixon administration has not sought to rehabilitate it. If anything, the administration has further dissipated this once central motivation, though without providing an effective substitute.

In the pages of Stanley Hoffmann's essay, these and still other doubts are forcefully elaborated. That they raise serious questions about the long-term domestic viability of the Nixon policy formulation is clear. It is not a criticism of Hoffmann's argument, however, to say that it depends on a number of factors that remain obscure. There is, of course, no question of the change in public outlook as a result of Vietnam. But there is a question of the deeper and more lasting significance of the change in public mood. To date, as already noted, the only indisputable lesson of Vietnam is of limited compass and, by itself, less than revealing about the constraints public opinion may place on policymakers in the future. Whether, for example, a strongly anti-interventionist mood persists will depend in part upon how Vietnam is seen in retrospect. It is quite possible that the nation's memory of Vietnam may yet turn out to be more favorable than its current assessment.

Nor is the public's increased inward orientation necessarily a liability for the Nixon policy reformulation. For the new policy does not need the kind of public support that foreign policy required during the period of the cold war. If anything, the "era of negotiation" might be endangered by this kind of public support. A policy that depends upon retaining maximum mobility and freedom of maneuver requires only a permissive public, not a zealous one. If it must choose between enthusiasm and apathy—though a permissive apathy—the latter would seem preferable.

This is not to suggest that the public does not understand the Nixon foreign policy, at least in the very proximate manner it understands any policy. After nearly five years, it scarcely seems plausible to assume that the budgetary implications of the new policy are still misapprehended by the public. Nor does it seem plausible to assume that the public misconstrues a strategy that places substantially greater emphasis on aerial and naval power to back up present commitments, while otherwise relying on indigenous forces supported by American military aid. No one can say with assurance how the public would react should this strategy be put to a test. But it might well receive public sanction or forbearance provided the use of American ground forces is avoided and, of course, provided the effectiveness of intervention can soon be made apparent. In the actual event, much would depend upon the persuasiveness with which a president could make a case for intervening. This would depend in part upon the continued willingness of the public to accept the president's assessment of what constitutes a vital security interest to be defended, if necessary, by force. And, as noted earlier, there is little evidence to suggest that, despite Vietnam, the deference and permissiveness that have long marked the public's attitude toward presidential judgment and initiative in foreign policy have substantially altered. A "stable structure of peace"—the requirements of which are equated with American security—may, therefore, continue to elicit sufficient public support for military intervention even though this structure is seen primarily in balance-of-power terms rather than in terms of anticommunism.

To be sure, the decline of anticommunism, so critical to the foreign policy consensus of the past generation, must be taken into account in any speculation on the future of American foreign policy. But the question persists whether the decline of anticommunism as the central rationale for acquiring the present American role and interests must leave policy without any viable alternative for maintaining the nation's global position. Interests acquired through one set of motivations may subsequently be maintained through quite different motivations. Indeed, nothing seems more common in the history of statecraft than unchanging interests supported by a changing rationale. In appealing to prestige and pride, to the uncertainties of a still dangerous world, and so on, the Nixon administration has certainly not been deficient in providing substitutes for anticommunism, though their effectiveness remains to be proved. These substitutes may no longer evoke the idealism and the enthusiasm of yesterday. But the visions—or illusions—of yesterday are in any event impossible to resurrect. Nor are they needed by a policy that is intent upon nothing so much as the maintenance of equilibrium and the status quo.

THE PAST

INTERVIEW WITH GEORGE F. KENNAN

In the "X" article you wrote: "Now the outstanding circumstance concerning the Soviet regime is that down to the present day this process of political consolidation has never been completed and the men in the Kremlin have continued to be predominantly absorbed with the struggle to secure and make absolute the power which they seized in November 1917. They have endeavored to secure it primarily against forces at home, within Soviet society itself. But they have also endeavored to secure it against the outside world." And you went on to state that the "characteristics of Soviet policy, like the postulates from which they flow, are basic to the internal nature of Soviet power, and will be with us, whether in the foreground or the background, until the internal nature of Soviet power is changed."

Do you view the principal themes of Soviet policy as essentially the same today as they were in 1947?

No. The conditions to which Soviet policymakers had to address themselves in 1947 have changed drastically over these twenty-five years.

In 1947 the Soviet Union, though seriously exhausted by the war, enjoyed great prestige. Stalin's hold on the international Communist movement was monolithic and almost unchallenged. There was still, in the major Western countries and to some extent elsewhere, a strong contingent of pro-Soviet intellectuals and fellow travelers who were amenable to Soviet influence and could be counted on to give general support to Soviet policies. All around the Soviet frontiers, on the other hand, there was great instability. This applied to East Asia as well as to Europe and the Middle East. For the Soviet leadership this presented both opportunity and danger: opportunity for taking advantage of this instability, danger that if they did not do so, others would. Their foreign policy, in these circumstances, was directed to two main objectives: one, the elimination, to the extent possible, of all other great-power influence—and this meant primarily American influence—everywhere on the Eurasian land mass, so that the Soviet Union would overshadow everything that

"An Interview with George F. Kennan" was published originally in *Foreign Policy*, Number 7, Summer 1972.

was left, in power and prestige; and, two, the achievement and consolidation of effective strategic glacis in east, south, and west.

Compare that with the situation the present generation of Soviet leaders has before it today. The international Communist movement has broken into several pieces. They retain, beyond the limits of their own military occupational power, the overt loyalty of only a portion of it. This is a not insignificant portion; but the facade of solidarity can be maintained today only by extensive concessions to the real independence of the respective Communist parties. Meanwhile, a great deal of the erstwhile liberal following in other countries, disillusioned by Soviet repressive measures at home and in Eastern Europe, has lost confidence in Soviet leadership. As a military power the USSR has great prestige—greater, in fact, than in 1947—but as a political power it has less than it did then.

The instability in the areas surrounding the Soviet Union has in part disappeared. The Chinese and Japanese have put an end to it in East Asia. Economic recovery, NATO, and the movements toward unification have largely done so in Western Europe, although there are disturbing symptoms of an underlying instability in Western Germany and a state of semichaos in Italy that is only slightly less alarming because it is chronic.

The East Asian glacis was largely taken away from them by the Chinese. The Middle Eastern one they are gradually gaining; but it is precarious, undependable, and expensive to keep. The European one, that is, the satellite area of Eastern and Central Europe, they continue to hold (Yugoslavia excepted) either by occupying it or by overshadowing it militarily. It is flawed by a certain potential instability in the form of the positions taken by the Rumanians; but it has won acceptance in the West and does not appear, at the moment, to be seriously threatened. It may be said, generally, that the southern and western glacis are fulfilling their function, as does the remaining one—Outer Mongolia—in East Asia; and the Soviet leaders undoubtedly derive from this fact a certain heightened sense of security.

The effort to expel American influence and presence from the Eurasian land mass has also been largely successful, though rather by the force of circumstance than as a response to any-thing the Russians themselves have done. Yet the result is only in part satisfactory from the Soviet point of view. In northeast Asia the Americans never did play a role, except in South Korea and Japan; and they have now largely forfeited their influence over the Japanese. On the other hand, Russia now finds herself confronted there by two local great powers—China and Japan—both capable of making more trouble for her in that region than the Americans ever did. In the Middle East the American presence and influence are pretty well eliminated everywhere except in Israel, Jordan, and Saudi Arabia. As for Western Europe: the American guaranty remains, as does the American military presence. Moscow would still like to eliminate both—just to be on the safe side. But the need for doing so has been reduced by the general Western acceptance of the Soviet hegemony in Eastern Europe. And agreements concluded with the Brandt government will relieve the Soviet leaders of their greatest single anxiety: that of an association of American military power with a *revanchiste* and revisionist Western Germany.

If, then, today the Soviet leaders have a sense of military in-security, it is not—for the first time in Russian history—pri-marily with relation to stronger forces just beyond their land borders but rather in relation to the nuclear weapons race, which is a subject in itself. Where they really feel most insecure is politically. The Chinese inroads on their inter-national prestige and on their influence in the world Commu-nist movement have really hurt and alarmed them, because they leave them no alternatives except isolation or alliance with capitalist countries, which could undermine the legiti-macy of their power at home. They are also insecure at home, because they are dimly conscious, as was the czar's regime seventy years ago, that they have lost the confidence of their own intellectuals and don't know how to recover it. Finally, there is the continuing hostility of the populations in most of Eastern Europe to the Soviet hegemony, a hostility that even with full control of the media for over twenty-five years they have not been able to overcome.

What, in the face of these environmental conditions, are their policies? These no longer represent a unified whole or reflect any unified concept. The party priesthood exerts itself mightily to recover ground lost to the Chinese in the foreign

Communist communities. The foreign office pursues a policy of détente with France and Germany and Italy in order to prove to the Chinese that Russia has an alternative to good relations with them and can easily arrange for security on her western front. The military-industrial complex, as real there as in Washington, struggles to match the United States in the cultivation of nuclear weaponry. The hotheads in their military establishment appear to be obsessed with the hope of breaking the long-standing supremacy of the Anglo-Americans on the high seas, and this strikes me, incidentally, as the most irresponsible and dangerous, at the moment, of all Soviet undertakings, comparable to the kaiser's effort to outbalance the British in naval forces before World War I.

These policies present a sharp contrast to those of 1947. The Soviet-American conflict has been largely removed geographically from the Eurasian land mass and relegated to the struggle for the control of the high seas and the fantasy world of nuclear weaponry. A great part of the energy of Soviet foreign policy is today devoted to the effort to "contain," politically, another socialist state—China. The anti-American propaganda and the competition with the United States for favor and influence in the Third World continue; but this is more of a force of habit than a policy, and the few successes achieved to date have come from American mistakes far more than from Soviet brilliance. "World revolution" has simply faded out of the picture as a concrete aim of Soviet foreign policy. In general, the situation of the Soviet Union is such that were it not for the dangerous nuclear and naval rivalry, the outside world, and particularly the United States, would have little more to fear from Russia today than it did in 1910. The ideological factor makes itself felt today almost exclusively in the Soviet relationship to the French and Italian Communist parties, which, if they were to come into power, would easily destroy NATO and upset the power balance in Europe. But these parties are reflections of long-term internal crises within the respective countries, and their influence cannot be treated as primarily a problem of international relations.

In what ways, if any, has "the internal nature of Soviet power" changed so as to affect Soviet policy?

Stalin was well aware that the legitimacy of his ascendancy in the party had never been wholly accepted by his comrades, that he had killed millions of people and virtually decimated the party in his effort to crush opposition, that he had thus provoked great potential contumacy, and that his rule rested overwhelmingly on fear. His successors are in a different position. Being largely men brought into the seats of power only toward the close of the Stalin era, they are not saddled with the same sense of guilt. Most surprisingly, furthermore—to us and to them—it turns out that the system itself is now strong enough to bear most of the weight: it does not have to depend on their charisma, as in Lenin's case, or their capacity to terrorize, as in Stalin's. Of course, they oppress the restless intellectuals. These people challenge the sense of orthodoxy that seems, to any Russian governmental mind, essential to the stability of the system. The Soviet leaders are simply acting, here, in established Russian tradition. But they are the first rulers of the Soviet Union who find themselves in the pleasing position of being able to be borne by the system—to ride along on it—instead of having to carry it; and for this reason they feel more secure than did Lenin, who died before the system was consolidated, or Stalin, who felt it necessary to dominate it by raping it. I think, therefore, that *inner* security plays less of a role in their psychology than it did in that of their predecessors, but there is strong sense of *external* insecurity, particularly with relation to the Chinese. No Leninist-Marxist can endure being outflanked to the left, and this is what the Chinese have repeatedly done to the Soviets.

Would you today continue to emphasize "the internal nature of Soviet power," rather than the international environment, as the most pertinent factor in the making of Soviet foreign policy?

No, for the reasons just given. But an exception must be made for the challenge presented by the Chinese. The position of Moscow as the "third Rome" of international Communism is little short of essential to the carefully cultivated Soviet image of self. Take it away, and the whole contrived history of Soviet Communism, its whole rationale and sense of legitimacy, is threatened. Moscow must oppose China with real desperation, because China threatens the intactness of its own sense of identity—of the fiction on which it has made itself dependent and without which it would not know how to live.

What are the implications for American policy of these changes in Soviet internal politics and external policies?

What all this means for Soviet-American relations is this: that the United States, having accepted the Soviet domination of Eastern Europe as well as the situation in all of Asia other than its southeastern extremity, has today, for the first time, no serious territorial-political conflict with the Soviet government, the one exception being the Middle East. But the Middle Eastern situation is, by common agreement, not worth a war between the two powers, and both hope to avoid its leading to one. This means that today the military rivalry, in naval power as in nuclear weaponry, is simply riding along on its own momentum, like an object in space. It has no foundation in real interests—no foundation, in fact, but in fear, and in an essentially irrational fear at that. It is carried not by any reason to believe that the other side *would*, but only by a hypnotic fascination with the fact that it *could.* It is simply an institutionalized force of habit. If someone could suddenly make the two sides realize that it has no purpose and if they were then to desist, the world would presumably go on, in all important respects, just as it is going on today.

There is a Kafkaesque quality to this encounter. We stand like two men who find themselves confronting each other with guns in their hands, neither with any real reason to believe that the other has murderous intentions toward him, but both hypnotized by the uncertainty and the unreasoning fear of the fact that the other is armed. The two armament efforts feed and justify each other.

Admitting that it is unreasonable to expect either side to disarm suddenly and unilaterally, one must still recognize that this curious deadlock, devoid of hope, replete with danger, is unlikely to be resolved just by carefully negotiated contractual agreements: these latter will have to be supported by reciprocal unilateral steps of restraint in the development of various forms of weaponry.

If one could begin to work this process backward, and eventually reduce the armed establishments of the two countries to something like reasonable dimensions—for both have, of course, ulterior military obligations and commitments as well—then there is no reason why the Soviet Union should be considered a serious threat to American security.

Should this happen, however, the United States would do well not to indulge itself in unreal hopes for intimacy with either the Soviet regime or the Soviet population. There are deeply rooted traits in Soviet psychology—some of old-Russian origin, some of more recent Soviet provenance—that would rule this out. Chief among these, in my opinion, are the congenital disregard of the truth, the addiction to propagandistic exaggeration, distortion, and falsehood, the habitual foulness of mouth in official utterance. So pernicious has been the effect of fifty years of cynicism about the role of objective truth in political statement that one begins to wonder whether these Soviet leaders have not destroyed in themselves the power to distinguish truth from falsehood. The very vocabulary in which they have taught themselves to speak, politically, with its constant references to the American "imperialists" and "monopolists," is confusing and offensive and constitutes in itself a barrier to better international understanding. Add to this the hysterical preoccupation with espionage, and the role that the continued fear of foreigners and the effort to isolate the Soviet population is allowed to play in the conduct of Soviet diplomacy, and one is obliged to recognize that it is simply unrealistic for Americans to look for any great intimacy or even normalcy, as we understand it, of relations with the Soviet Union. As is also the case with China, though for somewhat different reasons, relations can be reasonably good, but they must also be reasonably distant; and the more distant they are, in a sense, the better they will be.

In the "X" article you emphasized the vulnerability of the Soviet system, suggesting "that Soviet power, like the capitalist world of its conception, bears within it the seeds of its own decay." In fact you seem to have expected "either the breakup or the gradual mellowing of Soviet power." In retrospect, was this a realistic assessment or wishful thinking on your part? And, in 1972, would you tend to emphasize the Soviet system's strengths rather than its weaknesses?

I think there *has* been a very considerable mellowing of Soviet power. However little we may like the Soviet regime's internal policies, and admitting that there has recently been a considerable revival of the role of the secret police within the system, only someone who had never known the heyday of

Stalin's rule could fail to recognize the enormous difference between the conditions of his time and this one.

This mellowing, I think, has been a source of strength rather than weakness for the Soviet regime over the short term. But any form of despotism faces, ultimately, its own dilemmas. One cannot help but notice how similar is the situation of the Soviet regime of 1972 to that of the czar's government in, say, 1912. It has lost the confidence of the intellectuals. It is faced with a strong hard-line Stalinist opposition, chauvinistic and anti-Semitic, and comparable to the czarist reactionary-mon-archists, which operates from *within* the official establishment; and it is faced with a liberal-democratic opposition, comparable to the old Kadet and moderate-socialist parties, which operates essentially from outside the system. Czardom dragged along, in essentially this situation, for several decades and then fell only when weakened by a long war and a foolish imperial couple. But the effect of modern communications has been in many respects more revolutionary than the ideas of Marx and Lenin, and whether this same longev-ity-by-pure-bureaucratic-inertia will be granted to the Soviet regime no one can tell. The great average age of the present Soviet leadership is also a source of potential instability. If I had to guess, I would say that the dangers confronting these present leaders are considerably greater than they themselves realize.

In your Memoirs: 1925-1950 *you speak of containment as a political rather than military undertaking and express regret over the militarization of American foreign policy. Looking at the history of the past twenty-five years, though, wouldn't you agree that American military power has had a great deal to do with the containment of what you once called Soviet aggressive tendencies?*

This is an extremely difficult question. That we have taught the Soviet leadership something of our own obsession with military strength—have taught them, that is, to think in American-Pentagon terms—have caused them, too, to be hypnotized by the nuclear weapons race—I do not doubt. We also have to recognize that armaments are powerful not just in their actual use, or in support of overt threats, but also in the shadows they cast—particularly over fearful people. The Western Europeans, in particular, have a *manie d'invasion,* and I suppose it is true that if we had not eventually created some sort of compensatory ground forces, they would—in political terms—have tended ultimately "to commit suicide for fear of death." I concede, therefore, that there was need for the creation of something resembling NATO in Western Europe. But I don't think this was a reason for putting economic recovery and other constructive purposes into the background, nor was it a reason for pretending to ourselves, over two decades, that the Russians were longing to attack Western Europe and it was only we who were deterring them from this mad purpose. Finally, I do not think the nuclear weapon was at all essential as a factor in the creation of this necessary balance. The thesis that Western Europe could never be defended against Russia by conventional means is so out of accord with all historical, economic, cultural, and demographic realities that it did not deserve to be taken seriously. The nuclear weapon is, as Stalin correctly observed, something with which you frighten people with weak nerves. We have rendered a fearful and historic disservice—to ourselves and to the world at large—by pinning our own concept of our security, and indeed the security of the entire Western world, on this ghastly, sterile, and unusable weapon, which is incapable of serving any coherent political purpose.

The expansion of Soviet influence in world affairs could take three forms: (1) direct military aggression, (2) political expansion through the seizure of power by a Communist party controlled by Moscow, or (3) diplomatic expansion through the increased influence of the USSR in other societies by virtue of military and economic assistance, treaties, trade, cultural relations, and the like. Your notion of containment was originally concerned primarily with the possibility of the second type of Soviet expansion, although it was misinterpreted to be directed primarily against the first. In recent years, however, Soviet expansion has taken primarily the diplomatic form: increasing naval deployments in the Mediterranean and Indian oceans, military and economic assistance to India and Arab countries, treaties with India and Egypt, expanded trade relations with many Asian and Latin American countries. Should this expansion of Soviet influence be of major concern to the United States? What policies should the United States adopt in relation to this "moving outward" by the Soviet Union?

It seems to me that what you are saying in this question is that Russia is behaving suspiciously like a great power. You list a number of things she is doing: naval deployments in distant oceans, military and economic aid programs, treaties with Egypt and India, expanded trade relations with many countries. Correct. But is there any reason why a country of Russia's size and economic potential should *not* do these things? Are there, in fact, any of them that we do not do— any of them in which we have not set the example?

It seems to me that those who see a danger in these activities are predicating, just as in the case of the weapons race, some underlying political conflict that may not be there at all. I admit that Soviet activities in many of these countries are impregnated with anti-American attitudes, and one of their objectives, if not the leading one, seems to be at least the discrediting and the isolation of the United States—a purpose at which, I must say, we connive with an adeptness little short of genius. As a traditionalist who does not believe that this country is well constituted, anyway, to play a very active role in world affairs, I find myself less frightened than others over the fact that Soviet policies are so inspired.

It would be a very sad and hopeless situation if we were to convince ourselves that the peace of the world depended on the ability of the rest of us to prevent the Soviet Union indefinitely from acting like a great power. Would it not be better to avoid assuming that all Soviet activities are aimed primarily against us—unless, at least, it is proved otherwise—and to see whether there are not some areas of assistance to other nations, and constructive involvement with their affairs, where we and the Russians could work together instead of separately?

In saying these things one must, I suppose, make a certain exception with respect to Soviet policies in the Middle East. In addition to the program of naval expansion and maritime espionage this seems to me to be the only area of Soviet foreign relations that has been marked both by evident lack of coordination in Moscow and by certain signs of a disturbing adventurism. If one were to be asked to guess at the motives of Soviet policy from the surface appearances, one could only conclude that Soviet policy toward the Arab countries was based on a serious desire to gain total control over this area and to exclude every form of Western influence. Given

the existing dependence of Western Europe on Middle Eastern oil, this represents a serious and even dangerous challenge to the security of the Western European, and one which
seems poorly to accord with the prudence shown in other
areas of the Soviet government's foreign relations. Soviet
policymakers might do well to remind themselves that not
every fruit that seems about to fall is one that it is desirable
to pick.

In Memoirs: 1925-1950 *you wrote: "What I said in the X-Article was not intended as a doctrine. I am afraid that when I
think about foreign policy, I do not think in terms of doctrines. I think in terms of principles." There has been much
talk recently about the desirability of the United States' following a "balance of power" policy. Do you think this is an
appropriate and useful principle to guide U.S. policymakers
in the future? What other principles would you recommend?*

If a "balance of power policy" means using American influence, wherever possible, to assure that the ability to develop
military power on the grand scale is divided among several
governmental entities and not concentrated entirely in any
one of them, then I think that I favor it. But only with two res-
ervations.

First of all, I think it should not be cynically conceived, and it
should not, above all, be taken to mean pushing other people
into conflict with each other. In this, I am fully in accord with
what I understand to be the view of the present administration.

But second, I would not overrate our power to affect these relationships. Twenty-five years ago we did have very considerable power to affect them, particularly in Europe, and this
lay behind some of my own views about disengagement, because I thought that a better balance could be created
between Russian power and a united Europe than between
Russian power and a divided one. Today, except for our role
in NATO, and such influence as we might have—or might
have had—on the situation in the subcontinent of India-Pakistan, our possibilities are decidedly limited.

A curious balance of power already does exist today in East
Asia, as between the Russians, the Chinese, and the Japanese. So long as the Russians remain strong enough to defend their own Far Eastern territories, plus Outer Mongolia,

as they are today, this should assure peace along the Russian-Chinese border; and anxiety lest Japanese industrial power be added to the resources of the other party should cause both Russians and Chinese to cultivate good and peaceful relations with the Japanese. This situation is not our doing, and it needs no stimulation from us; but it serves our interests, and we should be careful not to disturb it.

In the "X" article you wrote that the ability of the United States to influence internal developments in the Communist nations, and therefore the policies they pursue, varies according to "the degree to which the United States can create among the peoples of the world generally the impression of a country which knows what it wants, which is coping successfully with the problems of its internal life and with the responsibilities of a World Power, and which has a spiritual vitality capable of holding its own among the major ideological currents of the time." Do you still believe this to be so? Given these criteria, how would you assess the record of the past twenty-five years?

I do believe this to be so, but it is here that I consider we have failed most miserably. We simply have not faced up successfully to our own internal problems, and we have lost, just since World War II, a great deal of our value and our potential influence as an example to other peoples. So obvious is this that if, thinking about the worldwide loss of American prestige and influence in recent years, one asks whether the Russians have succeeded in setting us back, one has to give the answer: no—we and the Russians have each defeated ourselves; neither was up to its own pretensions of earlier years.

How well do the Nixon-Kissinger policies for dealing with the Communist nations seem to fit the notions that underlay your own thinking at the time of the "X" article and subsequently?

The Nixon-Kissinger policies fit the conceptions of the "X" article, it seems to me, only indifferently.

Those policies continue to give great attention, geographically, to what I viewed in 1947, and have always viewed, as a secondary area from the standpoint of our interest: Southeast Asia.

While the SALT talks are certainly a significant and welcome step in advance, a great deal of American governmental attention and energy continues to be riveted to the sterile and dangerous effort to excel the Russians in the nuclear arms race. That had no place in my scheme of things.

There is undue emphasis on China, from which we have very little to gain in terms of world policy, and a certain slighting, in my view, of Japan.

You may say that much of this is not responsive to your question, which involved our dealings with the Communist nations directly. But it has always been true that the secret of successful dealings with Russia itself—and the same now goes for China—is the proper handling of our relations with the remainder of the world that lies between us.

Finally, there is the obvious partiality for summit meetings with Communist leaders, a procedure that may have its domestic-political dividends but that I regard as at best irrelevant, and potentially pernicious, to a sound handling of relations with the great Communist governments.

So far as the Soviet Union itself is concerned, I do not see a great deal that the Nixon administration could do that it is not now doing. I think—though it may not be of major importance—that we should at once agree to the cessation of underground testing. I think that we could well take certain further unilateral measures of restraint in the development of nuclear weapons and their carriers, with a view to encouraging the others to do likewise. I think we should press talks with the Russians to see whether we could not agree with them on putting a stop to the childish and dangerous mutual shadowing of naval vessels that now goes on all over the high seas. I think we should bend every effort to develop technical collaboration with them—in space activities as well as in international environmental undertakings. We should keep in communication with them—constantly—concerning the situation in the Middle East, with a view to avoiding misunderstandings. Beyond that, there is not much we can do.

In the light of its subsequent misinterpretation, do you regret having written the "X" article?

No—not on balance. I regret having written it exactly the way I did. But it was meant to sound—and did sound, I think, at the time—a hopeful note, urging people to believe that our differences with the Soviet Union of Stalin's day, while serious indeed, were not ones that could be solved only—or, indeed, solved at all—by war. Well, we have struggled along for another quarter of a century, and there has been no war—at least not between us and the Russians. And there is even less reason to think one necessary today than there was then.

The importance of the "X" article was, of course, distorted out of all reasonable proportion by the treatment it received at the hands of the press. The American mass media produce upon any given event an effect analogous to that produced on a man's shadow by the angle of the sun—causing it normally to be either much greater or much less than life size. In the case of this particular article it was much greater.

But the principle enunciated in it—that our differences with the Russians are not ones that it would take a war to solve— is still sound. What we need mostly to do is to free ourselves from some of our fixations with relation to the military competition—to remind ourselves that there is really no reason why we and the Russians should wish to do frightful things to each other and to the world—and to address ourselves vigorously, and with some degree of boldness, to the enormous danger presented by the very existence in human hands, and above all the proliferation, of weapons such as the nuclear ones. Somewhere between the intimacy we cannot have—either with the Russians or the Chinese—and the war there is no reason for us to fight, there is a middle ground of peaceful, if somewhat distant, coexistence on which our relationship with the great Communist powers could be considerably safer and more pleasant than it now is. We cannot make it so by our own efforts alone; the Russians and Chinese will have to help. But we could do better, in a number of respects, than we have been doing.

THREE COMMENTS ON THE "X" ARTICLE

W. Averell Harriman:

George Kennan's "X" article had a significant impact on American public opinion. The anonymity of the signature "X" created mystery and added to its public attention.

The piercing directness of his analysis of the dangers to us of Soviet conduct added to its force.

The policy of the Truman administration was, of course, already set and was supported on a bipartisan basis in the Congress under Senator Vandenberg's leadership.

The Truman Doctrine, with aid to Greece and Turkey, had already passed Congress. Secretary of State Marshall had made his historic proposal to the European nations in his Harvard address.

Winston Churchill's Iron Curtain speech, delivered at Fulton the year before, had jarred many Americans. Public opinion toward the Russians had been changing from our wartime attitude of our "Gallant Allies." The discussion aroused by the Mr. "X" article contributed to a public understanding of what Stalin was up to and gained support for President Truman's policies.

For my part, I never accepted Kennan's "Containment Policy" as outlined in his article. President Truman himself, as I recall it, never used that expression in any public statement. I believed we should try to check and roll back Stalin's aggressive Communist influence wherever feasible.

This we did successfully through aid to Greece and later in Western Europe. I have no doubt Stalin expected Western Europe to fall under his sway through the growing strength of the Communist parties, particularly in France and Italy, and was only turned back by our initiative in the Marshall Plan and later by NATO.

On the other hand, President Truman refused to become embroiled in China in support of Chiang Kai-shek. Though fiercely criticized at the time, history now accepts the wisdom of his restraint. In addition, his Point Four Program was a constructive move to help alleviate conditions of human misery in the underdeveloped countries in which Stalin himself told me Communism bred and thrived.

"Three Comments on the 'X' Article" was published originally in *Foreign Policy*, Number 7, Summer 1972.

Two years earlier, in May 1945, at the United Nations Conference in San Francisco, I had expressed my views of dealing with Stalin in off-the-record talks with a number of editors and commentators. I said that we had to realize that Kremlin objectives and ours were irreconcilable, but we would have to find ways to compose our differences in order to live without war on this small planet. The Kremlin, I explained, wanted a world of Communist dictatorships, with the oracle in Moscow, whereas we believed our security and welfare were best served by governments responsive to the will of the people. Although some of those I talked with understood and agreed, others were shocked. At one meeting two men left the room, refusing, they said, to listen to any more of my warmongerings.

My approach at the time was that we should have our guard always up, but the hand for negotiations ever extended. I still believe this. Greater and more valid opportunity for constructive agreements exists today than under Stalin.

Arthur Krock:

There is evidence that only shortly before his death did President Franklin D. Roosevelt realize the ghastly error of his conception of Stalin's USSR as a cooperative postwar ally. But as late as February 1946, when the new and uninformed President Truman was still trying to base U.S.-Russian policy on what he supposed to be his predecessor's, Stalin delivered the speech that was a declaration of total and unending world war to destroy the capitalistic system. Even then the Truman administration was slow to abandon the dream of postwar cooperation with the USSR, until it received, a few days later, a realistic analysis of Stalin's meaning from George F. Kennan, U.S. counselor of embassy in Moscow. James Forrestal, then secretary of the navy, showed me his copy of the analysis, and with evident pleasure because it conformed to his own—and then minority administration— view of what to expect of the postwar policy of the USSR.

When I read the Mr. "X" article in *Foreign Affairs*, its similarities with the Kennan paper of 1946 were so striking that I had no doubt of its authorship, a deduction that Forrestal confirmed when I told him of it, a deduction I published as a fact.

The effect of the 1946 analysis was more important than the *Foreign Affairs* presentation, because the latter articulated a policy that the 1946 telegram had helped to set in motion. For the analysis was the basic source of what became the U.S. policy of "containment" that eventually took concrete form in the Truman Doctrine—the Greek-Turkish aid legislation, the North Atlantic Alliance and NATO, Point Four, and the Marshall Plan. And though the Doctrine was executed beyond its purpose, and Kennan's intent, by U.S. military intervention in areas outside its immediate security interest, the February 1946 Kennan analysis—which his subsequent Mr. "X" article in the July 1947 issue of *Foreign Affairs* expanded into an informal White Paper—provided the official ground for the reversal of U.S. policy toward the USSR from appeasement to containment. But more importantly, as aforesaid, it effected an administration and popular consensus on the policy reversal that Forrestal, Harriman, and Clifford in particular had sought from the time Stalin's USSR showed its true world design at the organization of the United Nations at San Francisco in 1945.

Dean Acheson:

George Kennan's containment article was a description of what was happening anyway. He did not cause it. . . . George reminded me of an old horse my father used to have that would pull our buggy around. We'd go over an old clapboard bridge, and the horse would just stop to turn around to see the noise he was making. Of course, when he stopped, so would the noise. Then he would go on faster . . . and more noise, of course . . . stop, turn around again, and so forth until he got across the bridge, never realizing what the stir was about. The "X" article was a perfectly fine article. Then Walter Lippmann decided that he didn't like it. Well, it was as if God had looked over at George's shoulder and said, "George, you shouldn't have written such a bad article." They thought that containment applied everywhere, but it was nothing of the kind.

HOW CONTAINMENT WORKED

by Chalmers M. Roberts

The wartime alliance between Moscow and Washington was turning into cold war when George F. Kennan's containment thesis appeared in the famous "X" article, "The Sources of Soviet Conduct." Some rationale for new policies had to be found. Containment did so.

The key to the Kennan article was its timing. His famous telegram from Moscow on February 22, 1946, analyzing the Kremlin's behavior, in Louis J. Halle's words, "came at a moment when the [State] Department, having been separated by circumstances from the wartime policy toward Russia, was floundering about, looking for new intellectual moorings." The significant addition of the "X" article, as Halle put it, "was a word and a concept." The word was *containment*. The concept was that postwar Russia's "expansive tendencies" could be contained by American policy and if so contained would, over time, be modified in a way that would lessen or minimize the seeming threat to the United States. The goal certainly was satisfactory, whatever one's reading then was of the threat. The method, containment, seemed within both reason and the capability of a war-weary America. Containment thus charted a course for an indefinite period ahead without calling for a renewal of violence by a government and public anxious to turn to the pursuits of peace. It would protect that hard-won peace.

I would argue that containment remains to this day the principal basis of American foreign policy. Of course, it has gone through both phases and evolution. But it seems to me that the Nixon Doctrine of the current administration rests on what the government and the public took to be the fundamentals of Kennan's thesis: keep Soviet power from running over us and our allies and friends, hoping that in time the Kremlin's revolutionary fervor would wind down and the Soviet Union would turn into a normal great power in its relationship with the United States. The Nixon principle of moving from "an era of confrontation" to "an era of negotiation" must assume that kind of relationship.

"How Containment Worked" was published originally in *Foreign Policy*, Number 7, Summer 1972.

In his *Memoirs: 1925-1950,* twenty years after publication of the "X" article, Kennan wrote that "all that the X-Article was meant to convey" was this: "Stand up to them . . . manfully but not aggressively, and give the hand of time a chance to work." In the "X" article he had written that "it is clear that the main element of any United States policy toward the Soviet Union must be that of a long-term, patient but firm and vigilant containment of Russian expansive tendencies." And: ". . . it will be clearly seen that the Soviet pressure against the free institutions of the Western world is something that can be contained by the adroit and vigilant application of counter-force at a series of constantly shifting geographical and political points, corresponding to the shifts and maneuvers of Soviet policy, but which cannot be charmed or talked out of existence. . . ." Finally: ". . . the United States has it in its power to increase enormously the strains under which Soviet policy must operate, to force upon the Kremlin a far greater degree of moderation and circumspection than it has had to observe in recent years, and in this way to promote tendencies which must eventually find their outlet in either the breakup or the gradual mellowing of Soviet power. . . ."

The trouble with Kennan's prescription, as with all doctrines, was that different people read words differently. Kennan's own quarrel with the fate of containment springs from this—with what is meant by "stand up" and "manfully" and "not aggressively," to use his summation, or by "application of counter-force" and "firm but vigilant containment," to use his original words. Such language as the latter phrases, he wrote in his *Memoirs,* "was at best ambiguous, and lent itself to misinterpretation in this respect." But it was no more so than, say, the National Security Action Memoranda of several administrations, as revealed in the Pentagon Papers. Doctrinal prose always reads that way. What counts is the meat put on the bones.

What Kennan sent home from Moscow in his dispatches and the thoughts of his "X" article simply were prescient of Moscow's postwar policy. Andre Fontaine in his *History of the Cold War* concludes that "the division of Europe really dates" from the month of July 1947, the very moment Americans were absorbing the "X" article and learning who was its author. But Kennan was not alone in trying to plumb the Kremlin. The previous September, 1946, a young lawyer at the White House named Clark Clifford had written for Presi-

dent Truman a long analysis of "American Relations with the
Soviet Union" (printed in full as an appendix to Arthur Krock's
Memoirs) along lines similar to Kennan's, though lacking his
insights into the Kremlin. Clifford, whose own beliefs from
that day until early in 1968 stimulated the containment policy
of Democratic administrations, concluded that the United
States "must, as a first step toward world stabilization, seek
to prevent additional Soviet aggression." Clifford had far less
hope than Kennan of a breakup or mellowing of Soviet power.
But he did argue that "our best chances of influencing Soviet
leaders consist of making it unmistakably clear that action
contrary to our conception of a decent world order will re-
dound to the disadvantage of the Soviet regime whereas
friendly and cooperative action will pay dividends. If this position can be maintained firmly enough and long enough the
logic of it must permeate eventually into the Soviet system."
In the March before the September when Clifford wrote those
words Truman had sat on the platform in Fulton, Missouri, as
Winston Churchill spoke of an Iron Curtain descending
across the continent of Europe.

All these thoughts faced the test of reality on February 24,
1947 when the British tossed to Washington the problem of
Greece, the result of which was the Truman Doctrine. We
know that by then Kennan's ideas (though they had not yet
surfaced in the "X" article), the Clifford memorandum (likewise secret), and the Churchill warning all were in the bureaucratic mix. The State Department draft for the president's
speech had him saying that "I believe that it should be the
policy of the United States to support free peoples who are
resisting attempted subjugation by armed minorities or by
outright pressures. . . ." Truman scratched out "should" and
inserted "must" before he delivered the address to a joint
session of Congress. Aid began to flow to Greece and Turkey
and, in time, to many other places. Soon Kennan's Policy
Planning Staff was privately lamenting what it called "the
damaging impression" the public had of the Truman Doctrine, that it provided a worldwide blank check. Less than
three months after the Truman Doctrine came the Marshall
Plan. In the public eye, both were effective steps to implement containment.

But containment of what? Kennan felt Truman was too
sweeping, but it can be argued that the president simply was

taking Kennan at his word when he had spoken of confronting Soviet power "at every point where they show signs of encroaching upon the interests of a peaceful world." Truman thus spoke in a worldwide sense. Kennan later said he thought it had been understood that he meant only areas "vital to our security." But he didn't say so. Clifford didn't say so. Nor had Churchill for that matter. And nobody defined what areas were "vital to our security."

After all, the Kremlin then was Stalin and Communism was monolithic. Kennan later argued that the doctrine of containment "lost much of its rationale with the death of Stalin and with the development of the Soviet-Chinese conflict." Yet even as late as 1966, while testifying before the Senate Foreign Relations Committee, Kennan said that "the policy of containment certainly has relevance to China, but it is a question of what and where and what lies within our resources." Then he added: "If we had been able to do better in Vietnam, I would have been delighted, and I would have thought that the effort was warranted."

Kennan provided the word and the concept for all those in Washington struggling with the same problem. He verbalized better than most. While the course already had been set, he provided both logic and justification. He initially intended to apply containment to the Soviet Union alone, but if the words just quoted mean anything, then it appears that he was willing to apply containment worldwide once Communism turned out to be polycentric.

When the Republicans came to power in 1953, Dulles extended containment by means of what his opponents termed pactomania. He spoke of "international Communism," and he surrounded it with a complex of treaties covering the Sino-Soviet periphery. In the Republican platform of 1952 Dulles had written that the new administration would "mark the end of the negative, futile, and immoral policy of 'containment' which abandons countless human beings to a despotism and Godless terrorism. . . . The policies we espouse will revive the contagious liberating influences which are inherent in freedom."

The Republicans Continue to Contain

Containment to Dulles was static; liberation would be dynamic. But when the test came with the Hungarian rebellion, both Eisenhower and Dulles shrank back from liberation; they stuck to containment. Dulles went to "the brink of war," but he described the "art" of that policy as not going over the brink. Eisenhower and Dulles stood fast in two crises over Quemoy and Matsu. Mao retreated; therefore he had been contained, though China was not "liberated." Dulles acceded to the "loss" of half of Vietnam, though he had recommended military intervention to contain Communism in Indochina. Eisenhower visualized falling dominoes and put the United States behind an "independent" South Vietnam to contain Ho Chi Minh.

John F. Kennedy came to power proclaiming that every nation, "whether it wishes us well or ill," should know that "we shall pay any price, bear any burden, meet any hardship, support any friend, oppose any foe to assure the survival and the success of liberty." The public cheered. What better verbalizing of containment had there ever been? Laos would not be allowed to fall. Berlin would be held against Nikita Khrushchev's threats. Communism—international, fragmented, polycentric, or whatever—would be contained. There was no more talk of liberation, especially after the Bay of Pigs.

General Maxwell Taylor was sent off to Saigon to determine, as Kennedy put it in his letter of instructions, how best "eventually to contain and eliminate the threat" to the independence of South Vietnam. Taylor reported back to the president that the United States was "facing a problem of major proportions in deciding how to cope with a new and dangerous technique for bypassing our traditional political and military defenses"—in short, it had to deal with a breach in containment.

Lyndon Johnson carried on lest the containment line be so breached that the United States, as he was wont to put it, end up defending the beaches at Honolulu. Dean Rusk worried out loud about the future with its "billion Chinese . . . armed with nuclear weapons with no certainty about what their attitude toward the rest of Asia will be." The loss of Vietnam, said Rusk, would mean that Peking's "primitive, militant doctrine of world revolution" would not stop there. "I should think," he concluded, "they would simply move the problem to the next country and the next and the next." In Vietnam, containment of Communism, which was viewed as Moscow and Peking directed, was the only answer because "these are appetites and ambitions that grow upon feeding."

Truman had given up on negotiating with the Russians. All they understand, he remarked, is "an iron fist." Eisenhower tried the summit path but concluded that the new Kremlin leaders sought the permanent division of Europe, at the least. In 1955 Dulles rejected an overture from Peking; he wanted only to contain, not to deal with, China. Kennedy met with Khrushchev only to face what he took to be a Berlin ultimatum. Jointly they peered over the brink in Cuba. After that Kennedy denied a desire for a "Pax Americana," and he came to terms with Moscow on the limited test ban treaty. The Kremlin's power at least had been contained in the missile crisis; perhaps the treaty would contain the arms race. The void that followed Kennedy's assassination, as General Taylor saw it, was "particularly noticeable in foreign policy, where old slogans in support of the containment of Communism and the principles of the Truman Doctrine are no longer sufficient to rally public support for actions entailing public sacrifice." Kennan had never spoken of such sacrifices.

Eisenhower's efforts at summitry, Kennedy's American University speech, and Johnson's efforts to begin the Strategic Arms Limitation Talks (SALT) all represented realizations that containment had to mean more than just the "adroit and vigilant application of counter-force" in a military and/or economic sense. It meant the acceptance of at least the rudiments of Kennan's own belief that diplomacy should be the primary tool.

In due course Richard Nixon came to the White House. The man who was to be his chief foreign policy advisor, Henry A. Kissinger, had proclaimed in his 1957 book *Nuclear Weapons and Foreign Policy* that "the basic requirement for American security is a doctrine which will enable us to act purposefully in the face of the challenges which will inevitably confront us." And: "In any conflict the side which is animated by faith in victory has a decided advantage over an opponent who wishes above all to preserve the status quo." Once in power Kissinger the conceptualist and Nixon the old cold warrior combined to move from "an era of confrontation" to one of "negotiation." The United States would not be "a pitiful helpless giant," but it would lower its worldwide profile—if only because the American public demanded it by now. Superiority in arms would give way to sufficiency, if only because the money was running out. How to tie together such changes in an understandable bundle? By a doctrine, of course. Americans, both the public and its government, have a craving for doctrines. This is especially true for those who care about and pay attention to the nation's foreign policy. The president thus had no qualms about calling it the Nixon Doctrine.

The real problem was to find a new method of containment of Communism, now so clearly fragmented especially between Moscow and Peking, commensurate with a lessened American commitment abroad. The nuclear umbrella for allies and friends, dating from the Truman era, would continue. But friends and allies should provide the shock troops and appeal to the United States henceforth only in extremes. Washington would judge whether it would be in our national interest to become involved directly.

One may view the Nixon-Kissinger policy simply as the product of necessity. It is essentially a new form of the old containment policy, a new method of attaining the old end, in Kennan's words "stand up to them . . . manfully but not aggressively, and give the hand of time a chance to work." Nixon and Kissinger have not assumed that lions lie down with lambs. They simply are trying a new way, or rather reviving a very old way, to keep the lions contained so they cannot eat the lamb.

Did It Work?

Has containment worked? In Europe there is more stability than at any time since World War II, assuming Willy Brandt's *Ostpolitik* is not upset by the politics of Bonn. Berlin is defused. In Asia a new live-and-let-live arrangement is already visible, although its form remains shadowy. In the Middle East, Africa, and Latin America containment in the Truman Doctrine sense has been breached. But the development of national communisms, or more precisely of national socialisms, in such places as Chile, a number of Arab nations, and some of the African countries has done no irreparable harm to American vital interests. Only in Indochina has it been impossible thus far for the Nixon administration to disengage without accepting a major defeat of the old containment doctrine—therefore the effort to lessen the importance of Indo-china by a rapprochement with Peking and a new design in Asia.

In terms of raw power this is still a bipolar world. In terms of influence, economic and political, it has become *at least* five polar. Containment succeeded in preventing a bipolar clash, and it has aided in the development of the five-polar world by providing shields for both Western Europe and Japan. America has grown introspective, but not isolationist in the old sense of the years between the world wars. We may be unsure just where our frontiers lie. We have had it as the world's policeman. But we have not opted out of the world. In sum, Nixon has been conducting a rather orderly retreat in this disorderly world, based on his revamped version of the containment doctrine.

Of course, containment did get out of hand. It did so because the United States did not soon enough understand the reality of the post-Stalin developments within the Communist orbit. We did not as a nation perceive the peculiar circumstances of Ho Chi Minh's brand of Communism and·of such other ver-sions as Castro's. Pursuing containment to the extreme did lead to disaster in Vietnam and to major repercussions at home. We know the cost on both counts has been extreme, but we cannot yet determine the consequences.

Looking back over twenty-five years, it seems to me that the underlying concept of containment has worked. Containment began as a post-World War II policy. In the generation since, the initial concept has run its course. The initial post-World War II American dominance was unhealthy; today's balance of power is more rational. The excesses of pursuit of con-tainment, peaking in Indochina, have driven the United States to a new posture, of necessity.

Changes in policy tend to be cyclical and generational. I sus-pect that even if there had been no Vietnam, the United States by now, give or take a few years, would have been re-examining its policies. But because there was Vietnam, Nixon has had to attempt to ease the United States into a new world relationship.

I don't venture to guess how containment will appear on its fiftieth anniversary. But on this twenty-fifth birthday, George Kennan, for all his qualms about what succeeding adminis-

trations did to distort his word and his concept, can draw
more comfort than he may wish to concede from the role he
played in providing for so long the "intellectual moorings" of
American policy.

VIETNAM: THE SYSTEM WORKED
by Leslie H. Gelb

The story of United States policy toward Vietnam is either far better or far worse than generally supposed. Our presidents and most of those who influenced their decisions did not stumble step by step into Vietnam unaware of the quagmire. U.S. involvement did not stem from a failure to foresee consequences.

Vietnam was indeed a quagmire, but most of our leaders knew it. Of course, there were optimists and periods where many were genuinely optimistic. But those periods were infrequent and short lived and were invariably followed by periods of deep pessimism. Very few, to be sure, envisioned what the Vietnam situation would be like by 1968. Most realized, however, that "the light at the end of the tunnel" was very far away—if not finally unreachable. Nevertheless, our presidents persevered. Given international compulsions to "keep our word" and "save face," domestic prohibitions against "losing," and their personal stakes, our leaders did "what was necessary," did it about the way they wanted, were prepared to pay the costs, and plowed on with a mixture of hope and doom. They "saw" no acceptable alternative.

Three propositions suggest why the United States became involved in Vietnam, why the process was gradual, and what the real expectations of our leaders were:

First, U.S. involvement in Vietnam is not mainly or mostly a story of step-by-step, inadvertent descent into unforeseen quicksand. It is primarily a story of why U.S. leaders considered that it was vital not to lose Vietnam by force to Communism. Our leaders believed Vietnam to be vital not for itself, but for what they thought its "loss" would mean internationally and domestically. Previous involvement made further involvement more unavoidable, and, to this extent, commitments were inherited. But judgments of Vietnam's "vitalness"—beginning with the Korean War—were sufficient in themselves to set the course for escalation.

Second, our presidents were never actually seeking a military victory in Vietnam. They were doing only what they thought was minimally necessary at each stage to keep Indochina, and later South Vietnam, out of Communist hands. This

"Vietnam: The System Worked" was published originally in *Foreign Policy*, Number 3, Summer 1971.

forced our presidents to be brakemen, to do less than those who were urging military victory and to reject proposals for disengagement. It also meant that our presidents wanted a negotiated settlement without fully realizing (though realizing more than their critics) that a civil war cannot be ended by political compromise.

Third, our presidents and most of their lieutenants were not deluded by optimistic reports of progress and did not proceed on the basis of wishful thinking about winning a military victory in South Vietnam. They recognized that the steps they were taking were not adequate to win the war and that unless Hanoi relented, they would have to do more and more. Their strategy was to persevere in the hope that their will to continue—if not the practical effects of their actions— would cause the Communists to relent.

Each of these propositions is explored below.

1.   Ends: "We Can't Afford to Lose"

Those who led the United States into Vietnam did so with their eyes open, knowing why, and believing they had the will to succeed. The deepening involvement was not inadvertent, but mainly deductive. It flowed with sureness from the per- ceived stakes and attendant high objectives. U.S. policy dis- played remarkable continuity. There were not dozens of likely "turning points." Each postwar president inherited previous commitments. Each extended these commitments. Each ad- ministration from 1947 to 1969 believed that it was necessary to prevent the loss of Vietnam and, after 1954, South Vietnam by force to the Communists. The reasons for this varied from person to person, from bureaucracy to bureaucracy, over time and in emphasis. For the most part, however, they had little to do with Vietnam itself. A few men argued that Vietnam had intrinsic strategic military and economic impor- tance, but this view never prevailed. The reasons rested on broader international, domestic, and bureaucratic consider- ations.

Our leaders gave the *international* repercussions of "losing" as their dominant explicit reason for Vietnam's importance. During the Truman administration, Indochina's importance was measured in terms of French-American relations and Washington's desire to rebuild France into the centerpiece of future European security. After the cold war heated up and after the fall of China, a French defeat in Indochina was also seen as a defeat for the policy of containment. In the Eisenhower years, Indochina became a "testing ground" between the Free World and Communism and the basis for the famous "domino theory" by which the fall of Indochina would lead to the deterioration of American security around the globe. President Kennedy publicly reaffirmed the falling-domino concept. His primary concern, however, was for his "reputation for action" after the Bay of Pigs fiasco, the Vienna meeting with Khrushchev, and the Laos crisis, and in meeting the challenge of "wars of national liberation" by counterinsurgency warfare. Under President Johnson the code-word rationales became Munich, credibility, commitments and the U.S. word, a watershed test of wills with Communism, raising the costs of aggression, and the principle that armed aggression shall not be allowed to succeed. There is every reason to assume that our leaders actually believed what they said, given both the cold war context in which they were all reared and the lack of contradictory evidence.

With very few exceptions, then, our leaders since World War II saw Vietnam as a vital factor in alliance politics, U.S.-Soviet-Chinese relations, and deterrence. This was as true in 1950 and 1954 as it was in 1961 and 1965. The record of United States military and economic assistance to fight Communism in Indochina tells this story quite clearly. From 1945 to 1951 U.S. aid to France totaled over $3.5 billion. Without this the French position in Indochina would have been untenable. By 1951 the U.S. was paying about 40 percent of the costs of the Indochina war and our share was going up. In 1954, it is estimated, U.S. economic and technical assistance amounted to $703 million and military aid totaled almost $2 billion. This added up to almost 80 percent of the total French costs. From 1955 to 1961 U.S. military aid averaged about $200 million per year. This made South Vietnam the second largest recipient of such aid, topped only by Korea. By 1963 South Vietnam ranked first among recipients of military assistance. In economic assistance it followed only India and Pakistan.

The *domestic* repercussions of "losing" Vietnam probably were equally important in presidential minds. Letting Vietnam "go Communist" was undoubtedly seen as: opening the floodgates to domestic criticism and attack for being "soft on Communism" or just plain soft; dissipating presidential influence by having to answer these charges; alienating conservative leadership in the Congress and thereby endangering the president's legislative program; jeopardizing election prospects for the president and his party; undercutting domestic support for a "responsible" U.S. world role; and enlarging the prospects for a right-wing reaction—the nightmare of a McCarthyite garrison state.

U.S. domestic politics required our leaders to maintain both a peaceful world and one in which Communist expansion was stopped. In order to have the public support necessary to use force against Communism, our leaders had to employ strong, generalized, ideological rhetoric. The price of this rhetoric was consistency. How could our leaders shed American blood in Korea and keep large numbers of American troops in Europe at great expense unless they were also willing to stop Communism in Vietnam?

Bureaucratic judgments and stakes were also involved in defining U.S. interests in Vietnam. Most bureaucrats probably prompted or shared the belief of their leaders about the serious repercussions of losing. Once direct bureaucratic presence was established, after the French departure, this belief was reinforced and extended. The military had to prove that American arms and advice could succeed where the French could not. The Foreign Service had to prove that it could bring about political stability in Saigon and "build a nation." The CIA had to prove that pacification would work. AID had to prove that millions of dollars in assistance and advice could bring political returns.

The U.S. commitment was rationalized as early as 1950. It was set in 1955 when we replaced the French. Its logic was further fulfilled by President Kennedy. After 1965, when the U.S. took over the war, it was immeasurably hardened.

There was little conditional character to the U.S. commitment—except for avoiding "the big war." Every president talked about the ultimate responsibility resting with the Vietnamese (and the French before them). This "condition" seems to have been meant much more as a warning to our friends than as a real limitation. In every crunch it was swept aside. The only real limit was that our leaders were not prepared to run the risks of nuclear war, or even the risks of a direct conventional military confrontation, with the Soviet Union and China. These were separate decisions. The line between them and everything else done in Vietnam always held firm. With this exception, the commitment was always defined in terms of the objective to deny the Communists control over all Vietnam. This was further defined to preclude coalition governments with the Communists.

The importance of the objective was evaluated in terms of cost, and the perceived costs of disengagement outweighed the cost of further engagement. Some allies might urge disengagement, but then condemn the U.S. for doing so. The domestic groups that were expected to criticize growing involvement always were believed to be outnumbered by those who would have attacked "cutting and running." The question of whether our leaders would have started down the road if they knew it would mean over half a million men in Vietnam, over 40 thousand U.S. deaths, and the expenditure of well over $100 billion is historically irrelevant. Only presidents Kennedy and Johnson had to confront the possibility of these large costs. The point is that each administration was prepared to pay the costs it could foresee for itself. No one seemed to have a better solution. Each could at least pass the baton to the next.

Presidents could not treat Vietnam as if it were "vital" without creating high stakes internationally, domestically, and within their own bureaucracies. But the rhetoric conveyed different messages:

To the Communists, it was a signal that their actions would be met by counteractions.

To the American people, it set the belief that the president would ensure that the threatened nation did not fall into Communist hands—although without the anticipation of sacrificing American lives.

To the Congress, it marked the president's responsibility to ensure that Vietnam did not go Communist and maximized incentives for legislators to support him or at least remain silent.

To the U.S. professional military, it was a promise that U.S. forces would be used, if necessary and to the degree necesary, to defend Vietnam.

To the professional U.S. diplomat, it meant letting our allies around the world know that the United States cared about their fate.

To the president, it laid the groundwork and showed that he was prepared to take the next step to keep Vietnam non-Communist.

Words were making Vietnam into a showcase—an Asian Berlin. In the process Vietnam grew into a test case of U.S. credibility—to opponents, to allies, but perhaps most importantly, to ourselves. Public opinion polls seemed to confirm the political dangers. Already established bureaucratic judgments about the importance of Vietnam matured into cherished convictions and organizational interests. The war dragged on.

Each successive president, initially caught by his own belief, was further ensnarled by his own rhetoric, and the basis for the belief went unchallenged. Debates revolved around how to do things better, and whether they could be done, not whether they were worth doing. Prior to 1961 an occasional senator or Southeast Asian specialist would raise a lonely and weak voice in doubt. Some press criticism began thereafter. And, later still, wandering American minstrels returned from the field to tell their tales of woe in private. General Ridgway as chief of staff of the Army in 1954 questioned the value of Vietnam as against its potential costs and dangers and succeeded in blunting a proposed U.S. military initiative, although not for the reasons he advanced. Under Secretary of State George Ball raised the issue of international priorities in the summer of 1965 and lost. Clark Clifford as secretary of defense openly challenged the winnability of the war, as well as Vietnam's strategic significance, and argued for domestic priorities. But no systematic or serious examination of Vietnam's importance to the United States was ever undertaken within the government. Endless assertions passed for analysis. Presidents neither encouraged nor permitted serious questioning. Their having done so would have fostered the idea that their resolve was something less than complete, that they were not wholly committed to the objective of a non-Communist Vietnam, and after 1954 a non-Communist South Vietnam. It was this objective that drove U.S. involvement ever more deeply each step of the way.

2. Means: "Take the Minimal Necessary Steps"

None of our presidents was seeking total victory over the Vietnamese Communists. War critics who wanted victory always knew this. Those who wanted the U.S. to get out never believed it. Each president was essentially doing what he thought was minimally necessary to prevent a Communist victory during his tenure in office. Each, of course, sought to strengthen the anti-Communist Vietnamese forces—but with the aim of a negotiated settlement. Part of the tragedy of Vietnam was that the compromises our presidents were prepared to offer could never lead to an end of the war. These preferred compromises only served to reinforce the conviction of both Communist and anti-Communist Vietnamese that they had to fight to the finish in their civil war. And so more minimal steps were always necessary.

Our presidents were pressured on all sides. The pressures for victory came mainly from the inside and were reflected on the outside. From inside the administrations, three forces almost invariably pushed hard. *First,* the military establishment generally initiated requests for broadening and intensifying U.S. military action. Our professional military placed great weight on the strategic significance of Vietnam; they were given a job to do; their prestige was involved; and, of crucial importance (in the 1960s), the lives of many American servicemen were being lost. The Joint Chiefs of Staff, the MAAG (Military Assistance Advisory Group) chiefs, and later the commander of U.S. forces in Vietnam were the focal points for these pressures. *Second,* our ambassadors in Saigon, supported by the State Department, at times pressed for and often supported big steps forward. Their reasons were similar to those of the military. *Third,* an ever-present group of "fixers" was making urgent demands to strengthen and broaden the Saigon government in order to achieve political victory. Every executive agency had its fixers. They were usually able men whose entire preoccupation was to make things better in Vietnam. From outside the administration there were hawks who insisted on winning and hawks who wanted to "win or get out." Capitol Hill hawks, the conservative press, and, for many years, Catholic organizations were in the forefront.

The pressures for disengagement and for de-escalation derived mostly from the outside with occasional and often unknown allies from within. Small for most of the Vietnam years, these forces grew steadily in strength from 1965 onward. Isolated congressmen and senators led the fight. First they did so on anticolonialist grounds. Later their objections developed moral aspects (interfering in a civil war) and extended to nonwinnability, domestic priorities, and the senselessness of the war. Peace organizations and student groups in particular came to dominate headlines and air time. Journalists played a critical role—especially through television reports. From within each administration opposition could be found: (1) among isolated military men who did not want the U.S. in an Asian land war, (2) among some State Department intelligence and area specialists who knew Vietnam and believed the U.S. objective was unattainable at any reasonable price, and (3) within the civilian agencies of the Defense Department and among isolated individuals at State and CIA, particularly after 1966, whose efforts were trained on finding a politically feasible way out.

Our presidents reacted to the pressures as brakemen, pulling the switch against both the advocates of "decisive escalation" and the advocates of disengagement. The politics of the presidency largely dictated this role, but the personalities of the presidents were also important. None was as ideological as many persons around him. All were basically centrist politicians.

Their immediate aim was always to prevent a Communist takeover. The actions they approved were usually only what was minimally necessary to that aim. Each president determined the "minimal necessity" by trial and error and his own judgment. They might have done more and done it more rapidly if they were convinced that: (1) the threat of a Communist takeover were more immediate, (2) U.S. domestic politics would have been more permissive, (3) the government of South Vietnam had the requisite political stability and military potential for effective use, and (4) the job really would have got done. After 1965, however, the minimal necessity became the maximum they could get given the same domestic and international constraints.

The tactic of the minimally necessary decision makes optimum sense for the politics of the presidency. Even our strongest presidents have tended to shy away from decisive action. It has been too uncertain, too risky. They derive their strength from movement (the image of a lot of activity) and building and neutralizing opponents. Too seldom has there been forceful moral leadership; it may even be undemocratic. The small step that maintains the momentum gives the president the chance to gather more political support. It gives the appearance of minimizing possible mistakes. It allows time to gauge reactions. It serves as a pressure-relieving value against those who want to do more. It can be doled out. Above all, the small step gives the president something to do next time.

The tactic makes consummate sense when it is believed that nothing will fully work or that the costs of a "winning" move would be too high. This was the case with Vietnam. This decision-making tactic explains why the U.S. involvement in Vietnam was gradual and step by step.

While the immediate aim was to prevent a Communist victory and improve the position of the anti-Communists, the longer-term goal was a political settlement. As late as February 1947 Secretary of State Marshall expressed the hope that a "pacific basis of adjustment of the difficulties" between France and the Vietminh could be found.* After that, Truman's policy hardened, but there is no evidence to suggest that until 1950 he was urging the French not to settle with the Vietnamese Communists. Eisenhower, it should be remembered, was the president who tacitly agreed (by not intervening in 1954) to the creation of a Communist state in North Vietnam. President Kennedy had all he could do to prevent complete political collapse in South Vietnam. He had, therefore, little basis on which to compromise. President Johnson inherited this political instability, and to add to his woes, he faced in 1965 what seemed to be the prospect of a Communist military victory. Yet, by his standing offer for free and internationally supervised elections, he apparently was prepared to accept Communist participation in the political life of the South.

By traditional diplomatic standards of negotiations between sovereign states these were not fatuous compromises. One compromise was, in effect, to guarantee that the Communists could remain in secure control of North Vietnam. The U.S. would not seek to overthrow this regime. The other compromise was to allow the Communists in South Vietnam

*The New York Times, February 8, 1947.

to seek power along the lines of Communist parties in France and Italy, that is, to give them a "permanent minority position."

But the real struggle in Vietnam was not between sovereign states. It was among Vietnamese. It was a civil war and a war for national independence.

Herein lies the paradox and the tragedy of Vietnam. Most of our leaders and their critics did see that Vietnam was a quagmire, but did not see that the real stakes—who shall govern Vietnam—were not negotiable. Free elections, local sharing of power, international supervision, cease-fires— none of these could serve as a basis for settlement. What were legitimate compromises from Washington's point of view were matters of life and death to the Vietnamese. For American leaders the stakes were "keeping their word" and saving their political necks. For the Vietnamese the stakes were their lives and their lifelong political aspirations. Free elections meant bodily exposure to the Communist guerrillas and likely defeat to the anti-Communists. The risk was too great. There was no trust, no confidence.

The Vietnam war could no more be settled by traditional diplomatic compromises than any other civil war. President Lincoln could not settle with the South. The Spanish Republicans and General Franco's Loyalists could not have conceivably mended their fences by elections. None of the post-World War II insurgencies—Greece, Malaya, and the Philippines—ended with a negotiated peace. In each of these cases the civil differences were put to rest—if at all—only by the logic of war.

It is commonly acknowledged that Vietnam would have fallen to the Communists in 1945-46, in 1954, and in 1965 had it not been for the intervention of first the French and then the Americans. The Vietnamese Communists, who were also by history the Vietnamese nationalists, would not accept only part of a prize for which they had paid so heavily. The anti-Communist Vietnamese, protected by the French and the Americans, would not put themselves at the Communists' mercy.

It may be that our presidents understood this better than their critics. The critics, especially on the political left, fought for "better compromises," not realizing that even the best could not be good enough, and fought for broad nationalist governments, not realizing there was no middle force in Vietnam. Our presidents, it seems, recognized that there was no middle ground and that "better compromises" would frighten our Saigon allies without bringing about a compromise peace. And they believed that a neutralization formula would compromise South Vietnam away to the Communists. So the longer-term aim of peace repeatedly gave way to the immediate needs of the war and the next necessary step.

3. Expectations: "We Must Persevere"

Each new step was taken not because of wishful thinking or optimism about its leading to a victory in South Vietnam. Few of our leaders thought that they could win the war in a conventional sense or that the Communists would be decimated to a point that they would simply fade away. Even as new and further steps were taken, coupled with expressions of optimism, many of our leaders realized that more—and still more—would have to be done. Few of these men felt confident about how it would all end or when. After 1965, however, they allowed the impression of "winnability" to grow in order to justify their already heavy investment and domestic support for the war.

The strategy always was to persevere. Perseverance, it seemed, was the only way to avoid or postpone having to pay the domestic political costs of failure. Finally, perseverance, it was hoped, would convince the Communists that our will to continue was firm. Perhaps, then, with domestic support for perseverance, with bombing North Vietnam, and with inflicting heavy casualties in the South, the Communists would relent. Perhaps, then, a compromise could be negotiated to save the Communists' face without yielding South Vietnam.

Optimism was a part of the "gamesmanship" of Vietnam. It had a purpose. Personal-organizational optimism was the product of a number of motivations and calculations: career services tacitly and sometimes explicitly pressured their professionals to impart good news; good news was seen as a job well done, bad news as personal failure; the reporting system was set up so that assessments were made by the implementers; optimism bred optimism so that it was difficult to be pessimistic this time if you were optimistic the last time; people told their superiors what they thought they wanted to hear; the American ethic is to get the job done.

Policy optimism also sprang from several rational needs: to maintain domestic support for the war; to keep up the morale of our Vietnamese allies and build some confidence and trust between us and them; to stimulate military and bureaucratic morale to work hard.

There were, however, genuine optimists and grounds for genuine optimism. Some periods looked promising: the year preceding the French downfall at Dienbienphu; the years of the second Eisenhower presidency, when most attention was riveted on Laos and before the insurgency was stepped up in South Vietnam; 1962 and early 1963, before the strategic hamlet pacification program collapsed; and the last six months of 1967, before the 1968 Tet offensive.

Many additional periods by comparison with previous years yielded a sense of real improvement. By most conventional standards—the size and firepower of friendly Vietnamese forces, the number of hamlets pacified, the number of "free elections" being held, the number of Communists killed, and so forth—reasonable men could and did think in cautiously optimistic terms.

But comparison with years past is an illusory measure when it is not coupled with judgments about how far there still is to go and how likely it is that the goal can ever be reached. It was all too easy to confuse short-term breathing spells with long-term trends and to confuse "things getting better" with "winning." Many of those who had genuine hope suffered from either a lack of knowledge about Vietnam or a lack of sensitivity toward politics or both.

The basis for pessimism and the warning signals were always present. Public portrayals of success glowed more brightly than the full range of classified reporting. Readily available informal and personal accounts were less optimistic still. The political instability of our Vietnamese allies—from Bao Dai through Diem to President Thieu—have always been apparent. The weaknesses of the armed forces of our Vietnamese allies were common knowledge. Few years went by when the fighting did not gain in intensity. Our leaders did not have to know much about Vietnam to see all this.

Most of our leaders saw the Vietnam quagmire for what it was. Optimism was, by and large, put in perspective. This means that many knew that each step would be followed by another. Most seemed to have understood that more assistance would be required either to improve the relative position of our Vietnamese allies or simply to prevent a deterioration of their position. Almost each year, and often several times a year, key decisions had to be made to prevent deterioration or collapse. These decisions were made with hard bargaining but rapidly enough for us now to perceive a preconceived consensus to go on. Sometimes several new steps were decided at once but announced and implemented piecemeal. The whole pattern conveyed the feeling of more to come.

With a tragic sense of "no exit" our leaders stayed their course. They seemed to hope more than expect that something would "give." The hope was to convince the Vietnamese Communists through perseverance that the U.S. would stay in South Vietnam until they abandoned their struggle. The hope, in a sense, was the product of disbelief. How could a tiny, backward Asian country *not* have a breaking point when opposed by the might of the United States? How could they not relent and negotiate with the U.S.?

And yet few could answer two questions with any confidence: Why should the Communists abandon tomorrow the goals they had been paying so dear a price to obtain yesterday? What was there really to negotiate? No one seemed to be able to develop a persuasive scenario on how the war could end by peaceful means.

Our presidents, given their politics and thinking, had nothing to do but persevere. But the Communists' strategy was also to persevere, to make the U.S. go home. It was a civil war for national independence. It was a Greek tragedy.

4. After Twenty-Five Years

A quick review of history supports these interpretations. To the Roosevelt administration during World War II, Indochina was not perceived as a "vital" area. The United States defeated Japan without Southeast Asia, and Indochina was not occupied by the allies until *after* Japan's defeat. FDR spoke informally to friends and newsmen of placing Indochina under United Nations trusteeship after the war, but—aware of French, British, and U.S. bureaucratic hostility to this—made no detailed plans and asked for no staff work prior to his death. For all practical purposes Truman inherited *no* Southeast Asia policy.

In 1946 and 1947 the U.S. acquiesced in the reestablishment of French sovereignty. Our policy was a passive one of hoping for a negotiated settlement of the "difficulties" between Paris and the Vietminh independence movement of Ho Chi Minh. To the south, in Indonesia, we had started to pressure the Dutch to grant independence and withdraw, and a residue of anticolonialism remained in our first inchoate approaches to an Indochina policy as well.

But events in Europe and China changed the context from mid-1947 on. Two important priorities were to rearm and strengthen France as the cornerstone of European defense and recovery in the face of Russian pressure and to prevent a further expansion of victorious Chinese Communism. The Truman Doctrine depicted a world full of dominoes. In May 1950, before Korea, Secretary of State Acheson announced that the U.S. would provide military and economic assistance to the French and their Indochinese allies for the direct purpose of combating Communist expansion.* After years of hesitating, Truman finally decided that anti-Communism was more important than anticolonialism in Indochina.

Acheson admits that U.S. policy was a "muddled hodgepodge":

The criticism, however, fails to recognize the limits on the extent to which one may successfully coerce an ally. . . . Furthermore, the result of withholding help to France would, at most, have removed the colonial power. It could not have made the resulting situation a beneficial one either for Indochina or for Southeast Asia, or in the more important effort of furthering the stability and defense of Europe. So while we may have tried to muddle through and were certainly not successful, I could not think then or later of a better course. One can suggest, perhaps, doing nothing. That might have had merit, but as an attitude for the leader of a great alliance toward an important ally, indeed one essential to a critical endeavor, it had its demerits, too.**

*Department of State Bulletin, May 1950, p. 821.

**Dean Acheson, Present at the Creation (New York: W. W. Norton, 1969), p. 673.

Several months after the Korean War began, Acheson recalled the warning of an "able colleague": "Not only was there real danger that our efforts would fail in their immediate purpose and waste valuable resources in the process, but we were moving into a position in Indochina in which 'our responsibilities tend to supplant rather than complement those of the French.'" Acheson then remembers: "I decided, however, that having put our hand to the plow, we would not look back."* He decided this despite the fact that he "recognized as no longer valid an earlier French intention to so weaken the enemy before reducing French forces in Indochina that indigenous forces could handle the situation."**

5. The Eisenhower Administration

President Eisenhower inherited the problem. Although with Vietminh successes the situation took on graver overtones, he, too, pursued a policy of "minimum action" to prevent the total "loss" of Vietnam to Communism. Sherman Adams, Eisenhower's assistant, explains how the problem was seen in the mid-1950s:

If the Communists had pushed on with an aggressive offensive after the fall of Dienbienphu, instead of stopping and agreeing to stay out of Southern Vietnam, Laos, and Cambodia, there was a strong possibility that the United States would have moved against them. A complete Communist conquest of Indochina would have had a far graver consequence for the West than a Red victory in Korea.†

Apparently the president felt he could live with Communist control in the restricted area of North Vietnam, away from the rest of Southeast Asia.

Eisenhower did not take the minimal necessary step to save *all* of Indochina, but he did take the necessary steps to prevent the loss of most of Indochina. He paid almost all the French war cost, increased the U.S. military advisory mission, supplied forty B-26s to the French, and continued the threat of U.S. intervention, first by "united action" and then by forming SEATO. In taking these actions, Eisenhower

*Ibid., p. 674.
**Ibid., pp. 676-77.
†Sherman Adams, *Firsthand Report* (New York: Harper & Row, 1961), p. 120.

was deciding against Vice-President Nixon and Admiral Radford, chairman of the Joint Chiefs of Staff, who favored U.S. intervention in force, and against General Ridgway, chief of staff of the Army, who opposed any action that could lead to an Asian land war. He was treading the well-worn middle path of doing just enough to balance off contradictory domestic, bureaucratic, and international pressures. The Vietnamese Communists agreed to the compromise, believing that winning the full prize was only a matter of time.

In public statements and later in his memoirs President Eisenhower gave glimpses of his reasoning. At the time of Dienbienphu, he noted, ". . . we ought to look at this thing with some optimism and some determination . . . long faces and defeatism don't win battles."* Later he wrote, "I am convinced that the French could not win the war because the internal political situation in Vietnam, weak and confused, badly weakened their military position."** But he persevered nevertheless, believing that "the decision to give this aid was almost compulsory. The United States had no real alternative unless we were to abandon Southeast Asia."†

The Geneva Conference of 1954 was followed by eighteen bleak and pessimistic months as official Washington wondered whether the pieces could be put back together. Despite or perhaps because of the pessimism U.S. aid was increased. Then, in the fall of 1956, Dulles could say: "We have a clean base there now, without a taint of colonialism. Dienbienphu was a blessing in disguise."‡ The years of "cautious optimism" had begun.

President Eisenhower kept the U.S. out of war because he allowed a territorial compromise with the Communists. More critically, he decided to replace the French and maintain a direct U.S. presence in Indochina. With strong rhetoric, military training programs, support for Ngo Dinh Diem in his re-

*Public Papers of the Presidents, Eisenhower, 1954, p. 471. This remark was made on May 12, 1954.

**Dwight D. Eisenhower, Mandate for Change (New York: Doubleday, 1963), p. 372.

†Ibid., p. 373.

‡Emmet John Hughes, The Ordeal of Power (New York: Dell, 1962), p. 182. Eisenhower himself wrote that in 1954 "the strongest reason of all for United States' refusal to respond by itself to French pleas was our tradition of anti-colonialism" (in Mandate for Change, p. 373).

fusal to hold the elections prescribed by the Geneva accords, and continuing military and economic assistance, he made the new state or "zone" of South Vietnam an American responsibility. Several years of military quiet in South Vietnam did not hide the smoldering political turmoil in that country, nor did it obscure the newspaper headlines that regularly proclaimed that the war in Indochina had shifted to Laos.

6. The Kennedy Administration

The administration of John F. Kennedy began in an aura of domestic sacrifice and international confrontation. The inauguration speech set the tone of U.S. responsibilities in "hazardous and dangerous" times.

Vietnam had a special and immediate importance that derived from the general international situation. Kennedy's predictions about dangerous times came true quickly—and stayed true—and he wanted to show strength to the Communists. But it was also the precarious situation in Laos and the "neutralist" compromise that Kennedy was preparing for Laos that were driving the president deeper into Vietnam. In Sorensen's words, Kennedy was "skeptical of the extent of our involvement [in Vietnam] but unwilling to abandon his predecessor's pledge or permit a Communist conquest. . . ."[*]

Kennedy had to face three basic general decisions. First, was top priority to go to political reform or fighting the war? On this issue the fixers, who wanted to give priority to political reform, were arrayed against the military. Second, should the line of involvement be drawn at combat units? On this issue the fixers were more quiet than in opposition. The military and the Country Team pushed hard—even urging the president to threaten Hanoi with U.S. bombing. Some counterweight came from State and the White House staff. Third, should the president make a clear, irrevocable, and open-ended commitment to prevent a Communist victory? Would this strengthen or weaken the U.S. hand in Saigon? Would it frighten away the Communists? What would be the domestic political consequences?

Kennedy's tactics and decisions—like Eisenhower's—followed the pattern of doing what was minimally necessary. On

[*]Theodore Sorenson, *Kennedy* (New York: Harper & Row, 1965), p. 639.

the political versus military priority issue, Kennedy did not make increasing military assistance definitively contingent on political reform, but he pointed to the absence of reform as the main reason for limiting the U.S. military role. On the combat unit issue, according to biographer Sorensen, "Kennedy never made a final negative decision on troops. In typical Kennedy fashion, he made it difficult for any of the pro-intervention advocates to charge him privately with weakness."* On the third issue, he avoided an open-ended commitment but escalated his rhetoric about the importance of Vietnam. While he did authorize an increase of U.S. military personnel from 685 to 16,000, he did so slowly, and not in two or three big decisions. He continually doled out the increases. He gave encouragement to bureaucratic planning and studying as a safety valve—a valve he thought he could control. He kept a very tight rein on information to the public about the war. In Salinger's words, he "was not anxious to admit the existence of a real war. . . ."** By minimizing U.S. involvement, Kennedy was trying to avoid public pressures either to do more or to do less.

The president would make it "their" war until he had no choice but to look at it in a different light. He would not look at it in another light until Diem, who looked like a losing horse, was replaced. He would not gamble on long odds. But it is not clear what he expected to get as a replacement for Diem.

With the exception of much of 1962, which even the North Vietnamese have called "Diem's year," the principal Kennedy decisions were made in an atmosphere of deterioration, not progress, in Vietnam. This feeling of deterioration explains why Kennedy dispatched so many high-level missions to Vietnam. As Kennedy's biographers have written, the president was not really being told he was winning, but how much more he would have to do.

Writing in 1965, Theodore Sorensen summed up the White House view of events following the Diem coup in November 1963:

The President, while eager to make clear that our aim was to get out of Vietnam, had always been doubtful about the optimistic reports constantly filed by the military on the progress of the

*Ibid., p. 654.

**Pierre Salinger, *With Kennedy* (New York: Doubleday, 1966), pp. 319-29.

war. . . . The struggle could well be, he thought, this nation's severest test of endurance and patience. . . . He was simply going to weather it out, a nasty, untidy mess to which there was no other acceptable solution. Talk of abandoning so unstable an ally and so costly a commitment "only makes it easy for the Communists," said the President. "I think we should stay."*

7. The Johnson Administration

Lyndon Johnson assumed office with a reputation as a pragmatic politician and not a cold war ideologue. His history on Southeast Asia indicated caution and comparative restraint. And yet it was this same man who as president presided over, and led the United States into, massive involvement.

Three facts conspired to make it easier for Johnson than for his predecessors to take the plunge on the assumed importance of Vietnam. First, the world was a safer place in which to live, and Vietnam was the only continuing crisis. Europe was secure. The Sino-Soviet split had deepened. Mutual nuclear deterrence existed between the two superpowers. Second, the situation in Vietnam was more desperate than it ever had been. If the United States had not intervened in 1965, South Vietnam would have been conquered by the Communists. Third, after years of effort, the U.S. conventional military forces were big enough and ready enough to intervene. Unlike his predecessors Johnson had the military capability to back up his words.

In sum, Vietnam became relatively more important, it was in greater danger, and the United States was in a position to do something about it.

At Johns Hopkins in April 1965 the president told the American people what he would do: "We will do everything necessary to reach that objective [of no external interference in South Vietnam], and we will do only what is absolutely necessary." But in order to prevent defeat and in order to keep the faith with his most loyal supporters, the minimum necessary became the functional equivalent of gradual escalation. The Air Force and the Commander in Chief, Pacific (CINCPAC) pressed hard for full systems bombing—the authority to destroy ninety-four key North Vietnamese targets in sixteen days. Johnson, backed and pressured in the other di-

*Sorenson, op. cit., p. 661.

rection by Secretary McNamara, doled out approval for new
targets over three years in a painstaking and piecemeal fashion. Johnson accommodated dovish pressure and the advice
of the many pragmatists who surrounded him by making
peace overtures. But these overtures were either accompanied with or followed by escalation. Johnson moved toward
those who wanted three-quarters of a million U.S. fighting
men in Vietnam, but he never got there. Guided by judgments
of domestic repercussion and influenced again by
McNamara, the president made at least eight separate
decisions on U.S. force levels in Vietnam over a four-year
period.* For the "fixers," who felt that U.S. conduct of the
war missed its political essence, and for the doves, who
wanted to see something besides destruction, Johnson
placed new emphasis on "the other war"—pacificiation, nation building, and political development—in February 1966.
Johnson referred to this whole complex of actions, and the
air war in particular, as his attempt to "seduce not rape" the
North Vietnamese.

The objective of the Johnson administration was to maintain
an independent non-Communist South Vietnam. In the later
years, this was rephrased as "allowing the South Vietnamese
to determine their own future without external interference."
As the president crossed the old barriers in pursuit of this
objective, he established new ones. While he ordered the
bombing of North Vietnam, he would not approve the bombing of targets that ran the risk of confrontation with China
and the Soviet Union. While he permitted the U.S. force level
in Vietnam to go over one-half million men, he would not
agree to call up the Reserves. While he was willing to spend
$25 billion in one year on the war, he would not put the U.S.
economy on a wartime mobilization footing. But the most
important Johnson barrier was raised against invading Cambodia, Laos, and North Vietnam. This limitation was also a
cornerstone in the president's hopes for a compromise settlement. He would agree to the permanent existence of North
Vietnam—even help that country economically—if North
Vietnam would extend that same right to South Vietnam.

In order to sustain public and bureaucratic support for his policy, Johnson's method was to browbeat and isolate his op-

---

*See the Chronology in U.S. Senate Foreign Relations Committee, *Back-
ground Information Relating to Southeast Asia and Vietnam*, March 1969.

ponents. To the American people he painted the alternatives to what he was doing as irresponsible or reckless. In either case the result would be a greater risk of future general war. The bureaucracy used this same technique of creating the bug-out or bomb-out extremes in order to maintain its own members in "the middle road." The price of consensus— within the bureaucracy and in the public at large—was invariably a middle road of contradictions and no priorities for action.

President Johnson was the master of consensus. On Vietnam this required melding the proponents of negotiations with the proponents of military victory. The technique for maintaining this Vietnam consensus was gradual escalation punctuated by dramatic peace overtures. As the war was escalated without an end in sight, the numbers of people Johnson could hold together diminished. The pressures for disengagement or for "decisive military action" became enormous, but with the "hawks" always outnumbering—and more strategically placed than—the "doves."

Johnson knew he had inherited a deteriorating situation in Vietnam. Vietcong military successes and constant change in the Saigon government from 1964 to 1966 were not secrets to anyone. Throughout the critical year of 1965 he struck the themes of endurance and more-to-come. In his May 4, 1965 requests for Vietnam supplemental appropriations he warned: "I see no choice but to continue the course we are on, filled as it is with peril and uncertainty." In his July 28, 1965 press conference he announced a new 125 thousand troop ceiling. Moreover, the president then went on to say: "Additional forces will be needed later, and they will be sent as requested."

Talk about "turning corners" and winning a military victory reached a crescendo in 1967. At the same time a new counter-point emerged—"stalemate."* The message of the stalemate proponents was that the U.S. was strong enough to prevent defeat, but that the situation defied victory. Hanoi would continue to match the U.S. force buildup and would not "cry uncle" over the bombing. The Saigon government and army had basic political and structural problems that they were

---

*R. W. Apple, "Vietnam: The Signs of Stalemate," *The New York Times,* August 7, 1967.

unlikely to be able to overcome. Stalemate, it was urged, should be used as a basis for getting a compromise settlement with Hanoi.

These arguments were not lost on the president. At Guam, in March 1967, while others around him were waxing eloquent about progress, the president was guardedly optimistic, speaking of "a favorable turning point, militarily and politically." But after one of the meetings he was reported to have said: "We have a difficult, a serious, long-drawn-out, agonizing problem that we do not have an answer for."* Nor did the president overlook the effects of the 1968 Tet offensive, coming as it did after many months of virtually unqualified optimism by him and by others. He stopped the bombing partially, increased troop strength slightly, made a peace overture, and announced his retirement.

In November 1963 Johnson is quoted as saying: "I am not going to be the President who saw Southeast Asia go the way China went."** In the spring of 1965 Lady Bird Johnson quoted him as saying: "I can't get out. I can't finish it with what I have got. So what the Hell can I do?"† President Johnson, like his predecessors, persevered and handed the war on to his successor.

8.   Where Do We Go from Here?

If Vietnam were a story of how the system failed, that is, if our leaders did not do what they wanted to do or if they did not realize what they were doing or what was happening, it would be easy to package a large and assorted box of policy-making panaceas. For example: fix the method of reporting from the field; fix the way progress is measured in guerrilla war; make sure the president sees all the real alternatives. But these are all third-order issues, because it is not true that the U.S. political-bureaucratic system failed. It worked.

Our leaders felt they had to prevent the loss of Vietnam to Communism, and they have succeeded so far in doing just

*Quoted in Henry Brandon, *Anatomy of Error* (Boston: Gambit, 1969), p. 102.

**Tom Wicker, *JFK and LBJ* (New York: Penguin Books, 1968), p. 208.

†Lady Bird Johnson, *A White House Diary* (New York: Holt, Rinehart and Winston, 1970), p. 248.

that. Most of those who made Vietnam policy still believe that they did the right thing and lament only the domestic repercussions of their actions. It is because the price of attaining this goal has been so dear in lives, trust, dollars, and priorities, and the benefits so intangible, remote, and often implausible, that these leaders and we ourselves are forced to seek new answers and new policies.

Paradoxically, the way to get these new answers is not by asking why did the system fail, but why did it work so tragically well. There is, then, only one first-order issue: how and why does our political-bureaucratic system decide what is vital and what is not? By whom, in what manner, and for what reasons was it decided that all Vietnam must not fall into Communist hands?

Almost all of our leaders since 1949 shared this conviction. Only a few voices in the wilderness were raised in opposition. Even as late as mid-1967 most critics were arguing that the U.S. could not afford to lose or be "driven from the field," that the real problem was our bombing of North Vietnam, and that this had to be stopped in order to bring about a negotiated settlement. Fewer still were urging that such a settlement should involve a coalition government with the Communists. Hardly anyone was saying that the outcome in Vietnam did not matter.

There is little evidence of much critical thinking about the relation of Vietnam to U.S. security. Scholars, journalists, politicians, and bureaucrats all seem to have assumed either that Vietnam was "vital" to U.S. national security or that the American people would not stand for the loss of "another" country to Communism.

Anti-Communism has been and still is a potent force in American politics, and most people who were dealing with the Vietnam problem simply believed that the Congress and the public would "punish" those who were "soft on Communism." Our leaders not only anticipated this kind of public reaction, but believed that there were valid reasons for not permitting the Communists to take all of Vietnam by force. In other words, they believed in what they were doing on national security "merits." The domino theory, which was at the heart of the matter, rested on the widely shared attitude that security was indivisible, that weakness in one place would only invite aggression in others.

What can be done?

The president can do more than presidents have in the past to call his national security bureaucracy to task. He can show the bureaucracy that he expects it to be more rigorous in determining what is vital or important or unimportant. Specifically, he can reject reasoning that simply asserts that security is indivisible, and he can foster the belief that while the world is an interconnected whole, actions can be taken in certain parts of the world to compensate for actions that are not taken elsewhere. For example, if the real concern about Vietnam were the effect of its loss on Japan, the Middle East, and Berlin, could we not take actions in each of these places to mitigate the "Vietnam fallout"?

None of these efforts with the bureaucracy can succeed, however, unless there is a change in general political attitudes as well. If anti-Communism persists as an overriding domestic political issue, it will also be the main bureaucratic issue. Altering public attitudes will take time, education, and political courage—and it will create a real dilemma for the president. If the president goes "too far" in reeducating public and congressional opinions about Communism, he may find that he will have little support for threatening or using military force when he believes that our security really is at stake. In the end it will still be the president who is held responsible for U.S. security. Yet, if our Vietnam experience has taught us anything, it is that the president must begin the process of reeducation, despite the risks.

THE PLAIN LESSONS OF A BAD DECADE
by John Kenneth Galbraith

The decade of the sixties, in the absence of a massively successful revisionist exercise, will be counted a very dismal
period in American foreign policy. Indeed, next only to the
cities, foreign policy will be considered the prime disaster
area of the American polity and it will be accorded much of
the blame for the misuse of energies and resources that
caused trouble in urban ghettos and alienation and eruption
in the universities. The result was very dim in contrast with
the promise.

The promise was bright—"Let the word go forth . . . to friend
and foe alike," President Kennedy said in his inaugural address, and no one doubted the power and not many the wisdom of the word. The prestige of foreign policy in 1961 was
enormous. No one much cared about who was to run the
Treasury. It mattered greatly who was to be the secretary, or
under secretary, or even an assistant secretary of state, although there were enough of the latter to form a small union.
In the early months of the new administration, numerous
quite marvelous ideas were spawned for strengthening or improving or revising our overseas affairs. There was to be an
expanded and reorganized aid program, a Grand Design for
Europe (subject to some uncertainty as to what that design
might be), the Alliance for Progress, the Kennedy Round, a
Multilateral Force, the Peace Corps, counterinsurgency, an
expanded recognition of the role of the new Africa, a dozen
other enterprises that did not achieve the dignity of a de-
cently notorious rejection.

Now, ten years later, one looks back on a seemingly uninterrupted series of disasters: the comic opera affair at the Bay
of Pigs, the invasion of the Dominican Republic to abort a
Communist revolution that had to be invented after the fact,
severe alienation throughout Latin America, broken win-
dows, burned libraries, and more or less virulent anti-Ameri-
canism elsewhere in the world—over everything else, the

"The Plain Lessons of a Bad Decade" was published originally in *Foreign
Policy*, Number 1, Winter 1970-71. It later appeared in *Economics, Peace,
and Laughter*. Copyright © 1971 by John Kenneth Galbraith. Reprinted by
permission of Houghton Mifflin Company.

brooding, frustrating, endlessly bloody, infinitely expensive, and now widely rejected involvement in Indochina.

So it seems in retrospect. And at least one of the successes of these years seems a good deal less compelling when one looks back on it. In the Cuban missile crisis President Kennedy had to balance the danger of blowing up the planet against the risk of political attack at home for appeasing the Communists. This was not an irresponsible choice: to ignore the domestic opposition was to risk losing initiative or office to men who wanted an even more dangerous policy. There is something more than a little wrong with a system that poses a choice between survival and domestic political compulsion. The missile crisis did not show the strength of our policy; it showed the catastrophic visions and the resulting pressures to which it was subject. We were in luck, but success in a lottery is no argument for lotteries.

2

Yet not everything in these years went wrong. Our relations with Western Europe and Japan caused no particular pain; these had been the theaters of ultimate misfortune in the twentieth century, always assuming war to be such. And, during the sixties, relations with the Communist countries improved both in vision and in reality.

When the decade began, the official vision of the Communist world was still that of a political monolith—the word was still much used—relentlessly bent on the destruction of what few were embarrased to call the Free World. If there were divisions within the Communist world, they were presumably on how best to pursue the revolution. Foreign policy vis-à-vis the Sino-Soviet bloc, as it was still called, was accordingly a facilitating instrument for a larger conflict. During his long tenure as secretary of state, Dean Rusk was criticized for his conviction that foreign policy was subordinate to military convenience. But if conflict with the Communist world was the great and inevitable fact, the Rusk view was at least consistent. Diplomacy, like truth, is an early casualty of war.

But that vision has now dissolved. True believers are still to be found in the more airless recesses of the Pentagon. Retired chairmen of the Joint Chiefs; Joseph Alsop, Kenneth Crawford, one or two other aging sages; cold war diplomats solemnly contemplating the world over their martinis in the

Metropolitan Club—all still evoke the Communist conspiracy
on which their fame and fortune were founded. They rejoice
in anything that seems to suggest a revival of the conflict;
they try to warn a generation that does not share their wisdom. But their audience dwindles; and amusement replaces
even nostalgia in what remains. The terrible fact obtrudes.
The Communist world is as relentlessly plural as the non-
Communist world; China and the Soviet Union are much farther from coordinated action than France and the United
States. On the record, too, the Communist powers are cautious—rather more cautious perhaps than the government of
the United States—about risking disaster in pursuit of an
idea. One must sympathize with those whose lives were
predicated on the theory of a more unified and heroic Communism. They might be called the walking wounded of the
cold war.

The cold war vision of Communism always owed much to
men whose place in the American pantheon and whose self-
confidence of outlook substantially exceeded their information. But there has also been change in the substance of
world affairs. When the decade began, the United States and
the USSR were each equipped with weapons capable, even at
the lowest levels of military expectation (then more sanguine
than now), of destroying each other and most of the world
between. At the end of the decade, each was capable of destroying the other from five to fifteen times over. The difference to a population already dead is not decisive. Mean-
time—and here one can speak with certainty only of the
United States—there has been a considerable accretion of
knowledge both about the insecurity inherent in the weapons
race and the unwisdom of leaving the contest under the control of the armed services and the affiliated weapons indus-
tries. It would be optimistic to suggest that this control has
yet been broken. But the emergence of the Pentagon and its
power as a political issue is one of the major developments of
the late sixties. It is something for which one could hardly
have hoped at the beginning of the decade.

Meanwhile, tension between the two superpowers has diminished in other respects. In the United States there is not
quite the same conviction of total economic and social success that there was in 1960—at the crest of the Keynesian
revolution. One senses similar doubts in the Soviet Union. In

our case, at least, self-doubt is a valuable antidote to evangelism—with its capacity both to offend and endanger. At the beginning of the decade, to accept coexistence with world Communism suggested a slightly defective moral stance. Among the custodians of the then current foreign policy cliché, gathering for the ritual discussion at the Council on Foreign Relations, a suggestion along such lines induced a raised eyebrow. Perhaps Khrushchev was coming through a bit too well. That existence and coexistence are identical, few now doubt. That the great industrial societies have common requirements in planning, industrial discipline and organization, and common disasters in environmental effects is at least being discussed. Richard Nixon in the fifties spoke the lines of a militant cold warrior; it was on this theme and its domestic repercussions that he founded his political career. John F. Kennedy was at least moderately in the opposition camp. Yet enough has changed in the last ten years so that Nixon's expressions as president on the Communist menace are both fewer and more pacific than were those of Kennedy. No one will argue, where Mr. Nixon is concerned, that he is responding to anything so simple as a change in conviction.

Difficult problems remain between the United States and the Soviet Union. No bilateral relationship that depends on or is associated with capacity for reciprocal destruction can be regarded with equanimity—or considered stable. Circumstances and politics have given us different and relentlessly hostile friends and clients in the Middle East—a problem area that I am deliberately passing over in this article. Still, the larger fact remains. It was not our relations with the Soviet Union that made our foreign policy in the sixties the mess that we have come, not incorrectly, to consider it.

3

The disaster area of our foreign policy has been in what the knowing unite in calling the Third World. It was here—in Cuba, the Dominican Republic, in minor degree in the Conyo, and most of all in Indochina—that the mistakes were made or the disasters occurred. Had it not been for the policy in these parts of the world, Lyndon Johnson would have remained president of the United States, the wishes of his wife notwithstanding, and Dean Rusk would have continued as secretary of state or, at a minimum, found honorable retirement as president of a college well on the Establishment side of the Mason-Dixon Line. The Third World has been their and our foreign policy trap. On the visible evidence, this has been true also of the Soviet Union. If anyone from the Soviet foreign office has recently been assigned to Ulan Bator, it has not been for his handling of relations with France, Germany, Britain, or the United States. Indonesia, North Korea, and, above all, China were where Soviet policy went off the rails. Again the Third World.

Foreign policy is a gentlemanly profession that sets much store by tradition and continuity, even in error. Far better, one knows, to continue error than to lower the prestige of a great nation (or its servants) by changing course and thus confessing the mistake. Accordingly, introspection, and even thought, are held in low esteem in the diplomatic estate. However, even brief reflection on the recent history of our relations with the Third World suggests that we have made policy on the basis of a startling succession of wrong assumptions. That this is so will even be conceded. The assumptions being wrong, the results caused deep trouble. What remains to be recognized is that a shift in assumptions, from wrong to right, would produce better results. Such recognition does not come easily, as I shall presently argue. A bureaucracy defends, even with righteousness, the wrong assumptions if they are the ones on which it is operating. But first let me list what we have learned from dealing with the Third World in the last decade. Four lessons seem clear:

1. We have learned, first of all, the limits on our power in this part of the world. Following World War II, in Western Europe we developed a Marshall Plan syndrome. This view held that the United States could always work wonders in other countries. Our capital, our energy, our economic system, our idealism, our business statesmen, our special standing with a benign God, all combined to produce such capacity. It seemed so in Europe after World War II. There, economic organization or the capacity for such organization, industrial skills, technical competence, highly developed public administration and services already existed. The only missing ingredients were capital and people with the special blessings of Providence. When these were supplied by the United States, the miracle predictably followed.

Elsewhere, we have now learned in the hardest of schools, things are different. Where the preexisting European ingredients of success are missing, the power to work miracles is, not surprisingly, nonexistent. Governments can be influenced, but where governments are weak and their power negligible, the power implicit in so influencing them is also predictably negligible. Where organizational, administrative, and technical capacity and skills are lacking—where, in short, there is no industrial base or experience—the economy does not respond to an infusion of capital. For capital is not the missing ingredient. In the colonial era, European powers had a substantial influence on the inner life and development of the Third World countries. This they obtained by *creating* a structure for colonial administration, and having done so, they did not influence, they governed. Given this public framework, industrial, railroad, and modern agricultural development could be induced in reasonably predictable fashion if policy so prescribed. Such a solution is no longer allowed. Thus it has come about that the superpower that seeks to intervene in the Third World remains the victim of the organizational, administrative, and technical vacuum that, after all, is what tends most to distinguish this World.

2. The next lesson that we have learned, or more precisely are relearning, is that Communism and capitalism are concepts of practical significance only at an advanced stage in industrial development. In poor rural societies they have only a rhetorical relevance. Capitalism is not an issue in a country that has yet to experience capitalism, and neither is Communism as an alternative. The Third World consists by definition of poor rural societies—that is what undeveloped or underdeveloped countries are. It follows that whether such countries call themselves free, free enterprise, capitalist, socialist, or Communist has, at the lowest levels of development, only terminological significance. They are poor and rural, however they describe themselves. For the appreciable future, they will so remain. Even by the crudest power calculus, military or economic, such nations have no vital relation to the economic or strategic position of the developed countries. They do supply raw materials. But even here the typical observation concerns not their power as sources of such supply but their weakness as competitive hewers of wood in the markets of the industrially advanced countries.

It is hard to see now why so much tension developed in the fifties and early sixties over whether such countries would follow the Communist or non-Communist pattern of development. That alternatives to capitalism only become interesting after there is capitalism (and associated industrialization) was eloquently affirmed by Marx more than a century ago. That capitalism is only an issue if there is capitalism is a proposition not, in its essentials, difficult to grasp. In part, no doubt, our error was the result of a fantastic overestimate (as it now seems) of the speed of economic development in the Third World: Latin American, African, and Asian countries would soon be industrialized; therewith they would become military powers. To global strategists, a relentlessly amateur calling which the United States nurtured in alarming numbers after World War II, it seemed important, accordingly, that ideological affiliation be not with Moscow but with Washington and lower Manhattan. We now know—a few special cases such as Formosa and Israel apart—that the process of development is infinitely slow, that the ultimate organization of these societies is far too academic a question to influence the policymaking even of the most passionate ideologue. By the time India, sub-Sahara Africa, and most of Central or South America are industrialized to anything approaching present Western European levels, even greater changes will have occurred in the United States and the Soviet Union.

But it is a mistake to look for complex reasons for the error when simpler ones avail. American foreign policy in the fifties and sixties was made by men to whom a difference between capitalism and Communism was the only social truth to which they had access. That the difference is one thing in Europe or the United States and something very different in the Congo, Vietnam, even Cuba, was well beyond their reach. Often there was even a measure of pride—tough-mindedness it was called—in rejecting such complications.

3. Next, we have learned that although the inner life and development of the Third World is beyond the reach of the power of a superpower, and equally beyond its visible self-concern, the effort to influence that development brings into being a very large civilian and military bureaucracy. Colonial power was exercised rather simply through a line of

command that, in general, gave orders. Working indirectly by way of the hearts and minds of a people requires a much more massive table of organization. This is partly because such influence is disappointing in effect, and the normal bureaucratic answer to frustration and noneffect is to get more money and more men and build a bigger organization. Military missions, military advisers, active military formations in the more tragic instances, counterinsurgency teams, pacification teams, technical assistance teams, advisers on aid utilization, auditors and inspectors and other instruments against indigenous larceny, information officers, intelligence officers, spooks—the list extends indefinitely. Where, as in Vietnam and Laos, the frustration has been nearly total, the bureaucratic input has been all but infinite. But elsewhere as well, in Asia and Latin America and in lesser degree in Africa, the sixties saw the deployment of a huge American military, counterinsurgency, intelligence, diplomatic, public information, and aid establishment designed to influence potentially erring governments and people away from Communism.

4. Next, we have learned that an overseas bureaucracy, once in existence, develops a life and purpose of its own. Control by Washington is exiguous. Control by the Congress is for practical purposes nonexistent.

This is partly because of the nature of its task. A government that is being seduced by a superpower wishes, at a minimum, to have the deed done in private. So also a foreign politician. Decency has its claims. Surveillance of Communists, or more active military operations to put down subversion, also requires public reticence. It is axiomatic that in such matters one does not show one's hand to the enemy. Secrecy is also occasioned by the intrinsically high failure rate in these operations. Much of the work of our intelligence and military missions abroad is only possible because no one is aware of how little is obtained for the outlay involved. But secrecy is not the only protection from public scrutiny. The sheer number and variety of such overseas operations in all their different national settings, coupled with the revolving-door nature of higher Washington officialdom, also foster anonymity. Few men in the executive branch remain in office long enough to have knowledge of the affairs of which, nominally, they are in charge. Legislators who must rely on such men for knowledge have even less. This autonomy is combined, in turn, with the tendency for any bureaucracy, military or civilian, in the absence of the strongest of leadership, to continue to do whatever it is doing. This is a matter of the highest importance, one that explains the most basic tendencies of our foreign policy. It calls for special attention.

4

The tendency of bureaucracy to find purpose in whatever it is doing is superbly revealed by the experience of the past decade in Vietnam. Without exception, every reason originally offered for our intervention there has dissolved. Some have now become ludicrous. This is not the parochial view of an opponent of the war; not even the defenders of the conflict affirm the original reasons for the venture. None now say, though it was doctrine in the early sixties, that our action in Vietnam was in response to a probe deliberately directed from Moscow against a weak point on the perimeter and to be resisted, accordingly, as a matter of global strategy. That the NLF carries the banners of Vietnamese nationalism is now generally (if not quite universally) accepted. Once it was asserted that vital American strategic interests were involved— that, quite literally, if we did not fight in the jungles of Vietnam we would soon be assaulted in the Philippines or even on the beaches of Hawaii. Now that contention is offered only as an exercise in irony. Once it was held we were saving the fledgling democracy of General Thieu and Marshal Ky. An election was cited in support of the pretense. This vision, too, has become comic. In the late summer of 1970 much energy was expended on keeping Marshall Ky from coming to Washington for a political rally lest he remind Americans of the repressive, obscene, and incompetent dictatorship with which they have been aligned. Once there were the dominoes. Now to cite the domino doctrine is to remind people that it was the war itself that tumbled the first domino (or most of it) in Cambodia. Once it was held in its defense that, purpose aside, the war could readily be resolved by military means. Now the suggestion that the Pentagon was pursuing the chimera of military victory in Vietnam provokes an indignant denial. Once it was a defense of the war that it was a marginal exercise that the American economy could take in stride. That guns could be had with butter was the not excessively novel formulation. Now it is sound doctrine that the war caused the inflation of the latter sixties that still frustrates good economic management. And its conflict with sensible priority in resources use has become a cliché.

It is impossible to think of a case more intellectually inert than that for the Vietnam war. The bureaucracy, however, the military and intelligence bureaucracy in particular, operates not in response to national need but in response to its own need. The national need can dissolve and become ludicrous as in the case of Vietnam. But this does not affect the need of an army for the occupation, prestige, promotions that go with active military operations, or the need of the CIA for the interest, personal drama, excitement, and outlet for money that go with its Laotian adventures, or the need of the Air Force for bombing as a raison d'être. Since Korea we have been learning and relearning the lesson that strategic air power is ineffective against primitive agriculture or men moving at night along jungle roads. This has had little effect on Air Force doctrine, for it happens not to be what the Air Force needs to believe.

But it would be a mistake to picture bureaucratic need in terms of a too specific bureaucratic self-interest. A more important factor is pure organizational momentum. Bureaucracy can always continue to do what it is doing. It is incapable, on its own, of a drastic change of course. And the process by which it ensures its continuity—in the case of the Pentagon by which it prepares budgets, persuades the Office of Management and Budget, instructs its congressional sycophants—is itself highly organized. Thus the momentum. So it came about that after all national purpose in Vietnam had dissolved, and this was extensively conceded, bureaucratic purpose and momentum still served. The change in direction that is involved in stopping military operations, bureaucracy cannot accomplish. Dozens of other activities—military support to Latin American countries, staff services to SEATO and CENTO, bases in Spain, the radar watch in the Arctic, ABM, nuclear carriers, any number of cold war intelligence and countersubversive activities—owe much or all of their existence to the same momentum. Innocents imagine that when they have shown that purpose has evaporated, function will end. It is not so. Purpose is among the least of bureaucratic needs.

5

I do not, of course, suggest that a military and foreign policy bureaucracy, once launched on course, can never be diverted. The sixties were particularly favorable to its exercise of inertial power. The prestige of the military and foreign policy establishment, following the successes of World War II and the Marshall Plan, was high—far higher than now. The cold war panic led to a large delegation of power over the fearsome technology and clandestine maneuvering that seemed the only answer to the Communist menace. And this was the age of the Establishment in foreign policy—of the New York and Washington *genro* which had come to prominence in World War II, under the Marshall Plan, in the German occupation, and under John Foster Dulles. Although the impression was to the contrary, these statesmen had given little independent thought to foreign policy—it was their natural assumption that given their experience and high position in the community, they already knew. In consequence, men such as Dean Rusk as secretary of state, Allen Dulles and John McCone as heads of CIA, John J. McCloy and Dean Acheson as advisers at large were strongly and even uniquely compliant with the bureaucratic view. It added to their confidence and resulting acquiescence that the bureaucratic case was always couched in the resonant cold war platitudes which, as experienced men, they associated with sound policy. In the Johnson years it helped also to have a president who, though not lacking in either intelligence or will, was least experienced in the field of foreign policy and (from his congressional experience) had also a habit of acquiescence on military matters. But the inertial dynamic of the bureaucracy is the major explanation of the disasters of the decade. At the Bay of Pigs, in the Dominican Republic, in Vietnam, Laos, Thailand (as again in Cambodia), the bureaucracy showed its power to sweep the leadership into disaster and against all the counsels of common sense.

6

The lessons of the sixties, as regards foreign policy, are then both specific and self-reinforcing. What remains, as noted, is to act on them. The area where our course most needs correction is not Western Europe or Japan. Doubtless there are improvements to be made in both places, but the past has not been intolerable. Relations with the Soviet Union, including the indirect encounters in the Middle East and Germany, include a terrible component of latent risk. But it was not here in the last decade that we stumbled.

We stumbled in the Third World. In this World we cannot intervene, need not intervene, and we have intervened. The effort has required a large bureaucracy, military and civilian. This by its nature cannot be controlled. Acting where action is both impossible of effect and unnecessary, it has produced disaster. Given the nature of bureaucracy, there is great persistence in disaster. None of this, given the underlying circumstances, is altogether surprising.

The remedial action is also clear. It is greatly and promptly to contract our policy in Latin America, Africa, and Asia. This means specifically that we no longer stand guard against what is called Communism in this part of the world. It means that we no longer distinguish between governments that we like and those of which we disapprove. It means even more specifically that over the generality of Latin America, Africa, and Asia, military missions are withdrawn and military aid comes to an end. So also in all three continents do counterinsurgency, countersubversive, and intelligence operations. Remaining bases related to the defense of these areas are given up. It means that henceforth the raison d'être of aid and information programs is to assist economic development and inform countries as regards the United States; not to fight Communism. (I set very great and particular store by the continuing importance of foreign aid.) It means that in these countries we will return to orthodox diplomatic relations and the assistance in capital, technique, or volunteer manpower that an economically and technically advanced country finds it morally rewarding or economically advantageous to render to its less equipped neighbors. Not distinguishing between good and bad governments, we recognize all. We also trade with all. Our commercial relations, it is worth noting, will thus be freed from the incubus of suspicion that they reflect some larger imperial ambition.

Foreign policy, especially of the more belligerent sort, is regularly formulated with a view to rejoicing its author and audience with its therapeutic simplicity. But that is not my present intention. This is what must be done. It follows that, although the broad rule of nonintervention and nonpresence applies to all of the Third World, differing history will dictate a differing time schedule. Withdrawal from the Philippines and Korea will have to be negotiated. In the case of Korea withdrawal could be very slow. The SEATO treaty need not be denounced; it is sufficient that the Asian members know that it is being allowed to wither on the vine.

7

The strength of the nations of the Third World, in relation to the superpowers, lies in the absence of levers by which they can be controlled and the absence of power at the end of the levers. Without public administration there can be no control; there is no industrial society to be controlled. This accords immunity equally to effective intervention by the Communist powers and by the United States. Although one guesses that the Soviets have seen the impracticality of socialism without previous preparation, one cannot guarantee that such intervention will not be attempted. One can only be certain that Soviet and Chinese efforts to dominate these countries will encounter the same obdurate circumstances as have we. They will end, accordingly, in frustration not different from that of the United States in Vietnam or their own experience in Indonesia.

The course here urged does not mean that all will be well in the Third World. This World has no monopoly on peaceful behavior, occasional doctrine to the contrary notwithstanding. The possibility of struggle within and between nations and peoples remains. American withdrawal does not ensure good international behavior. Nor will it ensure greater reliance on collective reaction to attacks by one country on another, although that might be hoped. It accepts only the lesson of the last decade, which is that our intervention does us no good and, for the people involved, can make everything much worse.

Considerable movement along these lines has been implicit—though with an inconsistent commitment to earlier cold war rhetoric—in the so-called Nixon Doctrine. This is much to be welcomed. But it will now be clear that what is here proposed is no mere matter of announcing a change in policy. The present policy sustains and empowers a large bureaucracy that reacts to its own needs. The needed policy disestablishes this bureaucracy—indeed, one of the constraints on foreign policy in the future is that it must be of a nature that it is subject to political, as distinct from bureaucratic, control. (We cannot guide affairs in Laos; we do not need to do so; and we cannot, in any case, have a policy that requires that much delegation to the CIA.) None will doubt the extent of the exercise of presidential and other political authority that will be needed. It is not easy to associate the prospect with the passive tendencies of President Nixon. The proper policy toward the Third World requires not only new doctrine but also elimination of the need for a large part of the military, intelligence, and civilian bureaucracy that conducts the present policy. The survival of that bureaucracy depends on making policy on the wrong assumptions. It would be naive to imagine that these organizations will acquiesce easily in the change, however effectively they are proved in error and however ghastly the resulting experience. Not wickedness but the dynamics of big organization is involved. It is a far greater factor in our foreign policy than we have even begun to realize.

A STRANGE DEATH
FOR LIBERAL AMERICA?

by George Armstrong Kelly

In *A Room of One's Own* (1928) Virginia Woolf flits with a butterfly's vagrancy over the sere autumnal flowers of the Victorian garden—rebaptizing that lost time of song and passion. Why do the words not come through sweet and straight, laden with unambiguous love, as before? "Why," Virginia Woolf inquires,

has Alfred [Lord Tennyson] ceased to sing—
"She is coming, my dove, my dear"?
Why has Christina [Rossetti] ceased to respond—
"My heart is gladder than all these
Because my love is come to me"?
Shall we lay the blame on the war? When the guns fired in August 1914, did the faces of men and women show as plain in each other's eyes that romance was killed? . . . But why say "blame"? Why, if it was an illusion, not praise the catastrophe, whatever it was, that destroyed illusion and put truth in its place?

The music of Tennyson and Rossetti, Mrs. Woolf declares, hums itself in the ear—especially at luncheon parties. But you cannot remember two lines in a row from the best of the modern poets. They offer "a feeling that is actually being made and torn out of us," not a pleasure that can familiarly unfold. Why this abrupt dissonance, this terrible new disquietude? Was the loss of innocence also the dreadful collective tremor of mortality?

If English romance died beneath the guns of the Somme, its American version has been riddled along the road leading from Hiroshima to Cochinchina. Not that we ever romanced according to the manners of the British: no garden-party warblings for us, not in the New Jerusalem of Parrington or the "culture of flight" of Louis Hartz. To paraphrase Edward Shils, the English style has its privacy; ours has veered wildly between secrecy and publicity. It was predictable that the destruction of the American romance would be a bonesplitting affair.

Whatever metaphors Virginia Woolf may have used, it is not strictly true that the old Britain died in the trenches. In poli-

"A Strange Death for Liberal America?" was published originally in *Foreign Policy*, Number 6, Spring 1972.

tics it is obscure when anything dies (short of Carthage), though in both politics and pathology there are usually gathering symptoms of fatal disorder. Of these, England had at least three, going back into the final years of Victoria's reign. One was the advancing incapacity of British manufactures to compete with those of Germany and the United States in the free-market world, which led to a more aggressive foreign policy in the colonial areas.

A second was the incapacity of the traditional political style and party system of Britain to appease, represent, or keep pace with newly mobilized interests contained, for better or for worse, within the national structure. The burden of interaction between party leaderships and their increasingly unwieldy clienteles fell, for reasons presently to be canvassed, upon the Liberal party after its return to power in 1905. Following some brisk reformism, the Liberals ran up against a stone wall: the intransigence of the Tory-dominated House of Lords, and a dependence on the Irish Nationalists for their Commons majority. Little did the triumphant Liberals suspect that within a generation their party, riven by faction and misfortune, would abandon all expectation of governing the country! According to George Dangerfield's piquant book *The Strange Death of Liberal England*, "Beauty and Certainty and Quiet" died, not just with Rupert Brooke in the Aegean, but in those preceding years, when cretinous peers, manic suffragettes, rampant miners, and romantic Irish all conspired to kill the old order.

Dangerfield's thesis is probably as incomplete as Mrs. Woolf's, not simply because it makes short shrift of imperialism and foreign policy, but because (for chronological reasons) it ignores that central episode when the British ceased to be Gladstonian missionaries and Wellingtonian giant-killers, but became instead, in the words of the aging German historian Mommsen, "the performers of the hangman's office on the latter-day disciples of William Tell." [The third symptom of fatal disorder in England,] the Boer War of 1899-1902, qualifies as the British war in Vietnam, as C. L. Sulzberger pointed out recently. To pursue his words: "The cruel Boer War ruined the British reputation for international morality, lost the respect of foreign friends for a considerable period, and stirred up a hornet's nest of political opposition at home." Critics of this war, though by no means as strident and organized as our domestic opponents of Vietnam, were fond of stressing the fact that Britain and her loyal colonies brought to the struggle a population ratio of 50 million to 195 thousand. And for all the Englanders propagandized to believe that the Boers were, in the caustic words of the *Manchester Guardian*, "'hounds,' 'semi-savages,' 'cowards,' and 'utterly without honor,' who ought to be 'exterminated' and treated like plague-infected rats," there were more than a few who accepted the judgment of the Battersea M.P. John Burns that the Boers were "fighting under the greatest stimulus men can ever have—a deep religious motive, a patriotic impulse, and a love of liberty." "Gooks"—or "valiant peasants and workers"?

It is true that England survived the Boer War crisis (which lasted only three years) in tolerable shape. The final Liberal settlement of the war was so judicious that it gave to the white Afrikaaners an eventual political victory that all liberals of the present time deplore. The home-front wounds in England healed before new tests of moral and constitutional strength arose. Vicious and troubling as it was, the Boer War passed and could be, in some sense, redeemed by the prudent generosity of the Great Power toward the Afrikaaners. The Vietnam war [was long] upon us, with no "liberal" ending in sight. It [was] mixed up with all sorts of other problems that, with decent allowance for the time lag, make the "death of liberal England" and the incipient "death of liberal America" look more than casually alike. Can we not say that historical resemblance works on a large canvas, using sweeping brush strokes? Actually, the American situation looks the reverse of the British: beginning in a general war of unprecedented involvement (which seemed for a time to stamp the national destiny), it has proceeded backwards to the kind of condition in which the waning of English primacy started. The "American century" has been greatly foreshortened. But what we know empirically is that America perceived itself as taking over the British mission by stages, before and after World War II, with an equivalence of ideologies that fairly match the work of Gladstone and Salisbury to that of Wilson, Roosevelt, and Truman. The hypothesis is strong enough to be explored.

Does this mean an elaborate fitting of role to role? Shall Lyndon Johnson be Joseph Chamberlain? Lord Kitchener,

General Eisenhower? Is the "Eastern Establishment" the "Manchester Caucus"? Or is it "The City"? Is Sir Edward Carson, George Wallace? Is Stokely Carmichael, John Redmond? Is "Oom Paul" Kruger, Ho Chi Minh? Is Cecil Rhodes, the General Motors Corporation? How do the Humphreys and Muskies match up with the Harcourts and Bryces? Is Kate Millett, Emmeline Pankhurst? Where is labor (now)? Where were the young (then)? The comparisons are, to say the least, unlikely, but not so far outside mood and history as to be preposterous.

For a long while it was fashionable to analyze and polemicize the American crisis in terms of the "last pregnant example." For some this was Korea (in which Dean Rusk had been closely involved); for others it was Munich (how cheerful to think that America had produced neither a Chamberlain nor a Daladier!); for still others it was the Spanish Civil War of 1936-39 (which could be regarded as unconscionable foreign interference in a domestic struggle or blatant interference *on the wrong side*!).

Almost concurrently, some observers saw that the United States was assisting, then almost singlehandedly fighting, in a war that had belonged to the French in its earlier stages. If Vietnam was not exactly the same war at the same time, there could be no denying that it was in the same place, that the enemy was virtually the same and concentrated in more or less the same zones of the South, and that the ideological stakes were similar. And since the French had fought another war against nationalists in Algeria (in part according to principles taken from Vietnam), it became plausible to use both experiences in creating a model of "revolutionary war" in which large numbers of Americans were engaged. There was much reason in this exercise. General de Gaulle, fresh from his closing of the Algerian wound and long confirmed in the lessons of Southeast Asia, is purported to have warned President Kennedy away from military commitment in Indochina. Stanley Hoffmann has brilliantly summarized the true and false parallels between America's problem of extrication from Vietnam and de Gaulle's policies vis-à-vis the Algerian war in 1958-62.*

*Stanley Hoffmann, "Vietnam: An Algerian Solution," *Foreign Policy*, Number 2, Spring 1971.

President Nixon and his decision makers appear to have come to power in 1969 resolved to follow, flexibly, a "Gaullist" policy in Vietnam. The maxim was one of Machiavelli's favorites: if you cannot create policy for yourself, imitate the most creative example you can find. Nixon apparently intended to withdraw America from Vietnam, as de Gaulle had extricated France from Algeria, beneath the coverlet of a right-wing majority, and with whatever allies of convenience he could muster. But in the long run, Nixon did not or could not play at "Algeria." He moved into the "positions of strength" trap of the Cambodian excursion—not, perhaps, the American Dienbienphu, but possibly its functional equivalent. Hoffmann shows us conclusively why the scheme of the Algerian withdrawal is a frail parallel to lean on in Vietnam. But, more importantly, under the prodding of the military and the "Vietnam hands," Algeria ceased to be a model at all for the Nixon administration after Cambodia. There was soon no hypothetical referent, but only a model of the government's own making, which changed its outlines week by week.

For America, outpourings of knowledge—too little and late—about the zone of action where we were ravished of our "innocence" (if B-52s are innocent) must seem ingenuous. Nor can we attain final wisdom by studying the successes or failings of a power the global impact of which has not approached our own in the past generation. If history has anything to teach, our analytical bench mark should be the experience of another great power, troubled at home by social unrest and receding from the outermost limits of its foreign influence. If possible, it should be a great power close to us in culture and values. This is why I must return to the Boer War, the retrenchment of empire, the "strange death of liberal England," the guns of the Somme, and the stilling of the sweet tremolos of Alfred and Christina.

2

On March 1, 1894 the great Liberal W. E. Gladstone, then in his eighties, held his last cabinet meeting. Gladstone had steered the British vessel through stormy but prosperous seas, widened the electorate by parliamentary act, and left behind him a political legacy of "reform, retrenchment, and progress," tinctured with an ambiguous idealism in foreign policy and a subtle blend of Whiggishness and Radicalism in home affairs. What remained to the Liberals after Gladstone was a modestly gifted but cackling cohort of lesser personalities, divided roughly into nonconformist free-trade Radicals, great-magnate Whigs (verging on "Liberal imperialism"), and the Gladstonian middle. Only a year later, the Conservatives, led by the third Marquess of Salisbury, defeated the Liberals in the general election of 1895; Salisbury and his relative, Arthur Balfour, retained power until 1905.

The majority strength of the Conservative party in England was guaranteed by Joseph Chamberlain's Liberal Unionists. Chamberlain had begun his career as the Radical Mayor of Birmingham, but in time he turned himself into an efficient instrument of high British imperialism which, after 1895, he sustained from his key post as Minister of Colonies.

By 1895, the acme of imperialism was South Africa. The discovery of gold in 1886 in the southern Transvaal, that small and prim Boer state led by Paul Kruger, had launched an avalanche of freebooting entrepreneurs—American, British, German, Jewish, called collectively "Uitlanders" (outsiders) by the locals. These newcomers, with the power of development capital behind them, began to place irresistible pressure for commercial and political rights on the pastoral and Calvinist Boers. When British adventurers, apparently inspired by capitalist interests in Capetown and Johannesburg, launched the Jameson Raid on the Transvaal in 1895, the two Boer republics went into the European market for modern arms and concluded a defensive alliance with each other.

Chamberlain was accused of political involvement in the Jameson Raid, but a parliamentary inquiry exonerated him. This clearance could not have been managed without considerable Liberal complicity, since Chamberlain consistently refused to disclose any of the documents on the Jameson Raid. (Shades of the 1964 Tonkin Gulf Resolution?) The cogent Chancellor Bismarck had already predicted that South Africa would one day be the grave of the British Empire. A tactical but prophetic Chamberlain had in 1896 declared that "a war in South Africa would be one of the most serious wars that could possibly be waged . . . and would leave behind it the embers of a strife which I believe generations would hardly be long enough to extinguish." Cecil Rhodes, however, insisted that the Boers were only bluffing and would never fight. His judgment tended to prevail in Westminster, until the Boers made a precautionary attack on the British garrisons in Natal province in October 1899.

The word "escalation" had not yet been invented. But in June 1899 the British forces in South Africa numbered 10,000, and by 1901, according to official figures, 292,762 British troops had fought in South Africa, of whom 56,958 had been rendered *hors de combat.* It was not a glamorous war. One Tommy is quoted as telling another: "If I owned hell and South Africa, I'd live in hell and rent out South Africa." Comparable numbers and sentiments are not unfamiliar to us today. There are even parallels in the military circumstances. Though the war's first half was colonial-conventional, its second half was revolutionary-guerrilla, and the British retaliated by creating the concentration camp, building strategic blockhouses, and stringing about five-thousand miles of barbed wire over the veldt. When the Boers were at length compelled to surrender to the superior power in 1902, they were quite aware of the damage that had been inflicted on its reputation.

For a long time the Boers had hoped to survive by splitting the British home front. But neither the relatives of Tommy Atkins nor their social betters were heroically antiwar. In fact, many were "jingos," and it was the jingos who gave Salisbury and Balfour the "Khaki election" in October 1900. "The war," said Balfour, aping that familiar "end of tunnel" metaphor, "is now happily drawing to a close." Joseph Chamberlain played the Agnew part of his time: "A seat lost to the Unionist Government is a seat gained for the Boers." This theme was repeated incessantly up and down the country, and Chamberlain was bold to say: "There is nothing going on now but a guerrilla business, which is encouraged by these men [some of the antiwar Liberals and Labour]. I was going to say these traitors, but I will say instead these misguided individuals."

Thus, many of the same factors that stirred America's war drama were incipiently present: charges of patriotic delinquency or near treason, and even the "credibility gap." As Sir Henry Campbell-Bannerman, the leader of the opposition, declared in 1900: "Never has a war, great or small, been conducted with so little communication of authentic information as to its incidents and its policy." He compared government censorship to the autocratic measures of the Russian emperor and the Turkish sultan. Neo-isolationism was also an issue. When the jingos called John Morley a "little Englander," he countered: "They'll make England, as they call it, little enough before they are done with it." Along with Liberal defectors from the war policy, there were a few Tories, like Sir Edward Clarke, who called the war "a crime against civilization."

Atrocity was another theme. The publicist H. W. Massingham spoke of "tearing up a community by its roots . . . harrying women and children to their death or their ruin." His vision was cruelly confirmed by such military orders as Major-General Hamilton's in November 1900: "The town of Ventersburg has been cleared of supplies and partly burnt, and the farms in the vicinity destroyed on account of the frequent attacks on the railway line in the neighborhood. The Boer women and children who are left behind should apply to the Boer commandants for food, who will supply them unless they wish to see them starve." We hear of no My Lai; but the mores of the conflict were generally abased.

"How long will the civilized world tolerate . . . the shame of these transactions?" Lloyd George demanded. "Our empire," the former Liberal Prime Minister Lord Rosebery lamented, "is an object of the suspicion, jealousy, and hatred of the great mass of the nations of Europe at this moment." Sir William Harcourt went him one better: "We are the best-hated people in the world."

The ringing denunciations came from Liberal mouths, but the majority of Liberal politicians supported the government's war policy and suffered the tensions within their own party. There are, as one knows, "hard liberals" and "soft liberals." Britain at the turn of the century was no different from the contemporary United States in this regard. Some dared to object too late, or were perhaps headed off by the waning of the conflict. The "Khaki election" pushed the timid on to the defensive. Public opinion was not ripe in most quarters for an aggressive flock of doves. As Campbell-Bannerman declared in June 1900, a little pathetically: "Every vote of money, every financial or military arrangement that required our assent, was readily agreed to. Embarrassing questions were asked; it was not by us." In other words, the rhythm of the Boer War, in politics and in public opinion, distinctly resembles the American reaction to Vietnam during the first three years of heavy commitment. The British government was not forced to sustain illusions over a long haul, or to suffer widespread public doubt and civil disobedience. This goes far to distinguish the two episodes; it also prevented a more remorseless tearing of the liberal mind than actually happened in late Victorian England.

Nevertheless, the Liberals swept into office with an enormous and clear majority in 1906, partly due to a Unionist rift over protectionism. And they now had, as never before, a mandate for English "reform, retrenchment, and progress," under the neo-Gladstonian leadership of Campbell-Bannerman, with the fierce Lloyd George at one of his flanks.

It never quite came off, because the structures of the Liberal party, of Parliament, and of British politics in general interfered. The clear majority could arouse expectations, but give them only piecemeal satisfaction: the fate of Johnson's Great Society is not an absurd parallel. When the capable but hesitant Asquith took over in 1908, the Liberals seemed either unaware or incapable of dealing with the popular forces and particular groups pressing upon them. And the Conservatives were hardly disposed toward statesmanlike acts. Finally, in 1910 a closely divided election nullified earlier opportunities. The Irish Nationalists (their price: Home Rule) were made the brokers of English politics, and the country was polarized over its main constitutional and social issues. Was this impasse in any way a legacy of the Boer War? Only insofar as that war contributed an added dimension to the Liberal malaise. The historical differences in the party had been exacerbated by the linkage between positions on the war and social philosophies.

To an extent, the Liberals could innovate in the general area of democratization, but they could not lead. They were a self-conscious oligarchy that had not grasped the secret of mass politics. Nor could they concede the extinction of a century and a climate on which they had left such a vital imprint. They stood rooted in the shadowland between empire and the small merchant, between welfare and respectability, between government and nonconformist ethics, between politics and ideals. This did not destroy them yet—their end would come in the midst of World War I—but the theoretical seeds of division had been planted earlier.

Why and how Liberalism and liberalism failed England at this point has often been debated. Some say that liberalism, naturally identified with the political philosophy of the individual, had run its course. Others claim that liberalism was an "excluded middle" that could not survive between the stresses of the leaderly and mass principles. Still others assert that Liberalism expired because the competing parties usurped "liberalism" for themselves. And finally, some analysts blame the demise of the Liberal party on the weaknesses of Asquith and Lloyd George and the terrible toll of World War I. It is fairly sure that internal philosophical contradictions, combined with faults of leadership and organization, crippled this great organized doctrine. Liberalism, which fundamentally believes that the world is headed right, tends to come a cropper when the world is obviously going wrong. Its faith is too rough-and-ready, its view of human nature too simplistic to constitute a first-class theodicy. There is no supple dialectic to account for history's "dark moments," which then tend to seem an alarming conspiracy to liberals.

In the waning years of the England of Noyes's "Barrel Organ" and Elgar's "Cockaigne," liberalism both inherited and stimulated an English mess. It wanted the equal dignity of all; yet it was linked to baronial recipes flowing from Magna Carta. It wanted neatness; yet its economic ethics had made the world exceedingly untidy. It wanted a harmony of interests—but no jingoism, please!—and it found itself in a moderate version of class struggle. It wanted prosperity, but that unfortunately depended on the complacence of other nations. It wanted sanctuary beneath the abstract altar of Progress, but it discovered Nemesis there instead.

Consider Mr. Asquith, the Balliol aristocrat, confronting furious miners and dockers, suffragettes, and mercurial Irish Nationalists. This is a small sample of the worlds the Liberal politician was compelled to bridge. Asquith wished justice for his countrymen, but he did not want to have to smell them. And so, on the eve of World War I the Liberals stood on the brink of an army mutiny, suffragette violence of major proportions (including arson), Irish Civil War, a constitutional crisis, and eventual prospects of a general strike. Hands, it must be said, were gleefully rubbed in the Wilhelmstrasse. Then the guns of August spoke, and Lord Grey's lights went out all over Europe.

3

In a memorandum to Secretary of State Rusk written in the fall of 1964, W. W. Rostow spoke of the "limited but real margin of influence on the outcome [in Vietnam] that flows from the simple fact that we are the greatest power in the world—if we behave like it." An earlier study by Rostow, financed with the help of CIA money, was appropriately called *The United States in the World Arena*. The book is long but crisp, and by no means stupid. It contains an arresting appendix on the "national interest," a subject of much vogue in the Sputnik years. As an ambitious academician, Rostow's aim was twofold: to trace his own particular version of America's "national style" and arrival at world supremacy, and to prescribe strategies for the new involvement. America, argued Rostow, must not shrink from her global responsibilities by ceding either to "splendid isolation" or "soft" liberalism; and the application of power must be justified by the ideological meaning it bears. This idea corresponded well with the "muscular liberalism" of the Kennedy administration, of which Rostow became a member.

I do not mean to overstress Rostow's influence (though he remained close to the center of power for eight years), nor to denigrate his intelligence. In preparation for coming to power with Kennedy, Rostow was "with it"—he had half the truth, but he had not reasoned out the deeper consequences of the politics of the coming decade. He had much good company in his belief that Dulles's "massive retaliation" and its corollaries were a pious and dangerous bluff, that American forces were unfitted for the subtle task of "graduated deterrence," and that American diplomacy after Suez had become more reactive than creative. Unfortunately, the wider vision and new options that marked the innovative frenzy of Washington in the early 1960s were precisely those things that made our massive involvement on the Asian mainland technically possible. In 1954 the Joint Chiefs had reasoned that "the allocation of more than token U.S. armed forces in Indochina would be a serious diversion of limited U.S. capabilities." What changed their thinking? No doubt there were many political mutations in the next nine years, there was the florescence of the Soviet Third World strategy, and there was the Cuban experience. But there were also the changes in hardware and mobility and the increased will to put them to the test.

Under the aegis of Secretary McNamara and his "whiz kids" at the Pentagon, a military doctrine of "flexible response" was inaugurated. Although this flexibility was sometimes theorized in "limited" and "sublimited" war categories, it is difficult to believe in retrospect that the line between them was ever firmly drawn. A great irony is that McNamara's policy, intended as a more secure adjustment to changing European conditions, was made operational just in time to sink us irreparably in the morass of Vietnam. For the intensification of that involvement was greatly facilitated by the forces and strategies so fruitfully conceived by the defense opponents of the Eisenhower administration in the late 1950s: Maxwell Taylor, Thomas K. Finletter, Roswell Gilpatric, James Gavin, and others. It is not that essential perceptions about Asia changed, but that military capability and foreign policy aggressiveness had been boosted.

And so, from seminar and drawing board to practice, special forces, counterinsurgency doctrines, augmented troop transport, "sky cavalry," helicopter battalions, "civic action," and a new range of limited-war devices came into existence. Both the military and defense intellectuals were more than willing to put the new ideas to the test, given the right chance. The experience of Korea and preexisting notions about Chinese expansionism in Asia helped to exalt Vietnam to an Armageddon against the "Red peril." It has sometimes been claimed that Lyndon Johnson half stumbled into Vietnam while looking over his shoulder at graver issues like Berlin. But this is also the man who, as vice-president, reported to President Kennedy on May 23, 1961: "The battle against Communism must be joined in Southeast Asia with strength and determination to achieve success there—or the United States, inevitably, must surrender the Pacific and take up our defenses on our own shores."

At any rate the European "shield" had suddenly to be reconsidered as a Third World sword, with pragmatic modifications. The notion of "limited war," originally an inductive theorization of Korean events that was belatedly applied to a Europe where the potential enemy now disposed of varied nuclear weapons, was transferred back, willy-nilly, to the continent of its origins. In the wake of the almost total collapse of the South Vietnamese polity in the months immediately before and after the assassination of President Diem, the United States could not pretend, once it had chosen commitment, to be fighting a mere "brushfire" or even "revolutionary" war. It swiftly became "limited war *a outrance*," with the "hearts and minds of the people" getting rather short shrift, despite propaganda. As John Roche, who was closely involved with the Johnsonian phase of the war, wrote in October 1968: "The basic issue in Vietnam is this: Can a free society fight a limited war? That is, a strategic war, a war without hate, a war without massive popular involvement." Most of the empirical answers to these questions are now available.

Vietnam has not really been a counterinsurgent war from the American standpoint: that is why aspects of it have been so horrible. It must be said that America is probably congenitally inept, despite periodic Green Beret bravado, at fighting a "revolutionary war." It is not a revolutionary society, and its agents are not trained to think in such categories. It is also very opulent in technology and munitions. Its timeless doctrine of massive and superior firepower decides the issue in case after case. Vietnam can be described as a war of imperial policy fought under faulty premises. But the New Left and some of the "revisionist" historians go astray with the dazzling and vindictive adjective "imperialist." Vietnam has been fought as imperialists traditionally fight, but with only blood and mire, not gold, at the end of the rainbow. To carry through the "strong" imperialist thesis, it has been necessary to show a pattern of complicity going back to the Chinese Open Door and a rich discovery of oil off the Indochinese shores. But the oil strike comes much too late in the game to be a promising explanation. The truth is much simpler and less intelligent: people in Washington were actually persuaded to believe that the coasts of California would be in peril if Saigon fell, that "monolithic Communism" had to be shown a lesson, and, finally, that defeat would be ignoble and un-American, especially if it impugned certain reputations for sound judgment.

If in this sense Vietnam has been an imperialist war, it has also been a "limited war" of unprecedented scope, in the sense of prohibiting nuclear weapons, abstaining (at times) from territorial enlargement, and conducting a full range of political communications and tacit bargaining. Elements of the U.S. forces played at counterinsurgency. But the war has been chiefly fought by mobile conventional forces and massive air strikes, not by small covert groups. Thus, once it is granted that America had any business being in Vietnam in the first place, it is still quite valid to ask whether we had any clear idea of the kind of war we were fighting. After all, the legendary boy saved Holland by putting his finger, not his head, in the dike.

The implications sprawling across the complex face of the Vietnam war issue proceed from a common source of inspiration, and they suggest some of the puzzlement of liberalism. Of course, it is well known that mostly everyone in America, from William Buckley to Father Berrigan, is a liberal by some pedigree (laissez-faire and the right to resistance being sides of the same coin). But if we are not inquiring after ancient origins, only about present facts, the liberalism I speak of has been traditionally contained in the majority wing of the Democratic party, with some Republican spillover. Until recently, most experts in American politics have claimed that the presidency has been "liberal." We could debate that fact, but a more useful procedure might be to consider the British government of 1906-16, which called itself "Liberal." Despite the anachronism one would certainly find room for Rostows and Fulbrights (and even a few Buckleys and Berrigans) in such a movement. We cannot surmise what would have happened if the Liberals had had to wage the Boer War, but we do know that the British Liberal cabinet split over World War I. And we could apply some of that British soul-searching to the drawn-out months and years of policy making for Vietnam, when our own liberals were actually in power.

Liberalism, after all, has two chief dimensions that can abide each other so long as there is no good excuse to bring them into conflict. One is missionary zeal, centered in the cosmopolitan goals of the leading liberal nation. The other is the zeal for toleration and inwardness, every man his own priest, registered at the summit in a sort of impossible world church of self-fulfilling individualists. These caricatures, along with the theological context in which Americans think about their country, and the widespread expectation that American mores, whether private or paternal, would consummate world order in the twentieth century, provide some notion of how the American liberal psyche was torn on the rack of Vietnam.

For over a century liberals have known that they had to balance and belong to the middle, "the vital center," as Arthur Schlesinger, Jr. once called it. Fears of the Left trap them on the Right; a surge of the Right drives them leftward. Thus, it is not astonishing that, after a turgid resume of "domino theory," secretaries Rusk and McNamara should have informed President Kennedy late in 1961 that the "loss of South Vietnam would stimulate bitter controversies in the United States and would be seized upon by extreme elements to divide the country and harass the Administration. . . ." John Roche succinctly turned this impression into a theory when he wrote that "limited war was conceived of *by liberals* as *the liberal* alternative to massive retaliation and/or isolationism." This poses the question: *how total* can a "limited war" become without escaping its own "liberal" premises? The answer, as we now see it, is that "limited war" remains "liberal" (despite casualties, destruction, shame, and furious impotence) until "liberals" decide to desert their own creation and cross over to the opposition. Then it becomes most decidedly illiberal, especially since "illiberals" have been placed in charge.

It is perhaps no accident that the original protest against a war that liberals had escalated, if not made, came from a curious coalition of realist conservatives like Hans Morgenthau and exuberant leftists trying to rejuvenate the American radical tradition. Marriages are sometimes made not in heaven but in extremity. It is also perhaps no accident that the intelligentsia and a certain proportion of American upper-middle-class *bien-pensants* were attacking the war before the average American had begun to act on his creeping doubts. In part, the country was bewildered because it was liberal and because its liberal leadership had glimpsed the "end of the tunnel" on so many occasions, at least publicly. As Louis Harris wrote in 1967: "In essence, the *Newsweek* survey pictures a nation determined to persevere in what it believes is a grimly distasteful struggle for national security." However, a questionnaire mailed only a few months later to a highly intellectual group (members of the Society for the Psychological Study of Social Issues) elicited a response of 90 percent for positions more "dovish" than those of the administration. The year 1967 is really the demarcation between public tolerance of the war and public apprehension, with some eruption of civil disobedience; perhaps the Boer War might have begun to stimulate similar responses had it not reached a decisive conclusion after three years. Public moral concern surfaces when things are going badly, not when there is victory in the air.

In an essay published in 1971, Robert W. Tucker discriminates between two sorts of opposition to the Vietnam war. "To some—the more radical critics—America's purpose is suspect because it is seen as little more than a thin disguise for an imperialist policy, a policy that has grown out of repressive domestic institutions and necessarily reflects them. To others—the more conventional critics—the continued relevance of America's purpose is suspect because the world is seen as increasingly resistant to this purpose." This is indeed the way it looked once a horde of liberals had ditched the ship—a mass migratory movement that started in 1967. Here, the conspiracy theorist would mutter that the liberals want their bread wherever it can be buttered, and the conservative realist would fret that peace is being ideologized in the same fashion as was the war itself ("the loss of South Vietnam would make pointless any further discussion about the importance of Southeast Asia to the free world"—Rusk and McNamara to Kennedy, November 11, 1961).

One cannot help sympathizing with these plaints. The "come what may, the U.S. intends to win this battle" with which the Gilpatric task-force report launched the Kennedy administration has been gradually alchemized into parlor radicalism. As best exemplified by the heroics of Daniel Ellsberg, the liberals have recovered their conscience. Of course, there is virtue in recognizing an error and seeking to correct it. But the Dostoievskian "redemption by suffering" rings a little tinny through the charged air of exposure. If liberals cannot be right, then at least they must be righteous. However, there is still the collapse of a policy and the graves of the dead to account for.

It is interesting that the Vietnam protest began with the defection of those intellectuals whose links with the establishment were cursory. But from early 1968 it was fed by another kind of intellectual—technocrats, managers, and leaders of the dominant interest, many of whom, despite their original allegiance, became the most vocal. Eating one's cake and having it too? It is not as simple as that. There was stern self-reprobation in these *volte-faces*. But there was also a quotient of machiavellianism, or stay-on-topness. The Nixon victory could not have served the managerial intellectuals better, for it furnished an airtight excuse for their desertion.

It would be rash to deny that our disoriented liberals can succeed. In many ways they are the cleverest political animals in America and, miraculously, they are still in contact with the vital impulses of this disturbed country. We do not have the sometimes venal, sometimes unreflective political solidarity and deference of the British, the tact that could lead to a white-glove treatment of Joseph Chamberlain in 1897, a public stoicism toward General Haig's carnage in the mud in 1917, a teapot tempest in the very difficult days of Suez in 1956. We rise more furiously to our *causes célèbres* and exhaust great and enthusiastic passion along their simple surfaces.

The Pentagon Papers are important (to the realist) not because they show that our leaders failed us, which was already obvious, but because they go far toward showing *how*. If it is more salient to endure the pain of a retrospective learning experience than to indulge in the bliss of vendetta, then the release of the papers may have accomplished something. Above all, the documents show that our policymakers were prisoners of a liberal reading of American destiny, including the "terror of isolationism" and the "nightmare of appeasement," and that an old nobility of design melted into an ideology of mystification—not only public mystification but self-mystification.

The revelation of the documents has already qualified as a liberal act, uncovering liberal motives and educing liberal reactions about freedom of the press and why Ellsberg took this great personal risk. Most important, however, is the fact that the released papers are seven thousand pages long, and even *The New York Times* condensation requires considerable knowledge and stamina from the reader. In short, the battle of the "papers" has been fought, as usual, among intellectuals and the involved parties. The public, one guesses, has received bowdlerized impressions of what the Pentagon Papers contain and signify. If the public's temper is short and its political diligence spasmodic, this may not produce the effect that opponents of the "credibility gap" have hoped for. This is in the best liberal tradition of compromise: the public should "be informed," but the opinion leaders should "know." Though the general constituency, after years of heavy involvement in Vietnam, began to smell a fish, the Pentagon Papers are too recondite to banish the odor.

We began with an account of British Liberalism's "strange death." It is apparent that many of the signs are similar in contemporary America: the imperial mentality, the come-uppance of a peripheral war, dangerous distances between leadership and public, ethnic strife, militant feminism, social turmoil reflecting status and life styles, stirrings of economic malaise, the deterioration of symbolic idols, and so forth.

As in Georgian England, our best writers today approximate "a feeling that is actually being made and torn out of us." And there is the further, more ponderous issue of the recession of American power, not perhaps as measured in GNP, but as indicated in recent economic jolts, in the foreign aid imbroglio, in decay of national morale, in defects of leadership, in clumsiness of institutions, in losses of public-spiritedness. It was not an eager radical but an editor of *Foreign Policy*, Samuel Huntington, who wrote in 1967: "In the year 2000 the American world system that has been developed during the last twenty years will be in a state of disintegration and decay." And Alastair Buchan has recently asked: "Why does an international position based on such great, indeed continuously growing, physical strength appear to have lasted for so short a time?" It would be hard to prove that the liberals traded modest possibilities of world order for a chimera. However, their marriage of national theology to what Max Frankel calls "imaginative and cold-blooded techniques" has made the achievement of that order vastly more difficult.

Can we fault their repentance? There is a paradox here, which clearly separates the British case from the American. The British Liberals of the time of Rosebery, Campbell-Bannerman, and Asquith appear, in hindsight, to have been playthings of forces they could neither understand nor master.

Progressive in instinct, they were retrograde in technique. Our own liberals often betray the opposite failings, *faute de mieux;* yet, they are well placed to mediate the distance between new social predilections and old values (or what used to be called "rights") if they can shake Vietnam from their stringy hair.

The liberals, who have flailed each other and swapped sides on Vietnam, are both sincere and cynical enough to reconstitute a political class fit for modern times. Even while staring at the manifold perplexity of the globe through malprescribed historical goggles, they are well nigh all we have as a center of political gravity. We have no responsible conservatism, no imaginative socialism: we have only this gigantic symbol of a family quarrel. Thus I do not predict any "strange death of liberal America" in respect to political personnel. While involved in sincere repentance over Vietnam, our liberals are also engaged in a deeper hypocrisy than their doctrine permits them to fathom. One cannot fear their demise. One can only wonder what the next "liberalism" will look like in the age of mortality that we are now entering.

THE PRESENT
AND THE FUTURE

PRAGMATIC CONSERVATISM IN THE WHITE HOUSE

by Pierre Hassner

Had Metternich been born fifty years earlier, he would still have been a conservative, but there would have been no need to write pedantic disquisitions about the nature of conservatism. . . . He would still have played at philosophy, for this was the vogue of the eighteenth century, but he would not have considered it a tool of policy. . . . It is the dilemma of conservatism that it must fight revolution anonymously by what it is, not by what it says.
—Henry Kissinger, *A World Restored, The Politics of Conservatism in a Revolutionary Age*

They are not going home—yet. News of America's disengagement from the world may be slightly exaggerated. To a European who has been watching the greening of the American establishment with a mixture of amusement, disbelief, and dismay, that is the essential message of President Nixon's second State of the World report.

This reassurance was surely overdue. It has concerned foreign observers of the United States to see so many liberal senators attacking foreign aid, defense intellectuals applying as much energy to reducing strategic budgets when the Soviet Union is strong as they once did to increasing them when it was weak, radical establishmentarians arguing that the cold war was always an evil myth engineered by the military-industrial complex, and moderates claiming that East-West competition is obsolete despite the Brezhnev Doctrine, SS-9 missiles, and Soviet pilots in Egypt. It is nice to know there is one place left in the United States that is unimpressed with the news that balancing Soviet power is sinful or irrelevant. It does not hurt to know that this place is the White House.

This is said without irony. My relief is like that of the many other Europeans who hope for East-West reconciliation, but at the same time sleep more soundly each night knowing that Washington maintains a healthy skepticism about Soviet intentions and intends to "stick around" rather than announce the end of the postwar era and go home.

So we have pulled back from the era of negotiation and, if not exactly reentering an era of confrontation and cold war, at

"Pragmatic Conservatism in the White House" was published originally in *Foreign Policy*, Number 3, Summer 1971.

least have returned to one of division and containment. Of
course, we never really left it in the first place. One of the
most debatable concessions that the first (1970) State of the
World message made to the spirit of the times was its
clear-cut distinction between negotiation and confrontation.
It is the characteristic of our age that old confrontations
never die, although they sometimes fade away. They give way
to new ones, or at least to new unpredictabilities rather than
to stable settlements. But there was plenty of confrontation
left in the first report, and there is plenty of negotiation left in
the second. Indeed, the 1971 report includes not only an
overture toward Communist China but also acceptance (in
the Middle East) of the "expansion of Soviet influence in the
world" as "natural."

Yet the emphasis has unmistakably shifted. The second
message is formulated in much sterner and soberer tones.
Of the three components of a "stable structure of peace"
around which the 1970 message was organized (partnership,
strength, and willingness to negotiate), only one—partnership—has been upgraded in the 1971 message. It is now de-
signated "the core" and "the basic theme," the two other
components being merely "its adjuncts." The section on
Soviet-American relations, called "An Era of Negotiation" in
the first message, is titled "The Soviet Union" in the second.

Obviously, preoccupation with the Soviet Union and consoli-
dating existing alliances has gone up even as hopes of peace
through negotiation have gone down. While the change of
emphasis and tone is striking, it does not necessarily involve
a change of heart or even of mind. Like most high-sounding
and self-quoting American doctrines, Nixon's is a pragmatic
response to immediate pressures. It represents an attempt to
give some recognition both to the pressures of new (mostly
domestic) moods and to the constraints of old (mostly external) realities. Nineteen seventy's hope was that external realities (Soviet ambitions and allied strength) would undergo
enough of a favorable change to enable the United States to
achieve basically the same aims as before, or to maintain the
same international structure, while lowering its external posture and involvement in accordance with the psychological
mood and economic needs of the country. Nineteen seventy-
one's realization is that last year's hopes were misguided.
They have been replaced by the new hope (probably based on
the post-Cambodia and pre-Laos quietening of domestic op-

position) that domestic pressures have abated enough to permit American policymakers to maintain a role that persistent Soviet intransigence and allied weakness continue to make necessary.

From Maxis to Hot Pants

In the most perceptive comment made on 1970's message, James Reston wrote:

President Nixon's maxi-statement on American foreign policy is a little like the brilliant maxi-coats one sees swinging along the sidewalks of London these days; it is long, it covers a lot of territory, and it conceals the most interesting parts. The most interesting part of the Nixon Doctrine of "partnership" and "negotiation for peace" is what the other partners and the Soviet Union are prepared to do about it as the United States reduces its overseas commitments.

While nobody would dream of calling the new statement either short or hot, it does, like 1971's fashions, concentrate on showing the naked reality of the most interesting parts: the increase in Soviet moderation and allied effort is not sufficient to warrant a precipitate reduction in American commitments.

One is left, then, with the question of whether commitments and credibility can be maintained at lower psychological and economic costs. Obviously when the message was written, the belief was that in Asia enough substitution was taking place to reduce both types of costs to a tolerable level, while elsewhere realities were such that no disengagement was possible or desirable. Foreign policy has four main components: the pressures of domestic society, the views and objectives of policymakers, the strength and role of opponents, and of allies. The first and the last of these were crucial in 1970 (an increase in one calling for an increase in the other). But in 1971 the focus has returned to the second and especially the third components. The central question today is: how do American policymakers view "the relationship of major tension" and, to the extent that this is seen to be Soviet-American competition, how does it affect their view of America's relations with the rest of the world?

Oddly enough, the answer that emerges from this massive effort of rethinking and rewriting, from these hundreds of pages of messages and doctrine, lies in that most familiar and universal concept of American policy since World War II:

containment. Behind the modesty of the Nixon Doctrine, so unlike the missionary spirit of the Dulles and Kennedy eras, is a return to the original Truman Doctrine, the concept of holding the line until evolution makes allies more self-reliant and negotiations from strength more likely to influence the Soviet Union toward moderation. The ultimate aim is stability, the ultimate means negotiation, the immediate means military balance and socio-economic consolidation. The essence of the strategy is to be provisional and defensive. Partnership and regionalism should, as Walt Rostow said in 1967, provide a solution "somewhere between the far-flung responsibilities dating from the early postwar period and a return to isolationism." This solution requires "a stable structure of peace" based on regional balances.

Within this framework the novelties of the Nixon Doctrine are two: on the practical side, a more decided attempt than before (but more decided last year than this year) to decrease the military and political role of the United States, as compared to that of its allies, and, on the theoretical side, an attempt to formulate the post-World War II policy in pre-World War I terms, that is, to define containment and commitment, stability and structure, America's role and her environment, in terms of national interests and of balance of power, rather than in terms of ideological struggle, as in the late forties and the fifties, or of modernizing forces, as in the sixties. In the two Nixon messages the term "national interest" constantly recurs both as the criterion for American commitments and as the basis of the mysterious new "structure of peace."

But this, in turn, leads to two dangers. The theoretical danger consists either in believing, like Bismarck, that the national interests of historical states are self-evident and that domestic requirements can be ignored or manipulated, or in basing these interests, like Metternich, on a given ideological and social legitimacy. In the latter case, one asks revolutionary forces to conform to a legitimacy, to respect a status quo, and to practice a moderation that they are bound to challenge by their very essence.

A practical danger derives from this. Basing commitments on interests means reducing commitments if multipolarity increases and conflicts decrease. But if a hostile power, the Soviet Union, is expanding geographically and strategically without becoming more conciliatory, then we are back to global containment and to the bipolar balance of power, with the difference that the language of national interest gives a less genuine rationale for this global confrontation than the language of ideology. The danger is that a global confrontation seen predominantly from the point of view of *Realpolitik,* of diplomacy and of strategy, may become more militarized and undiscriminating than would be true in the case of ideological and social perspectives, which give more weight to domestic requirements and transnational forces.

This, indeed, is what seems to be happening. And this is why the present writer, who shares many of the assumptions of the American administration, is nevertheless deeply uneasy about the tendency of this message to see the state of the whole world in the light of the dialogue between two superpowers defending their national interests.

Conservatism and Change

The constraints of strategic deterrence, the growth of Soviet power, the uncertainty of Soviet intentions, the need for American commitment, detachment, patience, strength, and even unpredictability in any U.S.-Soviet negotiations had to be reemphasized if only to correct the emphasis of last year's message. But there are more things in heaven and earth than in the two messages and their shifting, yet static philosophy. They may be right on everything concerning the Soviet Union, and even Western Europe and the Middle East, on everything strategic, diplomatic, and even on everything immediately urgent and feasible, and yet be deadly wrong in their present view of the rest of the world and in their long-range view of where that world is going.

If it is true that any administration is bound to concentrate on immediate dangers and moves rather than on subterranean forces and on the year 2000, then the question arises whether these annual messages do not do more harm than good. Are they not too general and discursive to give any valid guidelines for policy decisions, yet too tied to immediate preoccupations to provide a useful guide to the challenges of the future?

What the presidential messages try to convey is less a doctrine than an attitude. This attitude is best defined as one of pragmatic conservatism. It may be true that pragmatic con-

servatism is better equipped than any rival approach to deal
with immediate issues of interstate relations. It seems, at
least, better than crusading messianism or economic-tech-
netronic determinism or moralistic pacifism as a tool for negotiating with an equally conservative, pragmatic, yet ultimately hostile power like the Soviet Union. On the other
hand, conservatism has great difficulty transcending the
state-to-state perspective and perceiving revolutionary situations. But if both the virtue and the limitation of pragmatic
conservatism lie in its tactical flexibility within an accepted
framework, isn't this attitude both the least likely to produce
a meaningful "doctrine" and the most likely to be hampered
in its freedom of movement by successive attempts to
formulate one?

The key to the view of the world on which the administration's attitude is based lies in its interpretation of diversity
and change. In both messages, as well as in earlier works of
Henry Kissinger, one finds identical formulations about the
need for adjusting to a more complex world, to military bipolarity instead of U.S. predominance, to political multipolarity instead of bipolarity, to consulting instead of dictating
to allies. On two levels—relations with allies and with rival
great powers—this evolution concentrates on interstate balances. But in "pre-Nixon" writings of Henry Kissinger,* one
occasionally encounters a deep awareness (which one sadly
misses in the two presidential messages) that a third level
may be becoming at least as crucial: the level of new
psychological and moral trends, which transcend national
barriers and may influence the balance of power more deci-
sively than any territorial or strategic shifts by affecting the
domestic evolution of nations and empires.

The Nixon Doctrine represents a genuine effort to accept
greater diversity in the world and, more important (since
Kennedy, too, wanted to make the world safe for diversity), to
accept that the implications of increased diversity are a decrease or at least a transformation in American leadership
and control. But this acceptance of diversity may have
started by overemphasizing the multipolar or polycentric dimension of diplomacy and by underemphasizing the other
challenge, that of increasing economic, social, ideological,

*Particularly in "Central Issues of American Foreign Policy," in *Agenda for
the Nation* (Washington, D.C.: The Brookings Institution, 1968).

psychological, and moral gaps within territorial units, between elites and masses, institutions and social forces, bureaucracies and competing groups, imperial powers and subordinate peoples.

While the first kind of diversity produces only limited and manageable change, if only because for the time being the world remains strategically bipolar, the second threatens to transform the meaning and the rules of the multipolar game—complicated planetary bargaining as well as tacit spheres of influence—just as much as of the bipolar one. It may be striking at the very nature of domination, of legitimacy, and of control.

Between the first and the second message, some of the enthusiasm for multipolarity seems to have abated. In some cases this is because its implications appear to be more destabilizing, or in greater contradiction with the persisting military bipolarity than was thought at first. The initiatives of allies are fine as long as, like de Gaulle, they strike revolutionary poses but fail to challenge the system of East-West relations effectively. They raise more problems and eyebrows when France is replaced by Germany. Germany's present loyalty to the West is beyond question, but its dialogue with the East introduces an element of movement in Europe that neither the United States nor anyone else in the West can control. In other cases, multipolarity just has failed to materialize, at least as far as new responsibilities are concerned, and the consequences of American disengagement seem to be less the appearance of new poles of power than of new areas of weakness: hence, a reaffirmation of the role and responsibilities of the United States, which seems to lead, by a kind of bipolar mirror, to a new recognition (and perhaps exaggeration) of those of the Soviet Union. While one stands up to the Soviet Union more and more, one also tends more and more to accept, in some cases to misperceive, and in others to encourage, its control over its allies. The return to containment seems to entail a trend toward tacit recognition of spheres of influence.

But in Asia, in Latin America, in Eastern Europe, gaps and conflicts between social trends and military structures and between the international balance and domestic aspirations seem to be making classical spheres of influence obsolete and explosive. This would seem to be the main problem that the present state of the world raises for the future. One can understand that elementary prudence would deter the president of the United States from speculating aloud about the comparative rate of decay of his authority and of Mr. Brezhnev's. But the result is that his message is only about one aspect of the world, perhaps not the most decisive. The farther away one gets, in the second message, from direct confrontation and negotiation with the Soviet Union, the more this weakness becomes apparent. Let us look at some specifics.

Soviet-on-the-Nile

On the Middle East issue one finds a balanced and competent analysis of the present situation, marked by great distrust of Soviet behavior along with a hopeful invitation addressed to the Soviets to join a stabilized structure based on balance, moderation, and cooperation. But what was justified in the bipolar and quasi-abstract nuclear world becomes more questionable in a world full of instabilities, divisions, and frustrations such as the Arab-Israeli conflict. There may be a twin misperception involved in expecting the Soviet Union to take a purely pacific and moderate view of national interest in the management of a Middle Eastern balance, and in suspecting the same Soviet Union of diabolical mischief either when it fails to cooperate as expected or when other local developments create a danger to stability. The first temptation (once described by Henry Kissinger as the typical conservative delusion, that of expecting revolutionary powers to cooperate in implementing a moderate version of the status quo) may not be unjustified as far as the Soviet Union's role in the area is concerned, since to some extent it is behaving more like a classical expansionist power than like a revolutionary one. But the ideological aspect involved in its commitment to "progressive" Arab regimes, and maintained by its competition with China, cannot be wished away. More important, local developments in the area create more frustrations and ambiguities than this vision seems to acknowledge. And this may be at the root of the other, more immediately relevant danger, that of exaggerating the Soviet Union's power and machiavellianism and underestimating local confusion. The violation of the cease-fire last autumn by the continued building of missile sites on the Suez Canal may just as easily be interpreted in terms of standard Soviet practice, combined with incompetence, as of a deliberate decision to humiliate the United States.

Even more characteristic is the U.S. interpretation of the Syrian move into Jordan as "the gravest danger to world peace since the administration came into office" and of Syrian withdrawal as due to American intimation of possible intervention. The whole episode is made to sound like a new Cuban missile crisis, another link in a chain of U.S.-Soviet confrontations. Yet this may be both inflating events out of proportion and interpreting them out of context. Crucial to the official interpretation is the degree of Soviet control over the Syrian decisions to get in and out of Jordan. To many observers the local dimensions of Jordanian resistance, Israeli threat, Syrian-Iraqui and intra-Syrian divisions appear as at least as important as the Soviet-American aspect. Soviet-American confrontation is certainly part of the Middle Eastern problem, but one wonders if local social transformations and nationalist upheavals are not definitely the more important part.

Insensitivity in the Orient

In Asia, the Nixon administration seems to have overcome the Chinese fixation of the Johnson presidency. Yet it does not seem to have quite abandoned a parallel Johnsonian illusion, that of Soviet cooperation in influencing North Vietnam toward moderation. One detects in the administration's general (and generally justified) dim view of Soviet behavior an irritation with the Soviet Union's failure to exert a pressure on North Vietnam that may be neither in her power nor in her interest. Conversely, the Asian version of the "structure of peace" (probably more explicit and imaginative than its counterparts for other regions) suffers even more than elsewhere from the implausibility of the conservative overvaluation of diplomacy and strategy.

A structure based on two pillars—the collective interest of Asian countries represented by regional groupings and the policies of the four major powers (the United States, the Soviet Union, China, and Japan)—is an ingenious construction based on some genuine realities. But can one imagine it working? Can one imagine each of these powers "adjusting its policies to the legitimate interests of the others"? Is

China's definition of legitimacy likely to coincide in the fore-seeable future with that of the United States and the Soviet Union? More important, isn't the Asian soil much too much of a quicksand to provide stable foundations for these two pillars? Do not regional differences, social revolutions, and national conflicts confine the effectiveness of this Asian version of the European concert of powers to a relatively abstract level?

The world is, in a sense, a diplomatic and strategic chessboard; but it may be more fragmented and more interdependent in terms of social, psychological, and moral perception and contagion than American policy assumes. Civil wars involving the bitter fight of emerging nationalisms are difficult to control by a continental concert, let alone to include in an intercontinental negotiation. Yet if local balances and bargains are often irreducible to regional—let alone to global—ones, the way specific experiences affect general attitudes and perceptions does have a global impact that is often irrational. For a global power affects others as much by what it becomes, or seems to be becoming, as by what it does.

This is why a European, however conscious he may be of his ignorance of local conditions, cannot avoid the subject of Vietnam, which figures so prominently in 1971's message. What the president says can provoke no violent reaction; it is so balanced, to the point of contradiction, that it gives equal grounds for acknowledging the achievement of Vietnamization, as compared to any other available policy, and for doubting its ultimate success. But on the broader issue of Vietnam's impact on America's relations with the rest of the world, especially with the Soviet Union, with Europe, and above all with itself, one cannot help both agreeing with the administration's preoccupations and being unhappy with its answers.

Surely the president is right in stating that in liquidating some vestiges of the past ". . . the method is crucial. Clearly we could not have continued the inherited policy on Vietnam. Just as clearly, the way in which we set about to resolve this problem has a major impact on our credibility abroad and on cohesion at home." Clearly, again he is right in fighting the belief "that the only antidote for undifferentiated involvement is indiscriminate retreat" and in wanting his policy not only to "reflect a changed public will" but also to "shape a new consensus for a balanced and positive American role." But the point is whether anything can do more harm to this credibility, this cohesion, this consensus, and this role than the war itself.

"Abrupt shifts are unsettling," but so is inability to extricate oneself from a war that is killing hundreds of thousands of people and is destroying the very domestic legitimacy on which any foreign policy, let alone any foreign intervention, must be based. A "reputation for unsteadiness" may isolate the United States. But so does a reputation of its leaders for moral insensitivity, of its intellectuals for political irresponsibility, and of its population for generalized distrust and disgust. After ten years of war, surely the danger is more in the second direction than in the first.

Commitments do have some interdependence, the global balance does have an important effect, but losses can be offset and commitments reaffirmed elsewhere after a retreat. The mortal danger to America's role in the world comes from a whole generation at home and abroad tending increasingly to view American power as immoral and imperialistic, or even, as Henry Kissinger has put it, to view management as manipulation, structural designs as systems of "domination," not of order. Precisely because nothing is more shocking to a European who is convinced of America's positive role in containing the Soviet Union and helping Western Europe than to see students and senators reinterpret NATO and the Marshall Plan, foreign aid and strategic deterrence, in the light of Vietnam, one would wish for a deeper understanding by the administration of the huge gap between its own view of international politics and the view held by an increasingly important proportion of its domestic and foreign constituency.

Immediate decisions may not necessarily be affected by a better moral perception of how war critics view the consequences of interventions in Cambodia and Laos, whatever their military logic, for the civilian populations of those countries and the image of America abroad. But the administration's interpretation of the world should at the very least take account of this pervasive moral criticism, and so should a report that, if it is to have any function at all, ought to prepare the beginnings of a common language with today's opponents of U.S. policy.

Myopia in Latin America

Nowhere is this kind of deficiency more glaring, and its future implications more disturbing, than in the section on Latin America. The report does pay what appears to be lip service to the growth of nationalism and to the need for a transformed relationship. Perhaps it is more than lip service. Given the blandness of the language, however, and its ambiguities and contradictions, can any Latin American be expected to find it responsive to his own perception of the hemisphere?

As nonrevolutionary a commentator as Raymond Aron has been struck by the way in which "psychological tensions between Latin American countries and the United States are hidden behind traditional formulas." There is no allusion to the role of multinational corporations, no discussion of tied loans, or of the proportion between new investments and re-exported profits. Writing in *Le Figaro*, Aron has pointed to the contradiction between Washington's alleged wish to accept governments as they are and its objection to Chile's relations with Cuba as a danger to the inter-American system. "As long as the president of the United States speaks in those terms," he commented, "Latin American states will feel they are not treated like partners. . . . In brief, President Nixon has not yet made the decisive step: to tolerate the same diplomatic autonomy from Latin American governments he tolerates from Western Europeans." There are two issues here: that of attitudes toward Marxist regimes and that of U.S. predominance.

On the first issue, it would seem that despite all the theoretical emphasis on polycentrism, any socialist government in Latin America is regarded as part of the Soviet threat, even if, as in the case of Chile, it came to power through free elections and does not pose any threat to the military security of the United States or to its strategic balance with the Soviet Union. One would have thought that even from the point of view of *Realpolitik*, it would be in the interest of the United States to encourage diversity, if not division, in the Communist camp. Has not the time come for peaceful coexistence with Cuba? Shouldn't the fact that other Latin American states have relations with Cuba be at least as tolerable to the United States as other Western states having relations with China? Doesn't this apply even more strongly to Chile?

This is not to say that the Allende regime is or is bound to remain democratic, or that the United States does not have to protect its economic and security interests. But if the turn from ideological cold war to a more moderate policy based on diplomacy and strategy is to be credible, then the apparent hardening toward the Chilean regime at the very time when it has gone out of its way to reassure the United States in terms of security is to be deplored. Perhaps the hostile turn taken by U.S.-Cuban relations was unavoidable no matter what the United States would have done. But clearly Cuba has learned some lessons, and Chile has learned them from Cuba. The only country that does not seem to have done so, even tactically, is the United States. Even if it does not do anything to overthrow the Allende regime, and even if the latter collapses from its own internal difficulties, the United States seems to be bent on taking the blame or the credit upon itself.

Beyond tactics, the fundamental issue is the basic social instability of Latin America and the pervasive belief among most Latin American elites that North American economic, military, and political domination is a crucial factor in their situation. If Vietnam is the most immediate tragedy, Latin America is likely to be the real future test of the Nixon Doctrine. If, as seems likely, other radical regimes appear in Latin America—some military, some civilian, some with and some without Communist participation, some through violence, some through elections—and if all have in common an anti-U.S. orientation and a challenge to U.S. economic interests, but a prudent attitude toward the military involvement of external powers like the Soviet Union, what will the attitude of the United States be?

Nowhere do the pressures of psychological tradition and of economic interest militate so strongly toward U.S. intervention, especially in the Caribbean. The nonproximity of any major rival military power makes such intervention even less justifiable in terms of security and power balance, but may make it seem less dangerous. Yet in terms of the United States' domestic consensus and external role, a Latin American Vietnam would be no less tragic than an Asian one.

One would think that perhaps the primary task of a State of the World message would be to educate the North American bureaucracy and public, on one hand, and the Latin American elites, on the other, into separating, as much as is possible, the military, diplomatic, economic, and ideological dimensions that the present inter-American system—just like the present anti-imperialist demonology—tends to lump together. Only a frank recognition that the United States is in an imperial situation in Latin America, and that this situation must qualitatively change if it is not to become explosive, can lead the way to improving North-South relationships. The United States has to protect its security interests and be economically involved, but should accept the political and social diversity of its southern partners, the existence of specific Latin American interests and ties distinct from hemispheric ones, and the pursuit by its neighbors of independent foreign policies as long as they do not lead to the military presence of other great powers. This is a far cry from what the Nixon message seems to be announcing.

Up Europa

A European is happy to acknowledge, by contrast, the frankness, lucidity, and good will of the section on Western Europe. The assessment of Europe's ambivalent desires both for greater independence and unity and for the continuation of American military presence is clear and accurate. The administration has correctly evaluated the likely consequences of unilateral troop withdrawals and the requirements of European defense. It has also analyzed in detail the long neglected economic issues likely to arise in relations between the European community and the United States.

If one compares the two messages of 1970 and 1971, the latter devotes much more space to Western Europe and is much more explicit in supporting European unity. Perhaps because it has become even more obvious that Europe will not significantly relieve the United States of part of its burden if it does not have a much greater degree of institutional unity, perhaps also because it is no longer de Gaulle who is the torchbearer of nationally independent diplomacy, the formulations about the advantages of a new unity come close to the pre-Nixon policy. Even the famous two pillars have made their reappearance! This whole section could have been written by George Ball.

On the other hand, equal emphasis is put on the likelihood that the progress of European economic unity will create

problems for the United States. The United States is not prepared to go a very long way in making economic sacrifices for
political gains, especially if the political gains are deferred
much longer. The whole issue of protectionism and of the
dangers of trade wars' poisoning political relations is
squarely and lucidly faced. The importance given to the famous citrus issue, the criticism of Common Market prefer-
ential agreements with African countries, the president's
stand on Japanese textiles and on monetary issues indicate
that the administration's policy will not necessarily be as
conciliatory (not to mention self-denying) as the Europeans
might wish and as the Nixon Doctrine might seem to imply.
But the general commitment to free trade and the awareness
that European economic unity itself offers the best path toward handling the difficulties it creates remains the dominant note.

This commendable return to an emphasis on West European
unity is accompanied, however, by a corresponding de-emphasis of detente, of German *Ostpolitik*, and of Eastern Europe. On each of these issues the indispensable positive
truths are repeated: that West European unity and East-West
reconciliation are complementary and not contradictory, that
Germany's attempt at normalization corresponds to a natural
evolution, that a real European detente must include Eastern
Europe, and that states like Rumania and Yugoslavia should
be able to have good relations with the United States without
offending anybody. But they are all said in about a sentence
each, and the emphasis is definitely on the negative: "The
momentum of individual approaches to the East" cannot be
allowed to put allies inadvertently in the painful position of
having to choose between their national concerns and their
European responsibilities; "the facts of history and geo-
graphy" do "create special circumstances in Eastern Europe," and "a divergence in social, political, and economic
systems between East and West" has to be recognized.

Clearly, the United States will (in principle) be responsive to
East European countries that believe they can afford to improve relations with it. Washington accepts the transformation of the Berlin talks from the discussion of practical improvements to assure Berlin's viability "into an indicator of
the possibilities of moving toward fruitful talks on broader
issues of European security." But even more clearly, great

hope is not placed in such broader talks. The United States is not ready to take initiatives toward them nor toward an evolution of the East European situation. Once again, Washington's eye is glued to the short range rather than the long range, to a conception of stability based on the balance of power rather than to a perception of larger trends of social and psychological evolution.

In the short run, and in terms of policy priorities, the United States is almost certainly right. While the building of Western Europe's unity and the transformation of its relations with the United States provide an immediate and inevitable challenge, the prospects for any real progress in relations with Eastern Europe are blocked by the rigidity of Soviet rule as demonstrated by the invasion of Czechoslovakia and by the doctrine of the Socialist community. Faced with this impasse, the easy way is a passive acceptance of the status quo. Any attempt at an active policy, even in the name of reconciliation, runs a grave risk of provoking East European instability, Soviet suspicions, and, eventually, repression. This would be especially true of any scheme initiated and spectacularly promoted by the United States. But de Gaulle's "Europe from the Atlantic to the Urals" or Brandt's *Ostpolitik*, while they have attracted less fire than "peaceful engagement" or "bridge building," have not had much more success in converting Moscow or Pankow to a more relaxed view of their security. So far, the policy of movement has produced results exclusively on the Western side.

Yet containment based on division is no permanent European settlement. The German quest for a new identity and role is irreversible, even if, for the time being, it is blocked or channeled by immovable barriers. The East European societies are in deep social and economic crisis, which can be solved only by economic and political reform and contained only by Soviet military force. This is why, no matter how limited immediate perspectives, there is something wrong with a report on the State of the World that has so little to say on the German problem, that does not mention the political hardening in the Soviet Union and Czechoslovakia or (except by the most indirect implication) the Brezhnev doctrine, nor even the events in Poland, and that views the future of East-West relations in Europe in an essentially negative and defensive framework.

If one thinks of the instabilities in and around Yugoslavia, or of the apparent acceleration of internal crises in Eastern Europe, there may be dangers in the not-so-distant future of new and violent conflicts. These can be averted only if the great powers are reassured (partly by each other) about their own security and interests, and if they in turn reassure their allies or satellites that they will have a substantial degree of domestic autonomy free from the threat of forcible intervention. The logic of the balance of power leads one to regard Eastern Europe as a Soviet sphere of influence just as it leads one to see Latin America as a North American sphere, the nature of the respective influence being, of course, as different as the imperial powers themselves. Yet true stability will be found only if these regions (and, for that matter, Southeast Asia), while remaining mindful of the security and economic interests of their powerful neighbors, can lead their own autonomous life without being isolated or threatened. Security and stability do not require a dismantling of alliances, but they do require a qualitative change in relations within some of them.

No Orgy

One does not expect the United States to invite the Soviet Union to participate in a joint orgy of self-denial. But it is precisely in policy statements like this presidential message, and in discussions of a possible European security conference, that the United States could give at least a distant sense of hope to some of America's most genuine friends: the East Europeans. An opportunity has been missed to declare opposition to the threat and use of force within alliances, to welcome a degree of interpenetration and mutual control between alliances, and to favor Western "contacts and moral pressure" in Eastern Europe comparable to the policy the report later recommends toward South Africa.

The report on the State of the World seems to me fairly effective in conveying the right degrees of warning and of reassurance to other major participants in the balance of power: the Soviet Union and America's allies. But it has nothing to say to those who look to the United States with real frustration or despair, whether out of disappointed hope like the East Europeans, or out of fear and hatred, like many Asians, Latin Americans, and, indeed, North Americans.

To be sure, these latter peoples do not represent much physical or diplomatic power. But they do count in that "psychological balance based on intangibles of value and belief" the
importance of which, Henry Kissinger declared in 1968,
"cannot be overemphasized." A "satisfied, advanced society," Kissinger continued, "puts a premium on operating
with familiar procedures and concepts" and "defines excel-
lence by the ability to manipulate an established framework."
But for the largest part of mankind, living in conditions of
minimum well-being and free choice, "the present becomes
endurable only through a vision of the future." Thus, Kissinger concluded, "equilibrium is not a purpose with which we
can respond to the travail of our world. . . . Our conception
of world order must have deeper purposes than stability. . . .
Whether such a leap of the imagination is possible in the
modern bureaucratic state remains to be seen."*

Until then, the value of an exercise like the latest State of the
World report must also remain in doubt.

*Ibid., pp. 606-614.

WILL THE BALANCE BALANCE AT HOME?
by Stanley Hoffmann

A new era of American foreign policy is obviously beginning. The cold war era is over. The reasons for its ending depend on whether we look at the world at large or at the American scene.

On one hand, the international system has drastically changed. Analyzing world affairs in bipolar terms may be relevant in a military sense, but it has become a hindrance to understanding today's world. The very unusability of the full panoply of force by the superpowers, the emergence of new nations, the intractability of various conflicts independent from the cold war, and the development of transnational links have strained or broken the blocs, multiplied the actors, and created new chessboards for them to play on.

On the other hand, in the United States, what precipitated not only the recognition of these facts but also a revulsion against the cold war era is the Vietnam tragedy. The international system would have changed even if the United States had never committed itself to the defense of Saigon. But the war in Vietnam made much more acute the problem that the transformation of the international system would have raised in any case—that of giving domestic roots to a new policy adapted to the new world. For the problem of foreign policy today, in any democracy, is twofold: how to devise a strategy that serves the nation's interests, and how to convince the nation that such a strategy deserves support. The external developments of the 1960s made obsolete the strategy that had been devised in the late 1940s. The war in Vietnam destroyed the consensus. In a way, this may have been a service—at what a price!—for it forced Americans to face the obsolescence of policy earlier than they probably otherwise would have. Given the solidity and stolidity of the elites' support for a stance that fitted in so well with the main features of the American style in foreign affairs, only an earthquake could destroy the consensus. But in another way,

"Will the Balance Balance at Home?" was published originally in *Foreign Policy*, Number 7, Summer 1972. Copyright © 1972 by Stanley Hoffmann. It will, in revised form, be part of *The Burden and the Balance*, to be published by McGraw-Hill.

the Vietnam earthquake, while accelerating the demise of the
old, may also have delayed beyond reason the appearance of
a new consensus.

When the Nixon administration came to power, it thus faced
a changed world and a chaotic nation. It has, bit by bit,
pieced together a new strategy that tries to address itself to
both problems. Instead of looking at the world as a bipolar
contest of blocs—however muted by the factors I have
listed—it envisages it as an emerging multipolar system, to
be structured and regulated by the balance of power. Instead
of relations of total enmity or total friendship, both inimical
to diplomacy, there would again be those fluctuating mixes
of common and divergent interests characteristic of eighteenth and nineteenth century European diplomacy. Ideology
would not disappear, but its external effects would be neu-
tralized: different political systems could coexist, since beliefs would be disconnected from behavior through voluntary
or necessary restraint. From the color of a given regime one
should no longer be able to deduce the nature of its alliances
and external pursuits.

The diplomatic game would be horizontal rather than ver-
tical: a great power would be more concerned with its maneuvers with and around the other major states than with the
courtship of the weak; it would, properly, worry about the designs of its equals rather than about the tantrums of the pyg-
mies. The management of the central concern of foreign
policy—how to limit the ambitions of one's rivals—would no
longer be entrusted to the technique that had dominated for
twenty years: the organization of a camp around a hegemonial leader, thereby condemned to anguish all over the world.
One could again count on other powers, not necessarily
one's allies, for the containment of one's rivals and worry
less about minor shifts or losses. Thus, mobility would be
restored to the diplomatic game, and changes in the international system would, once more, result from the playing of
the game itself rather than from "eyeball to eyeball" crises,
always too threatening to the game and the players.

Such a new strategy not only matches trends already apparent in the world, it also seems to correspond to the psychological conditions of the United States after Vietnam. Instead of a universal American presence on the front lines, the
new strategy promises self-restraint. After the colossal

strains of engagement, it points to some disengagement. After the delusion, or dream, of the "world mission," after the pretense of being the only nation with a sense of world responsibility, the teacher of all other nations, the new strategy proclaims that self-interest, not the activist idealism that leads to empire and disillusionment, will be the guiding principle—the cement of a new consensus around a policy that promises better results than those achieved by what I had called "Gulliver in the chain gang";* for there would be a double liberation: from the chain gang of the old, inflexible, and stalemated system, and from the posture of being Gulliver. The old strategy was often strident in its rhetoric, hectic in its effort to keep a domestic consensus behind far-flung military, economic, and diplomatic enterprises. The new strategy, after Vietnam, unfolds, on the whole, with coolness—either as a spectacle, as during the president's trip to China, or with magisterial discursiveness, as in Dr. Kissinger's yearly scholarly publication, the State of the World message, perhaps a relic of the "publish or perish" imperative—certainly not with the trumpet calls for mobilization characteristic of the Kennedy inaugural address, so insistently used by the Nixon administration as the symbol of the militancy it has discarded. The old strategy, geared to a single and simple imperative—anti-Communism—could afford the complexities of a highly splintered decision-making system. The new strategy, geared to the subtleties and shifts of the balance of power, requires a centralized and lofty machinery such as that of the National Security Council system.

What I would like to examine is the domestic side of the new foreign policy. This may not be the most interesting problem; analyzing whether it really meets the realities and the challenges of the international system, whether the world of the last third of the twentieth century is manageable in a Metternichian or Bismarckian way is probably more fascinating. But the most intelligently conceived strategy will fail if the domestic conditions are not ripe. Metternich's world outlasted Metternich, but the revolution of 1848 put an end to his policy; and it was the internal dismissal of Bismarck that led to a gradual dismantling of his grand scheme.

*Stanley Hoffmann, *Gulliver's Troubles, Or the Setting of American Foreign Policy* (New York: McGraw Hill, 1968).

The domestic side of the new policy can itself be discussed in two stages. First, what are the domestic prerequisites of success for a balance-of-power strategy; and if we find that the traditional prerequisites are out of reach, are modern equivalents available? Second, if we find that the strategy is not really well adapted to the outside world, that the new international system cannot be equipped with an eighteenth or nineteenth century transmission, motor, and brakes, what would be the likely internal repercussions?

Kissinger's NSC vs. Metternich's Diplomacy

The traditional internal prerequisites for a successful balance-of-power diplomacy are essentially two. One, to use the current jargon, relates to "bureaucratic politics"; the other, to the "linkage" of domestic politics with foreign policy.

The first prerequisite was that the nation's policy be formulated, and its interest defined, by a small, professional elite, coherent enough to provide the flexibility, negotiating skills, discretion, and imagination essential to that type of strategy, continuous enough to prevent sudden reversals not required by shifts in the outside world and to nurture traditions. In today's America, however, we run into two obstacles. Obstacle No. 1 is excruciatingly familiar: the problem of coordination. Despite the establishment of the National Security Council system, there is no end to the old headache of too many centers of decision, too many voices, too heavy a bureaucracy. To be sure, the National Security Council system under Henry Kissinger has introduced a modicum of order. But it has also created three problems of its own.

One, as pointed out recently by former U.N. Ambassador Charles Yost,* the kind of order that has been instituted is one that gives the military services an even greater weight in decision making than before—and they are not necessarily the most skillful practitioners of diplomatic flexibility.

Two, despite its expansion, the National Security Council staff cannot manage and control all foreign policy issues.** There are limits to what any such staff can do, and inevitably

---

*Charles W. Yost, "The Instruments of American Foreign Policy," *Foreign Affairs*, October 1971, pp. 59-68.

**See Destler, pp. 165-75, and Leacacos, pp. 176-90.

differences will emerge between the way in which it handles issues it considers important enough for itself and the handling of those it leaves to other agencies. If those it deems not vital enough for itself become crises, due to mismanagement, they may well turn out to be vital after all. As in the past, differences between agencies either lead to confusion (as was visible during the China debate in the United Nations General Assembly) or drift toward uncomfortable compromises between the positions developed by different parts of the bureaucracy (as over our Middle East policy, which provides always just enough aid to Israel to infuriate the Arabs, but in such doses as to perpetuate Arab hopes for a change in U.S. support of Israel; it also puts just enough pressure on Israel toward a settlement to annoy the Israeli government, but not so much as to force it to make major concessions). Or else these divergences necessitate presidential arbitration once they have become paralyzing or dangerous—such as the recent presidential decision, a compromise, between the State Department's "soft" and the Treasury's "tough" line on Latin American expropriations, and the president's dampening of Mr. Connally once the actual political repercussions and potential military impact of his aggressive foreign economic policies made it possible for the National Security Council to reassert its jurisdiction in this area. In the past, the guideline of national security interpreted in cold war terms provided some kind of criterion for reconciling differences. In a fluctuating balance-of-power world, such a criterion is far less evident, and each agency may develop its own definition of the national interest, depending, for instance, on the nature of its constituency. Both prereconciliation divergences and postreconciliation rigidities could be even more harmful, to a strategy that requires tact and mobility, than in the past. As of today, there are three centers of executive power under the president: the National Security Council system, the State Department—residually—and the Treasury—by default. An end to this perennial headache is hard to imagine. The logical solution proposed by many—a return to State Department primacy—demands not only a thorough rejuvenation and reorganization of Foggy Bottom (a not inconceivable but herculean task), but also an abdication by other departments and agencies of *their* foreign policy roles and branches: a rather unimaginable sacrifice. It is easier for all these departments and agen-

cies to accept the tutelage of the National Security Council—
a presidential outfit—than that of an equal like the State
Department.

The third problem created by the National Security Council
system is potentially even more serious. A deep crisis in
executive-legislative relations has been opened by the Vietnam war. This congressional (and especially senatorial) res-
tiveness would in any case complicate the formulation of the
new strategy, especially because any balance-of-power
policy, with its requirements of secrecy and discretion,
seems to demand at least as much executive control as the
policy of the recent past, and thus runs counter to the kind of
shared executive-legislative policymaking for which senatorial and other critics of the cold war docility or atrophy of
Congress in foreign affairs have been calling. To be sure, this
need not be a decisive obstacle: insofar as the controversy
centers around the war powers of the president and the new
strategy promises self-restraint, a balance-of-power policy
could in some way facilitate rapprochement. But nothing
guarantees that congressional priorities would be the same
as the executive's, and the new importance of the National
Security Council system gives an added dimension to this
problem: for the man who dominates the system cannot be
summoned before congressional committees. The solution
proposed by Francis Wilcox—a joint legislative-executive
committee on national security affairs*—is hard to conceive
as long as the special assistant for national security affairs is
on top of Mount Olympus, unreachable by Congress down
below, and the only executive *interlocuteurs* available to Congress are chaps whose policy role is marginal or fragmentary.

To sum up: the present NSC system, rather than restoring
the traditional conditions in which balance-of-power policies
were formulated, tends to add a new layer. A "traditional"
closed shop has been superimposed upon the heavy bureaucracy we have inherited from the cold war era. It also adds a
new irritant to those that executive preponderance and its
abuse had created in the eyes of many congressmen—thus
worsening the problem of achieving a new consensus, to
which I will turn in a while.

* Francis O. Wilcox, *Congress, the Executive and Foreign Policy* (New
York: Harper & Row, 1971), pp. 157 ff.

Elite Discontinuity

But first let me examine Obstacle No. 2 to the formulation of policy by a coherent and continuous elite: after the old problem of coordination, the new problem of continuity. Today we have, on one hand, a huge "foreign policy machine," dispersed, creaky, and minimally efficient, symbolized by what has repeatedly been called the State Department "fudge factory." Its heaviness is largely responsible for its decline; and yet it is there that continuity is found: *there* are the career officers and the country experts. Discarded for a variety of reasons—layering, low morale, addiction to mere reporting, timidity—the State Department has become the victim of a self-fulfilling prophecy: its neglect makes the charges true, and the internal impulses for reform have been recurrently smothered under the ashes.

On the other hand, there is, at the center, next to the president, a dazzling solo performance by a man who is unique, thus irreplaceable. But his performance is a problem as much as a promise. First, his working habits, as is well known, drive ordinary human beings out of his shop; their choice seems to be between making foreign policy (or rather, helping the foreign policy maker make it) and living. So they leave. Hence, in the closed shop I mentioned, continuity is not assured. Second, this would not be so serious if there were—as there was for over twenty years—a big reservoir of men, both within the government and outside (in the universities, the professions, business) from which one could readily draw for the formulation and execution of foreign policy. Today, it seems, the great postwar pond is almost dry: the Marshall Plan generation has retired, and the generation to whom the torch—the same cold war torch—was going to be passed, in JFK's words, has been decimated by Vietnam. Today there is only a skeleton crew that waits to step in. It is no insult to its competence to say that it is small in size, restricted in scope (by being in many instances more knowledgeable about military affairs than about foreign policy on a global scale), and uncertain in prospect (both because its chances in the near future are not so great and because its own cohesion, its own world view, are unclear). Prolonged exile from power could lead even to its dispersion. As for younger blood, it does not exactly run toward foreign policy.

In other words, the reestablishment of a consensus is in itself a prerequisite to the kind of continuity, to the creation of a foreign policy elite, that the new policy demands. It is not a *sufficient* prerequisite, because the grand solo performance on top is of a sort that does not need, or want, extensive participation, even if such an elite were more broadly available. But it is a *necessary* condition—and one of the results of the solo performance is, paradoxically, to discourage its emergence: why bother, if there is a man who "knows" and who does not exactly invite meddling? In the conditions of the eighteenth century or even of the post-Congress of Vienna world, the statesmen could draw on a seemingly permanent pool recruited by elite schools and largely based on birth. There is no such pool in the United States; and what provided an equivalent in the recent past—wartime experiences in international administration, the subsequent rewards, in prestige and positions, of "world leadership"—has faded. The substitution of a new policy makes the issue of recruitment for foreign affairs more anguishing for the long term, even if a great performer makes it less pressing in the short run.

Skillful Policy plus Clever Politics?

The second internal prerequisite for the success of the new policy is far more monumental. Traditionally, a balance-of-power policy was not merely formulated by the kind of elite described above, but also conducted in considerable isolation from domestic currents. There is a new view—part of the revisionist offensive—that explains that this is nonsense and that foreign policy was always largely a diversion from, if not the export of, domestic conflict. There is some occasional truth in this, but not much more. I am more struck by the continuity of foreign policy, despite party changes and social transformations and constitutional upheavals, than I am by the primacy of domestic conflict in foreign affairs. Even at Versailles—when the balance of power had collapsed—statesmen were concerned with one issue besides the specter of Bolshevism: the role of Germany. The deterioration or breakdown of the balance of power can indeed often be attributed to domestic turmoil or revolutions. But that proves my point: its success required insulation—which is precisely why, wrongly, theorists from Tocqueville to Lippmann have had doubts about the capacity of democracies to wage such a policy. Democracies could do so—as long as the parties were willing to leave foreign affairs outside the arena of fundamental disagreements and the electorate was willing to trust the foreign policy elite.

Obviously such insulation is a thing of the past all over the world. Today foreign policy is not so much the quest for the national interest outside, or the search for a "reason of state" for conduct abroad, as it is the external projection of national moods and concerns. That this makes the relevance of balance-of-power policies and techniques dubious is an important point, to which I shall return. But it does not doom the attempt by itself. For there remains the possibility of two "functional equivalents" of the old insulation. Assuming outside conditions are favorable, a balance-of-power policy could still be successful if it took into account, in its calculations and gambles, the domestic policies of those it tries to affect and if it obtained at home a consensus around the new vision of the world and the newly defined American role in it. The two questions one must raise are, therefore, these: Can we develop something we've never been good at—a diplomacy that is not merely skillful policy but also clever politics? Can we develop, around the balance of power and America's international interest as a player of that game, the deep support that previously existed first for isolationism and later for globalism?

The first problem is obviously connected with the one I have just discussed: the recruitment of a foreign policy elite. The "structure of peace" that the president wishes to build will require diplomats with considerable expertise about those internal forces, tensions, aspirations, atavisms of other nations that determine or at least influence the definition of their interests, or set limits to what can be demanded of them. The new policy, being less ambitious than the old, no longer requires from the United States a more or less subtle presence in, and manipulation of, the domestic politics of dozens of nations. But even if we decide to concentrate only on key countries, the subtle maneuverings of the balance we seek and the confrontation of national interests we encourage are not likely to lead to moderation unless we show greater skills in this respect than we have in the past. Recent developments do not appear encouraging. The way in which we have waged our reconciliation with China did a great deal to undermine the most pro-American government Japan is likely to have. The shock tactics that are part of the "billiard game" of balance-of-power strategy, in which one power acts by itself in order to force others to adjust, may fail if there are some reasons why those others simply cannot take the measures that the U.S. tactics aim at provoking, or must stick to the policies U.S. shoves aim at eliminating, or react with moves different from those our too purely "diplomatic" or "interstate" calculations expected. For instance, an attempt at applying the Nixon Doctrine to NATO that obliged West European governments to increase rapidly their contributions to the common defense would run into insuperable domestic obstacles, however justified such a redistribution of the burden would be from a global viewpoint.

This problem is particularly acute in a period of transition, when allies used to a certain style of American diplomacy are suddenly exposed to the rather more brutal tactics of the new strategy, not so much because the United States did not, in the past, also pursue its own interests, but because the soft veil of "community" is being torn away. What we need are diplomats aware of other nations' anxieties and neuroses. Having got used to a certain tone, and having sometimes seen in it a guarantee against shocks (such as those administered on August 15, 1971), allied governments and their political systems are likely to interpret tactical changes as strategic reversals and to react with far greater indignation than is "objectively" required: for we deal here less with realities than with perceptions.

This means that in such a period we may well face the special difficulty of being caught between two sets of external requirements of our new strategy. Serious changes in military and diplomatic "posture" are demanded by what might be called its new vision of interstate relations, whereas the need to take into account the domestic realities of others (especially our allies) requires that such changes be made prudently, lest they upset the very interstate balance we seek by destroying the internal balance of others. Should our allies believe, despite our protestations, that we are in effect walking out on past commitments, their reactions may, for reasons of a domestic nature, prove to be profoundly destabilizing and beneficial to those very rivals whom we are trying to balance. Only a very subtle and innovative kind of diplomacy could reconcile these different, often divergent sets of considerations.

It would be foolish to expect nations with a whole internal equilibrium arranged around a certain style of relations with the United States to understand at once, and not feel threatened by, the shift in U.S. strategy, just as it was absurd to believe, in the cold war era, that there would be easy harmony or automatic solidarity between us and our allies. The new strategy draws the consequences of the death of the latter illusion, but the way in which it does so shows the survival of another old fallacy: that of believing that what is evident to us—the primacy of anti-Communism yesterday, the need for a balance-of-power system today—is also evident to others and poses no special internal problems to them. What can be done about the training of our foreign affairs personnel so as to inculcate in them a greater awareness of other nations' internal problems, bureaucratic structures, constellations of parties and lobbies, and images of themselves and of others, is unclear, at a time when foreign language requirements are dropped, young people's interest in foreign countries is low, and student desire to join the Foreign Service is hardly visible. The foundations have a responsibility here: their spectacular and almost uniform shift of funds from foreign to domestic affairs has not been helpful, to put it mildly.

New Policy, No Consensus

This shift has reflected and underlined the collapse of the cold war consensus. Thus, we come now to the second problem: that of popular and elite support for the new policy. So far, this policy, while redefining America's role in the world, has merely aimed at, and partially succeeded in, cooling off the dramatic internal debate that accompanied the Vietnam tragedy. But it has not succeeded in establishing a new consensus. What is striking is that it has not really tried. The State of the World messages oscillate from pious generalities, usually unassailable except when they obstinately describe pre-Nixon policies as pure drift in the dark, to highly tactical and piecemeal accounts of recent decisions. The overall political rationale—by which I mean the set of political guidelines that would indicate what the new, allegedly "clear definition of our purpose" is and what kind of international system we have in mind—is missing. Once again, we find instead a set of moral attributes—moderation, fairness, compromise—that do not become more precise just because we proclaim that we no longer strike moralistic poses. Why is this the case? Is it because, in that past so well studied by Dr. Kissinger, the foreign affairs specialists not only did not worry about getting their acrobatics approved and supported by a wide public, but felt that the existence of a broad and active foreign affairs constituency might actually be a burden, because the game was so subtle and demanded such concentration as to rule out unprofessional kibitzers?

If this is the case, it is a misreading, both of the American political system and of twentieth century foreign policy in any democracy. This has never been a polity willing to entrust its role in the world to a group of experts without any questions asked. It would be particularly impossible to introduce such an "ideal" after Vietnam. For Vietnam has not only destroyed the old consensus, it has also put the American government—any American government—under suspicion. One of the most intriguing aspects of the recent turmoil is this: the more radical or vocal critics of our cold war policy have convinced themselves that it was through deception, through a deliberate obfuscation of the public and of Congress, through the machinations of the corporate establishment, through the pursuit of elitism on top, that we got into Vietnam. There was deception, to be sure, but more cosmetic than fundamental. What made Vietnam possible was the cold war consensus. It was that consensus, rather than the dubious tactics of the Johnson administration, that led to the Tonkin Gulf Resolution. Deception was used to protect the consensus from the impact of the disaster to which it had led. A greater willingness on the part of the past administrations to assuage their critics in the Senate, and greater candor in their treatment of public opinion, might in fact have made it easier for the government to preserve the consensus behind a doomed expedition: it would have improved the management of the war at home without achieving anything better on the ground. Today the government officials "responsible for Vietnam," whose mistakes I would be the last to condone, also serve as the public's scapegoats, just as petty war criminals in Vietnam, whose crimes deserve punishment, also serve as scapegoats for mass violations of the laws of war and the ethics of humanity that have been accepted as normal ever since World War II by the great mass of the people. Those who believe that the cold war villains are the momentum of the bureaucracy or the dynamics of American capitalism must still explain how the few succeeded so easily in carrying with them so many for so long.

Be that as it may, the result has been that no administration today could ask for "basic trust," however evident its determination to change the direction of American policy. Nineteen seventy-one was the year of the Pentagon Papers and the Anderson Papers. The assumption that the government is plotting strange things in the dark is still strong and has perhaps even been strengthened by Mr. Nixon's "Gaullist" uses of surprise and secret diplomacy. In effect, the administration does not face a choice between a return to insulated diplomacy and the restoration of a consensus, but between the latter and a paralyzing, destructive continuation of indifference and distrust. The new strategy still entails a major role in the world. Both indifference and distrust would be heavy obstacles for a policy that demands that the United States continue to be able, on various chessboards, in various parts of the world, and at various moments, to commit itself to a course of action, even if it is less often and less completely than in the past. Indeed, the very emphasis put on the pursuit of the national interest (for instance, in the economic and monetary fields) requires an effort at defining that interest in such a way that whatever bold moves the administration deems necessary *not* be undermined by dissent or by incomprehension at home—for instance, among the business community, on whom America's economic health depends, or in Congress, which still has the power of the purse. As another attempt at playing a balance-of-power game, de Gaulle's, has shown, the statesman's skill is of little avail if the public does not endorse his gambles and strokes—for example, his Middle Eastern policy of 1967 or his Canadian venture—or if it is unwilling to sacrifice domestic priorities to the international freedom of maneuver that it relished, and that flattered its vanity, but the costs of which it resented.

Who's for Balance?

The rebuilding of a consensus is, however, a most difficult
task. There are two major obstacles: one atavistic, one more
tied to the present. Anti-Communism has, for over twenty
years, provided a rationale and a cement. What doomed it,
domestically, even more than its increasing external
irrelevance, was the not-so-subtle shift that had taken place,
that got us stuck in Vietnam, and that Robert W. Tucker has
incisively analyzed.* In the late 1940s purpose had been a
function of security—our feeling (rightly or wrongly) threatened by the Soviet Union had, especially in the Truman
Doctrine, shaped the definition of our mission. Whereas in
the late 1960s security had become a function of our purpose—in the days of Dean Rusk and Walt Rostow we said we
couldn't feel secure unless the international milieu conformed to our specifications. But the demise of the old rationale should not obscure the fact that it appealed for a very
long time to many characteristics of America's style in foreign affairs. Anti-Communism seemed to synthesize our
various principles; it corresponded to a past experience that
associated involvement and crusading, commitment and
leadership; it allowed the mobilization of all our organizing
skills and of all our forms of busyness. In other words, while
it represented a shift to the most extreme activist end of
America's traditional pendulum, it provided for a temporary
fusion of what I have called elsewhere the instinct of violence
and the drive for harmony, or what others have called realism
and idealism. Indeed, it stretched both to their limits: it
clothed the former in the appealing garb of the latter, it gave
the latter the irresistible weight of the former, and it allowed
for a formidable expansion of American business, as the
practical servant of American ideals and the companion of
America's might.

It is far from clear that the pursuit of the balance of power and
of the national interest provides an adequate substitute. The
national interest is precisely what has to be defined. Anti-
Communism provided a simplistic but convenient shorthand
definition; remove it, and we seem adrift. The attempt to explain that from now on the national interest is to be seen as

*Robert W. Tucker, *Nation or Empire: The Debate Over American Foreign
Policy,* Studies in International Affairs, Number 10 (Baltimore: Washington
Center of Foreign Policy, 1968).

the establishment and maintenance of a proper equilibrium between the main powers, and as the advent of a moderate international system, may be appealing to specialists of international relations. But is it convincing to citizens whose tradition it is to see in the balance of power a sport of kings or a game of cabinets at the expense of their peoples, in a multipolar world a quicksand in which the United States could easily be trapped by cunning foreign leaders, in a world of harmony under a single set of principles and a common rule of law (ours) the only guarantee of moderation? The voice of Wilson is not dead. Tellingly enough, the few times President Nixon has tried to find a new rationale in his addresses to the public, it has been in Wilsonian, not in Metternichian, terms. The truth of the matter is that anti-Communism appealed to all varieties of American impatience: to those who believe that the only way of fighting an enemy is to seek for victory, that, so to speak, the alternative to world disarmament is escalation, as well as to those who believe that the purpose of America is to promote the American way of life, or American ideals, all over the world. The subtleties of the balance of power, the apparent coldness of a policy that gives up both the most extreme claims of force and those of evangelism, that tries to curb both disembodied idealism and the imperial strivings of a self-interest licensed by idealism, are not likely to strike a similarly responsive chord.

This would have been true at any time. It is particularly so today. For if the new rationale is not likely to appeal to the reservoir of activism in America, it is even less likely to appeal to that other reservoir: quietism, which gets filled by the waters that flow away from activism whenever the latter gets polluted. This is another manifestation of American impatience: if escalation does not work, get out altogether; if the idealism that tries to make the world look like America turns out corrupting, let America stop violating the world by removing herself altogether. So the gap between American foreign policy—old or new—and the public mood persists. The new policy offers a skillful, more modest, more flexible rationale for continuous involvement. The public mood is one of disinvolvement. What one senses, in Congress but also among many of the nation's businessmen, and among most students, is a kind of battle fatigue with the outside world, a desire to leave it alone in order that we be left alone. To some, the Nixon Doctrine is attractive insofar as it means a retreat; but once it becomes clear, in its budgetary implications especially, that it has another face, and implies a lasting world role, it may well cease to be so appealing. Others have denounced that face ever since the beginning.

From One Extreme to the Other

It may well be that a successful balance-of-power policy could gradually, through its achievements, restore a consensus around the middle of the American pendulum. Should, in particular, developments in the relations between the United States and its Communist rivals lead to concrete gains, a reduction of arms races, a modernization of old tensions, a settlement of protracted conflicts, both the maximalists and the minimalists would find themselves running out of anxieties. The current lowering of the decibel level in the public debate (except among foreign policy scholars and journalists who have been mining the rich revisionist quarry) has at least the advantage of allowing the grand solo performance on top to take place relatively unhindered. But the persistent angry dispute over how to settle problems in Southeast Asia, the Senate's reticence about foreign aid or American radio stations in Europe, the new suspicion of even aging defense hawks about the military budget shows that the current mood, while more permissive than destructive, is far from a consensus; and the restoration of one, as I have tried to show, is a *sine qua non* for external success and a prerequisite for the emergence of a new foreign policy elite.

But what would be the international repercussions of an unsuccessful balance-of-power policy? In my opinion, the split that I have just described would be magnified, and instead of a consensus around the middle of the pendulum, we might have a most unsettling oscillation between the two extremes: activism and quietism. There are many reasons for believing that the world of Metternich and Bismarck cannot be recreated in this century. While I cannot analyze them in detail in this essay, let me mention one symptom and three main factors, and examine their likely effects.

The world of the nineteenth century had its summit meetings, especially after wars. But they took place up there, far above the plodding crowds. Today even a balance-of-power policy that aims at restoring diplomacy—the art of protracted preparation and quiet negotiation and ambiguous formulation, and slow returns—cannot do without a very modern brand of spectaculars, which the press and television carry into every home. Now, especially in the American context, in which images feed stereotypes and emotions, such shows reactivate the never-dying aspiration for harmony, the generous and foolish illusion that friendship among peoples is just around the corner because deep down we're somehow all alike, the misleading belief that differences of regime and ideology are mere shaky superstructures that can't repress for long the basic humanity of us all. And, in some quarters at least, it revives a lingering paranoia that fears the trickery of foreigners and reveals a fascinating conviction that Americans abroad are born dupes. While the latter groups are neither very vocal nor very numerous, they run a kind of shelter into which the others, the hopeful ones, tend to take refuge when their high hopes have vanished and when the time has come to look for scapegoats responsible (since human nature is not) for the dream having failed once more. Today, while the president soberly warns of continuing differences and says that *his* highest dream is to make the world livable despite, not without, them, the exuberance of the shows and gullibility of the media turn the China visit into a moon landing and, literally, promise the moon. This does not suggest that, as some have argued, summitry is an evil thing—especially not in this instance, where it was probably the only way of changing a moldy policy and of dealing with a leadership in which only the summit matters. But this very fact underlines my point: *this* balance-of-power world is an original.

Reasons for Skepticism

Let us move on from the spectacle to the fundamentals. First, one reason for skepticism is the absence of a consensus on rules of the game between the major powers. Their behavior is constricted by nuclear interdependence and domestic priorities, but these are essentially outside, frequently unwelcome, constraints. In Vienna or Berlin, all the leaders of the European Concert could meet, however fragile their harmony; where, today, could one have a summit to which Brezhnev, Mao, Nixon, and their Japanese and European counterparts would all consent to come? The Soviet

Union shows no sign of accepting the kinds of limits that a true balance-of-power policy demands—such as the willingness to refrain from exploiting a rival's retreats. While seeking, here and there, a moderation of conflicting interests, it also seems to seek the kind of universal influence and presence the utility of which, indeed the necessity of which, for a greater power seems, unexpectedly enough, to be one of the two lessons the Soviets have learned from our teachings in the 1960s. (Only the other lesson, arms control, was intended.) The Nixon Doctrine on this side is matched by the Brezhnev doctrine on the other. Our retrenchment, if it is not matched by the reinforcement of our allies, is an invitation to our rivals to move in; yet that very reinforcement is an obstacle to our policy of détente. Of the five so-called major powers, one (Europe) does not yet exist, one (Japan) has not found a role, and one (China) happens to be neither a superpower yet nor a very likely practitioner of the balance of power should it become one. Under these circumstances, the United States may well be condemned to more intervention than the new strategy promises. The game of "flexible alignments," in order to succeed, has to be played by all or else the lone player becomes, indeed, a dupe. Perhaps there shall be no new involvements, although a precedent for them is being set in the Persian Gulf; but there could be more preservation of the old than was hoped.

Second, while misjudging somewhat the results that can be achieved among the major powers on the traditional chessboard of international politics—the strategic-diplomatic one—the new policy tends to apply the same principles to other chessboards on which they do not belong; some, like international trade and the international monetary system, are old but have gained tremendously in importance, both because of the relative decline of the strategic game in the nuclear age and because of the saliency of economic issues in this world. Other such chessboards, on which the players are private groups and multinational corporations as well as states, are new; they cover a multiplicity of industrial, scientific, and technological fields. For reasons that cannot be developed here, the Brechtian rules of the balance of power— "my gain is your loss, my aim is to balance you, I push my national interest and you push yours"—simply do not fit there. Mr. Connally has brilliantly shown what happens when one tries: it upsets not only these chessboards of interdependence, but also the traditional chessboard of strategic interaction. Now, the very suggestion that the same game can be played on all has one disastrous domestic implication: it gives a kind of license to various forces that interpret the national interest in highly aggressive or protectionist terms and see in the new approach a welcome shift away from the more internationalist or liberal attitudes of the recent past. Those who are primarily concerned with domestic priorities, whatever happens to world trade or to employment abroad or to international monetary stability, as well as those who want the United States to pursue a more brutal policy in exploiting sea resources or in defending its investments from nationalist seizures, can all find in the new primacy of the national interest, in the pursuit of "a more balanced monetary system and a more equitable trading environment,"* a permit to push things that run exactly counter to the hope of a moderate, stable, well-regulated world. The Hartke-Burke bill is an example. It is clear that, here again, the administration faces a dilemma. Either it emphasizes the break with the past and stresses its desire to lift the burdens associated with the cold war era, and thus plays the sorcerer's apprentice, or else it underlines the desire for a livable international system—but then it has to recognize that the era of entanglements continues and that domestic priorities and lobbies cannot take precedence over our responsibility, as the leading power on many of these chessboards, for making the system work. This in turn would upset all those who fear that economic involvements abroad could again serve as springboards for military ventures, or who see in them a blatant pursuit of economic imperialism and social repression.

Third, a policy that concentrates on the central balance—between major powers—underestimates several very important facts. Today's world has over 130 actors, whose existence, problems, and interrelations simply cannot be treated as a mere by-product of, or factor in, the central balance (this has been amply demonstrated by the India-Pakistan debacle of U.S. foreign policy). Also, all over the world, two other cardinal preconditions of a successful balance of power are gone: the distinction between public and private activities and the

---

*Richard M. Nixon, *U.S. Foreign Policy for the 1970s* II (Washington, D.C.: Government Printing Office, 1972), p. 7.

distinction between internal politics and foreign policy. But the state, however weak or sievelike, remains the major unit of decision; it is likely to try to protect itself vigorously against the threat of "penetration" or to promote itself by exploiting the domestic discords of others. Consequently, this planet is threatened less perhaps by what imperiled balance-of-power systems in the past—the formation of rigid blocs, the resort to force by the major powers—than by generalized chaos; less by the deterioration of the rules of the game, than by massive anomie; less by a failure of central management, than by unmanageability. Should this be the case, the debate would indeed be reopened between two groups. On one side would be those who think that in such a world American self-interest would best be served by its own brand of protectionism, by locking itself in its prosperous fortress, by "decoupling"—a fashionable word—its concerns from those of an anarchical world. On the other side there would be those who on the contrary believe, either out of idealism pure and simple or out of the same kind of realism that reigned during the cold war years, that only an active involvement in international transactions, in foreign aid, in worldwide programs, could stave off the peril—a new alliance of men concerned above all with our selfless responsibility to the "endangered planet" and of men worried first of all by the opportunities that chaos might provide to our chief rivals. Again, the delicate balance, the middle ground sought by the present policy, would be lost.

The Weakness of Stability

These three weaknesses can be summed up as one. The new policy shares with the previous one a central concept: the search for stability. Less rigid than the old approach to international affairs, it remains a bit too geometric, too mechanistic, too engineering. The quest for order is understandable—that is what any responsible foreign policy is about. But our idea of order remains, even today, wedded to a conception that makes of military interstate confrontations among the great powers the principal peril to be avoided. That it is a terrible peril, in the nuclear age, is obvious. But the very cataclysmic prospects of nuclear war among the major states, while they make deterrence essential, also make other kinds of perils more immediate. The new policy puts, on the United States, a dubious burden and a dangerous blinder: the burden of teaching others, who may not want them, the rules of our preferred game, the blinder of neglecting precipices and problems that simply do not enter our universe of discourse. Yesterday we were being told that the world was a single chain, or a single mine field, and that we had the responsibility of seeing that no mine blows off.Today we are told that peace is somewhat divisible and that we can relax a bit, but we are still told that we are the pacesetters in global self-restraint. What would happen in the United States if a policy that remains one of global concern (if not entanglement) should produce neither very tangible rewards nor the kind of stability it seeks? If reality turned out to be not the new big five but both the old big two (perhaps three) and the recently emerged one hundred-odd others? I fear the resulting cacophony and vendettas. Some would demand a new isolationism, either *a la* George Wallace, in order to stop wasting money on Hottentots who spit in our faces, or else in order to set up an oasis of domestic justice and prosperity in a hopeless world. Others would call for a new crusade, either to save the world from hunger, pollution, overpopulation, or industrial growth, or to defend our own far-flung positions. In a world without consensus an old association of order with military balances or with legal structures—so well analyzed by Robert Osgood many years ago*—is a permanent invitation to domestic dissent: between those who will find such an order too military and those who won't find it military enough, and also between those who will deem it too demanding altogether and those who will find it too timid or too selfish in its demands. For the world of today the balance of power familiar to students of history is the past; there is no future in our past. Should we try anyhow, there would be a past in our domestic future—the past of oscillation and "great debates."

More Gloomy Thoughts

These have been gloomy thoughts. I must end with a few more. Despite the orderly minds at the top, this remains, at home and abroad, a period of confusion. At a moment when

*Robert E. Osgood, *Ideals and Self-Interest in America's Foreign Relations* (Chicago: University of Chicago Press, 1953).

policymaking is more centralized, and in many ways more remote than ever, there is a clamor, born of the Vietnam tragedy, for a "popular" foreign policy, openly arrived at. But some of those who demand one really wish for no foreign policy at all; others expect from it feats of world-good-doing idealism that nothing in the makeup of middle America today allows one to anticipate; others have forgotten that in the absence of a strong consensus, or of the kind of decisive executive leadership that is precisely the opposite of what they wish, the people, the informed public, and Congress are likely to exhibit little more than perplexity. In such a mood what is most likely to break through the crust of confusion is the kind of protectionism or will to retrenchment that is least likely to help either the new strategy or, indeed, a stable world order.

One thing is clear to me: there is no fortress America in the last part of the twentieth century. While our involvement in world affairs must take different forms, less costly to ourselves and to others than those of the cold war years, and probably more varied, more imaginative, less traditional than those outlined so far by the administration, we shall not be able either to understand their necessity or to discern their shapes unless the public's interest for, and information about, the outside world is sustained. Indifference and the xenophobic reactions it breeds, illusions derived from ignorance and the self-accusatory excesses they engender—these are more than we can afford. Yet the amount and quality of information American citizens receive today about the outside world are seriously deficient. Television coverage, inevitably, cherishes crises and climaxes—wars, riots, floods, state visits, and the sampling of Chinese food by presidential palates. Often it has been daring and provocative, but, again, mainly around "hot" issues, like Vietnam, or in the dizzying form of rather simplified pro-and-con arguments precariously balanced on top of an issue. As for the press, with the exception of a very small number of fine papers and magazines, both the quality of reporting and commentary and the quantity of space devoted to the outside world have been declining, even though the earlier levels were never very high. Is it because a world that is obviously not our oyster and the complexities of which defy analysis ceases being interesting?

Whatever the reason, the fact is that outside a thin geographical area—the Northeast—this country has, materially, become almost insulated again. The disarray of the councils or associations that served as relays between the administration and the enlightened public in the cold war days, the shift in foundation concerns, the failure of academic centers of foreign policy studies either to grow or to broaden their fascination with models and computers so as to include the real world, the discredit that has (not always unfairly) affected think tanks at the service of the government or academics whose itch to advise the prince has often subverted their values and deadened their language—all of this makes the rebuilding of a consensus, the education of a general public that senses with relief the demise of the old but does not know what to expect, the recreation of a concerned elite, and the training of an adequate foreign policy personnel extremely difficult tasks. As long as they are not undertaken, the dangers and uncertainties of the outside world are likely to feed the demons and anxieties to which Americans have so often been addicted in the past.

THE ESTABLISHMENT
by Godfrey Hodgson

The American foreign policy establishment is now divided even on the question of its own existence.

McGeorge Bundy, for example, very much doubts whether there has ever been such a thing as the establishment. And this is surprising, for only a few years ago Bundy's name would automatically have been mentioned as the natural head of that mythical but very real entity.

When I talked to him recently in his office in the Ford Foundation's strangely Piranesian headquarters on 42 Street, he murmured learnedly about misapplications of Pareto's theory of the circulation of elites and then asked somewhat sharply where the establishment had been during the Eisenhower years. At the head of the State Department and the CIA, for a start, I suggested, in the persons of the Dulles brothers. Surely, he argued, like a very polite tiger moving in for the kill, any definition of the establishment that included both John Foster Dulles and Adlai Stevenson was so wide as to be meaningless. For Bundy, the establishment, "like 'intellectual,' is a word that confuses without defining."

Cyrus Vance, in his only slightly smaller office, looking out over the Statue of Liberty from a crisp new skyscraper at the lower tip of Manhattan, disagrees. And there are those who would say that Vance, after a distinguished career in the law, as deputy secretary of defense, and as a Vietnam peace negotiator, is poised to replace Bundy as the next chairman of the establishment. "I don't think the establishment is dead," he said. "I think it will continue to function, and usefully."

In his book-lined sanctum in the Littauer building at Harvard, decorated with some of the exquisite miniatures he brought back from his tour as ambassador in New Delhi, John Kenneth Galbraith disagrees with both Bundy and Vance. "The foreign policy elite was always the world's biggest collection of meatheads."

While in his office in Washington, the one with the view out over the White House which is said to impress his clients so

"The Establishment" was published originally in *Foreign Policy*, Number 10, Spring 1973.

much that it has helped him to become the highest-paid lawyer in the country, Clark Clifford recounts gloomily, though perhaps not without a certain lugubrious sense of justice done, how many brilliant reputations in the foreign policy establishment have been destroyed. Take A, he says. He had something of a reputation as a stragetic thinker. He was even, says Clifford, studying his fingertips, something of an oracle. Well, says Clifford, looking up, he has been crucified.

I suggested that it was above all the war that had destroyed the influence of the foreign policy elite. He looked at me with the faintly ironic pleasure of a teacher whose pupil has finally seized what to the teacher is a painfully elementary truth. "My friend," he replied, "you are so"—pause—"very"—pause—"right."

Fiction or Fact?

But can we afford to beg McGeorge Bundy's question out of hand? Is there, has there ever been, an American foreign policy establishment?

It was the British journalist Henry Fairlie who coined the phrase "the establishment," in its modern sense, in an article in the *Spectator* in the 1950s. He did not apply it, as it is too often loosely applied in America today, to the "upper class," or to the rich, or to conservatives. He coined it to describe a reality of political life in Britain as he saw it at the time: the group of powerful men who know each other or at least know someone who knows anyone they may need to know, who share assumptions so deep that they do not need to be articulated, and who contrive to wield power outside the constitutional or political forms: the power to put a stop to things they disapprove of, to promote the men they regard as reliable, and to block the unreliable—the power, in a word, to preserve the status quo. Fairlie was explicitly not thinking only of politicians: the editor of *The Times,* the archbishop of Canterbury, the top civil servants in Whitehall, and the most influential bankers in the City were members of his establishment, and not all cabinet members could make the same claim. On the other hand, membership for Fairlie was explicitly not a question of party politics. The true establishment man prided himself on his nonpartisanship, his ability to get on and work with right-minded fellows of either party.

The very existence of such undemocratic and cabalistic influences is profoundly shocking to many Americans; it
seems to negate the populist mythology of American democracy. No doubt this is one of the reasons why even many
who display the strongest establishment reflexes and characteristics are fond of scoffing in public at the very idea that
it exists. Back in 1966, for example, Flora Lewis of *The Washington Post* drew a deft dry point of John J. McCloy and Dean
Rusk at a black-tie dinner of the Council on Foreign Relations, rocking with dignified and apparently not altogether
displeased mirth at the notion that "the Council on Foreign
Relations is a member of the establishment."

And yet when Richard Rovere first imported Fairlie's term
into America, in a famous article in *The American Scholar* in
1961, it was John J. McCloy and Dean Rusk whom he chose
as presidents emeritus and incumbent, respectively, of the
establishment; and it was the Council that he named as "a
sort of Presidium for that part of the Establishment that
guides our destiny as a nation."

Rovere's piece was written as a spoof, decked out with fake
scholarly references in the manner of Stephen Potter's
Gamesmanship. He went so far as to say that the Council's
prestigious quarterly, *Foreign Affairs,* "has, in its field, the
authority of *Pravda* or *Izvestia.*" In those days, you had to be
joking when you compared any American institution to its
Russian counterpart.

But since Rovere's squib, the idea that there is indeed an
American establishment, and that it exercises influence particularly over foreign affairs, has taken root in earnest and
has become part of the common coin of political debate in
the United States. Nor is there anything original in the idea
that the foreign policy establishment should bear a large part
of the responsibility for the Vietnam war. Such books as
Noam Chomsky's *American Power and the New Mandarins*,
Richard J. Barnet's *The Roots of War*, and David Halberstam's *The Best and the Brightest*, for example, contain
elaborate discussions of that proposition. The corollary,
however, has not been so widely noted: that among the
casualties of the Vietnam war have been the unity, the credibility, the influence, and perhaps the survival in any recognizable form of the American foreign policy establishment.

What Is It?

What is the establishment? It is certainly not identical with the Council on Foreign Relations, which has become something of a whipping boy for liberal journalists (as well as for the lunatic right) and even the focus of a good deal of conspiracy theory. Its importance, both as the headquarters and as the test of membership in the establishment, has probably been exaggerated. And in any case, even if the Council was crucial at one time, as a result of the crisis of confidence brought on largely by the Vietnam war, it has considerably modified its attitudes and its membership.

There has also been a tendency to confuse the establishment and the upper class. It may help you to rise in the establishment if you have inherited wealth, or family connections with powerful men in it, or an Ivy League education. But many representative and influential establishment figures had none of these things, while many a millionaire alumnus of Harvard or Yale could not hope for membership. Typically, perhaps, the establishment man comes from that class that George Orwell, in one of his essays, identified as the backbone of the British Empire: the "lower upper middle class." Among the older generation of establishment leaders—Acheson, the Dulleses, Stimson, Lovett, McCloy—one does find a high proportion of graduates of the old, elite private preparatory schools and of Harvard, Princeton, and Yale. Since until recently those schools gave relatively few scholarships, charged high fees, and reserved a substantial proportion of their places for children of their own alumni, it follows that most of those older members of the establishment came from what are known in America as "old" or "good" families. But by no means would all of them have been called wealthy families. Both Dean Acheson and the Dulles brothers were the children of clergymen, and the typical establishment man of the older generation came from that kind of family: one that could afford to give its sons the inheritance of a superior education, but had little money to leave after that.

Among the younger men, as Bayless Manning, the head of the Council on Foreign Relations, pointed out to me, the catchment in geographic origin and social class has been much wider—if for no other reason, because the GI Bill after World War II and the Korean War allowed almost any young man of average intelligence who was keen enough about it to get to a good graduate school, where he could study law, the prime avenue to the seats of the establishment, or international relations. Even so, the proportion of even the younger men occupying key foreign policy jobs in America who are graduates of either Harvard or Yale is extremely striking in relation to the proportion of men from the same universities whom one would find in the more sought-after jobs in business or in politics.

Nevertheless, the foreign policy establishment, as I understand it, is defined not by sociology or education, and still less by genealogy, but by a history, a policy, an aspiration, an instinct, and a technique.

The history stretches back to Colonel House and the tiny group of businessmen and scholars with knowledge of Europe whom he gathered round him at Versailles for the Peace Conference in 1919. It continued with the efforts of a handful of Americans, most of them drawn from the international banking community in New York and from its lawyers, to combat the rising tide of isolationism after the Senate defeated membership in the League of Nations in 1920.

But historically speaking the crucial event was World War II. It was the war that brought together the three groups that make up the modern foreign policy establishment: the internationally minded lawyers, bankers, and executives of international corporations in New York, the government officials in Washington, and the academics.

Government service, especially in the Office of Strategic Services (OSS), forerunner of the CIA, gave a whole generation of intellectuals and academics a taste for power and an orientation toward government service which they have never lost. "We were kids," one of them, Carl Kaysen, later McGeorge Bundy's deputy in the White House and now the head of the Institute for Advanced Study at Princeton, once reminisced: "We were kids, captains and majors, telling the whole world what to do." When they went back to their law offices or their classrooms, they took with them contacts and attitudes they had learned with OSS. And they were all to meet again—George Ball, David Bruce, Allen Dulles, Arthur Goldberg, John Kenneth Galbraith, Arthur Schlesinger, Walt Rostow, Paul Nitze, and so on.

The dangerous complexities of military technology, strategic confrontations, and world power after World War II all reinforced this tripartite alliance. Moreover, there was a mood of national destiny and, after the Soviet Union acquired nuclear weapons, a sense of national danger. Both, incidentally, were nonpartisan. They were felt equally by largely Republican Wall Street and by the predominantly Democratic intellectuals in the great graduate schools. And, given the political weakness of the Democrats in the years 1945-48, they needed the bipartisan support that Republicans in key jobs could bring.

Each of the great decisions of American policy in the Truman years tied these same ties tighter. Bankers and professors took time off to work in the administration of the Marshall Plan, on NATO, or on rethinking strategic policy. A trickle of academics and lawyers began to go down to Washington as consultants, especially on these international programs.

The Establishment's Policy

But, more important than that, the grand strategy of the Truman administration was the establishment's policy. For the kernel of policy was simple: to oppose isolationism. That is the bedrock of the American establishment's thinking about the world. The experience of World War II had reinforced it, and had plaited a compatible strand to it. The American opponents of isolationism, to a man, felt that appeasement had been a disaster, and that the lesson to be drawn from the struggle against fascism was that there were those in the world who could only be restrained by force, that the use of force in international affairs might therefore indeed be justified, and that great powers must maintain the credibility of their willingness to use force. The policy of the establishment was anti-Communist: the capitalist right and the social democratic left within the coalition, Wall Street and Cambridge, could agree on that. An important qualification must be made. Establishment anti-Communism was essentially for export. One of the issues that distinguished the establishment from the right was the establishment's far lesser concern with domestic Communism: a distinction that had crucial consequences in the McCarthy era, when a conservative, nationalist anti-Communist like Acheson found himself attacked as if he had been a man of the left.

The establishment's favorite term for its own policy has been "liberal internationalism." The term "liberal" has been greatly devalued in American politics: what the establishment meant by liberalism was a tendency to advocate restraint, to dislike crude militarism or overbearing chauvinism, and to show sensitivity to the prickings of conscience. (Galbraith has called this, in tribute to the most prestigious of American private schools, "the Groton ethic.") But these liberal tendencies are, after all, relative. The establishment's style has been to deprecate chauvinism, and at the same time to press for American wishes to be respected and American strength felt around the world, to advocate restraint and yet to despise softness, to admire a willingness to use military power, to feel conscience but by no means to allow it to paralyze one into inaction.

The establishment's favorite European, Winston Churchill, called the American commitment to Europe in the Marshall Plan "the most unsordid act in history," and unsordid it certainly was. But it was also characteristic of the establishment to take on the burdens of world power with a certain avidity. George Ball once penetratingly observed that the Europeans had entered upon colonialism not so much for its economic advantages as for "the satisfactions of power." It was strange that he did not recognize the echo of his own contemporaries' feelings; for power—the unprecedented economic, military, and political power of the United States after 1945—was their birthright, and they found it highly satisfying. Colonialists they were not; they did not need to be. But the Bay of Pigs was the sort of thing they meant by internationalism, and so was Vietnam.

For their aspiration was quite simply to the moral and political leadership of the world. Once, many years later, after President Kennedy's death, his principal speech writer, Theodore Sorensen, used that very phrase: Americans should aspire, he wrote, to the "moral leadership of the world." That was 1968. By then the national mood, the intellectual fashion, had changed. The war had changed them. But that had been the core of the establishment's aspiration. Specifically, the American establishment wanted America to succeed Britain as the military and economic guarantor and moral leader of an enlightened, liberal, democratic, and capitalist world order.

"Britain had given up its role as the 'balance wheel,'" Townsend Hoopes put it to me in an interview. "The idea of a single Western coalition holding the world in balance against the infidel is fundamental to this particular establishment." (He added, and this is one establishment man whose changed attitude can be attributed with certainty to the Vietnam war: "This idea is now obsolescent.") The idea of a "power vacuum" into which it was the grim but grand duty of America to insert itself is fundamental to the establishment's perception of the world. And this idea springs from the notion of America as the lineal heir of Britain, and to a lesser extent of the other European powers, especially France.

The establishment's instinct has always been for the center. "If American politics have a predilection for the center," McGeorge Bundy has said, "it is a good thing." And he went on to list all the "major undertakings of postwar American foreign policy" and to claim that all had "turned upon the capacity of the Executive to take and hold the center." In this context he listed the Marshall Plan, NATO, the Kennedy Round, the Cuban missile crisis, "strategic strength," the test ban treaty, and even Middle Eastern policy as the policies of the center. The center is an interesting concept in politics: to some extent those who want to occupy it must find their positions defined for them by what others are saying. (We shall come back to this point.) But psychologically it is true, and important, that the characteristic men of the establishment—Stimson, McCloy, Acheson, Rusk, Bundy—have always seen themselves as the men of judicious, pragmatic wisdom, avoiding ideology and steering the middle course between the ignorant yahoos of the right and the impractical sentimentality of the left.

It has been said that one leitmotiv of the establishment has been the fear of public opinion. That is perhaps too strong. But it is true that the establishment's origins lay in the resistance to isolationist mass opinion. And it is also true that its historical opportunity lay not in electoral or congressional politics but in what C. P. Snow has called "closed politics." It has risen with the executive branch at the expense of Congress, and especially with the White House and the "national security" institutions created since 1945: OSD (Office of the Secretary of Defense), ISA (Office of the Assistant Secretary of Defense for International Security Affairs), and the CIA.

A Working Definition

The establishment has therefore developed a characteristic technique, a recognizable *modus operandi.* It has worked out of the public eye, and through the executive branch, especially through the White House. (It is almost part of the definition of the true establishment insider that he has never run for elective office. W. Averell Harriman, former governor of New York, is perhaps the exception that proves the rule; politicians would argue that he had little taste for the electoral process, and connoisseurs might argue that he was always too much of an individualist to be a typical establishment man. The fact that McGeorge Bundy once ran unsuccessfully for the Boston City Council is of merely archaeological significance; the mistake was not repeated.)

To come to a working definition, then: for me the foreign policy establishment consists of a self-recruiting group of men (virtually no women) who have shared a bipartisan philosophy toward, and have exercised practical influence on, the course of American defense and foreign policy. I would add that to qualify for membership a man must have a reputation for ability in this field that is accepted by at least two of three worlds: the world of international business, banking, and the law in New York, the world of government in Washington, and the academic world, especially in Cambridge, but also in a handful of other great graduate schools and in the major foundations. And I would further suggest that this group of men was in fact characterized, from World War II until the late 1960s at least, by a history of common action, a shared policy of "liberal internationalism," an aspiration to world leadership, an instinct for the center, and the habit of working privately through the power of the newly bureaucratized presidency.

To identify the existence of an establishment, of course, is not to assert that it is monolithic. Any elite will be divided in several directions: by tensions between the leaders and the outer rings of its membership, and between the older and younger generations, as well as by genuine intellectual disagreements, which are nevertheless capable of being reconciled in the framework of an overall consensus. To show that disagreements exist within a given group of men by no means proves that they do not constitute a group.

Those who are reluctant to admit the historical reality of the American foreign policy establishment lay heavy stress on the disagreements between its putative members. But these disagreements turn out on examination to have been largely tactical. Should we intervene now, or later? With advisers, or Marines, or troops? On the premises of action, in the assumption that nothing could be worse than letting South Vietnam "fall" to the Communists, the consensus was so nearly absolute that disagreement virtually guaranteed disbarment. Perhaps the most striking single impression one derives from reading the Pentagon Papers is that, through long years of constant, minute-by-minute debate of the immediately available options (How much pressure should we exert on Diem in return for our support? Should we bomb the North now, or only later? How many American troops, and how fast?) the most fundamental questions went by default.

From 1956 to 1965 virtually every member of the establishment endorsed the broad lines of U.S. policy in Southeast Asia. With certain exceptions, which I will discuss, there was no serious dissent within the establishment circles from the U.S. commitment to contain Communism in Asia as it had been contained in Europe, from the commitment to maintain South Vietnam independent of the North, in spite of the 1954 agreements; nor, indeed, at the level of tactics, was there noticeable dissent from the support for Diem or from the initial commitment of military aid and "advisers." And this was because it was a prerequisite for being taken seriously as a foreign policy adviser to the government to support the general policy of which these were specific applications: the policy of active intervention wherever required to defend "the Free World" against Communist encroachment, Communist subversion, and even native left-wing insurrection in the developing world.

Certain qualifications should be made. The first is that certain individuals with standing in the establishment did have the foresight to question the wisdom of the commitment in South Vietnam specifically. Both George Ball and John Kenneth Galbraith had done so privately to President Kennedy by the end of 1961, for example.

The second is that in a larger context the establishment had been divided, within the framework of its larger consensus about internationalism and anti-Communism, on the specific question of policy toward the Third World. A minority school of thought on the fringes of the establishment (led, significantly, by men like Adlai Stevenson and Chester Bowles who *had* held elective office) did constantly question the tendency of the mainstream to relate everything that happened in the Third World to the cold war; or at least they questioned the military emphasis of the mainstream of thought. Men like Bowles and Stevenson pressed for a more serious commitment to the United Nations (Bundy's center was content with mere "adherence" there) for heavier expenditure on development aid and for priority to be given to alliance with those developing countries—India or Chile—that seemed to promise some hope of evolving their own native forms of democracy, even if this might prove irritating to the United States, as against more militantly anti-Communist regimes such as those in South Korea, Pakistan (then), "China"—or South Vietnam.

But in truth the Stevenson-Bowles wing was neither very representative nor very effective. And it was decapitated by President Kennedy's appointments in 1960-61. Galbraith was exiled to New Delhi, where (by a historical irony that he particularly enjoys) he ended up in the Sino-Indian war being more closely involved in military conflict with China than any other American official since the end of the Korean War. Stevenson was embalmed alive at the United Nations. And Bowles was soon banished from the State Department and thence to India to replace Galbraith. That was what happened to the "soft line" men. "Tough-minded" and "hard-nosed" were the adjectives in vogue among the lawyers and the bankers, the systems analysts and "defense intellectuals," who congregated in Washington around Rusk, McNamara, Bundy, and Paul Nitze.

A third qualification should be made. The establishment was not in point of fact very interested in Vietnam as such. Harvard, for example, had no program for regional studies of Southeast Asia as it did for Soviet or Western European or Middle Eastern studies. There are still more classes in Tibetan than in Vietnamese there. The Council on Foreign Relations did not sponsor a research project on Vietnam until 1972, and for years one of the CIA's principal sources of information on North Vietnam was Professor Patrick Honey of the University of London. When I asked Professor Thomas Schelling, former acting head of the Center for International Affairs at Harvard (where the establishment's strategic doctrines were developed in the 1950s) about the doctrine of counterinsurgency, which became under McNamara in the Pentagon one leg of a three-legged strategy of "flexible response," he answered, apparently perfectly seriously, that counterinsurgency had been "sold" to Walt Rostow by the Marines.

But this perfectly genuine lack of interest in the details of the country to which American power was to be committed, with such fatal results both for the country and for American power, did not prevent the establishment's supporting, perhaps reluctantly but almost unanimously, the creeping commitment from the time of the Taylor-Rostow mission of November 1961 until the fall of Diem, which occurred two years later.

Nor did the advent of President Johnson, and the disappointments with the successor governments to Diem in Saigon and with the strategic hamlet program in the provinces, shake that support. Indeed, though Lyndon Johnson may have said that Ngo Dinh Diem was the Winston Churchill of Asia, those who knew him best are convinced that essentially he "bought" the war policy because it had the endorsement of "the Kennedy people," which in this context means the endorsement of the establishment. Only when American casualties were involved, and he felt honor bound to give American boys all the support he could, did Lyndon Johnson take the war for his own. In any case, right up to 1965, the year of decision, the overwhelming consensus of the establishment accepted without moral or intellectual doubt that the war would have to be escalated—if the only alternative was losing it. The commitment to "internationalism," the horror of "Munich," the "burdens" of world leadership, the intellectual rigidity of continuing to see the world in terms of a "Communist bloc," and now paradoxically the commitment to the presidency—in sum, the whole of the establishment's tradition propelled it tragically in the same direction, so that seven years ago virtually all establishment opinion was clustered around a single position: the commitment is inevitable, the war is necessary, escalation is justified, or the dominoes are forfeit, the war must be supported, and won.

Fragmentation of Consensus

Yet today the once neatly drilled soldiers of establishment opinion straggle along a continuum that stretches from the farouchely defensive to the penitential. This continuum can be roughly calibrated in a sequence of positions. Position Zero is that the war was justified and that no major *avoidable* mistakes were made in the way it was waged. Publicly, perhaps, only Walt Rostow and Dean Rusk stand with the late Lyndon Johnson even near Position Zero today, and both have paid the penalty with exile. Position One is that the war was indeed justified, but that grave mistakes were made in its conduct. Somewhere within a decimal point or so of that is McGeorge Bundy's position, as we shall see.

Position Two is that the war itself was a mistake. Clark Clifford, for example, now believes that. Indeed, he may be part way to Position Three, where he would encounter his law partner, Paul Warnke, who was one of Senator McGovern's national security policy advisers, and also George Ball. Position Three holds that not only the war, but the policy that led to it was mistaken, in the sense that it was a mistake to extend the policy of containing Communism from Europe to Southeast Asia; further, it holds that the policy of containment itself had at some point become mistaken, even if it was correct in the time of Stalin and up to the end of the Korean War. And Position Four, the penitential position, holds that the war, and possibly the policy that led to it, were worse than mistakes: they were crimes. That, for example, is Daniel Ellsberg's position today, and if ever there was a candidate member of the foreign policy establishment (MIT, the RAND Corporation, the Pentagon, the Council on Foreign Relations, and White House consultancy), it was Ellsberg.

Very few members of the establishment have moved as far as Position Four, and fewer even, perhaps, still cling to Position Zero. The most crowded stretches of the continuum, as might be expected, lie near the center. That is the establishment instinct.

This rather crude schema of a continuum helps, I believe, to chart the gradual fragmentation of a consensus. But it scarcely does justice to the complex analyses and rationales of what are, after all, highly subtle and intelligent men. It does not help us to understand, for example, the position of

one incontestable establishment man in the present administration, Henry Kissinger. If one looks at Kissinger's diplomatic strategy as a whole, one might put him somewhere
near Position Three. Yet, insofar as he actually waged the
war, some part of his mind would seem to be straggling back
around Position One. The fact is, of course, that the possible
positions that can be taken in regard to a problem of such
agonizing complexity cannot be regimented into so simple a
schema without distorting some of them to an almost comic
degree.

So a better way of understanding what the Vietnam war has
done to the establishment is to plot the breakup of consensus over time. One way of doing this is to look at five episodes that mark off the stages in the dissolving unity and
failing influence of the foreign policy establishment.

Episode I: The Rallying of the Paladins

As is well known, George Ball was the one major figure in the
inner foreign policy councils of the Kennedy and Johnson
administrations who openly articulated his misgivings about
the war. He did so for several reasons, the most compelling
of which was his feeling that Europe was the major theatre,
and Southeast Asia a costly distraction, for American power.
In October 1964, after the Tonkin Gulf incident, he circulated
to Rusk, Bundy, and McNamara a memorandum of his
"skeptical thoughts" (published in the *Atlantic Monthly* in
July 1972). In the summer of 1965, when the bombing of the
North had begun and the decision to commit U.S. ground
forces was being discussed, Ball returned to the charge,
writing a whole series of papers advocating the opening of
peace negotiations as an alternative to escalation. He also
brought in Dean Acheson and another prominent Washington
lawyer, Lloyd Cutler, gave them an office in the State Department, and asked them to propose an alternative to the escalation of U.S. ground forces.

Ball had been thinking along the lines of a negotiated formal
agreement, but the proposal Acheson and Cutler came up
with, and which Ball submitted to the president, was for a
political solution—in effect, a deal between the government
of South Vietnam and the Vietcong, which would allow the
United States to retire gracefully from the scene. Acheson

and Cutler proposed that the Vietcong should be invited to participate stage by stage in political life. First regional, then national elections would be held, with the Vietcong taking part. There would be a general amnesty, and a territorial deal, whereby in effect the Saigon government would refrain from rooting out the Vietcong from the areas it controlled and the Vietcong would not molest the areas that Saigon controlled.

The two lawyers did not expect that there would be any kind of signed agreement for a long time. Rather, they envisioned parallel actions by the two sides, progressively developing mutual trust, and leaving the two sides inside South Vietnam to find out what political support they had after the United States had withdrawn. If the Vietcong failed to go along, U.S. troop strength could be progressively built up as a negative inducement. It is interesting that, though the U.S. government cited North Vietnamese infiltration as one of the justifications of its subsequent decision to bring in U.S. troops, there were so few North Vietnamese regulars inside South Vietnam at the time that they did not then constitute the major stumbling block that they proved to be in the 1972 talks.

At first glance, this plan, which—given the realities of Vietcong strength in the South Vietnamese countryside—might have turned out to be little more than a discreet form of bugout, would seem highly inconsistent with the vigorously hawkish views for which Dean Acheson was known. At the time of their work together, however, Lloyd Cutler is quite clear that Acheson was deeply pessimistic about the possibility of winning a ground war in Vietnam and strongly in accord with Ball's view that it would prove a catastrophic diversion from more important issues. For Acheson, as for Ball and most of the great figures of the American postwar establishment, it was the Atlantic Alliance and Europe that was central to America's security and role in the world; Asia was important primarily insofar as it was an extension of the European confrontation with the Soviet Union (thus Korea, in the eyes of Acheson, Rusk, and company in June of 1950).

The Acheson-Cutler proposals were received with interest in Washington, and a young member of Ball's staff, Tom Ehrlich (who was later to succeed Bayless Manning as dean of Stanford Law School), was dispatched to Saigon to get the opinion of the Americans in charge there. In Saigon, Ambassador Maxwell Taylor and his deputy, U. Alexis Johnson, took a look at the proposals, branded them unacceptable, and sent Ehrlich back to Washington. For all practical purposes, the proposals were dead.

Having seen his attempt to find a political solution fail, Acheson's views seem to have hardened. In September 1965, for example, Acheson joined a committee sponsored by the prestigious establishment figure Arthur Dean, senior partner of the Dulles brothers' law firm, Sullivan & Cromwell, which strongly supported the president's policy. The best explanation for his change in 1965 is the same one that explains the behavior of several other senior contemporaries of Acheson (such as Ellsworth Bunker, but definitely not W. Averell Harriman): once American soldiers were being shot at in Vietnam, the great figures of the establishment, men who had lived through three major American wars in their lifetimes, saw no choice but to rally around the flag and around the president.

Thus, Acheson was the leading member of the first group of establishment advisers whom Lyndon Johnson convoked at the White House to discuss, among other things, Ball's case against the war. The other members of this small group from outside government included such powerful figures as Clark Clifford and John J. McCloy. But it was Acheson who took the lead. "The Moustache," as McGeorge Bundy reported to his staff the next morning, "was voluble."

Here was a test of the establishment's position, if an informal one. The president had called in what amounted to a steering committee of its elder statesmen to pass on his policies and, in effect, to deal with a rebellion on the part of Ball.

"All right, George," the president said when the group met in the Cabinet room, "give me your dissent." Ball made his now familiar argument, and the president polled the group. Unanimously, they supported his policy, including bombing North Vietnam. "They were for bombing the be-Jesus out of them," one eyewitness recalls. The matter disposed of, the elder statesmen fell to reminiscing to the president about Korea. That had been a far stickier business, they seemed to feel, which most of them had lived through; and that had gone off all right in the end, and so would this nasty little war in Vietnam. "Stick to it, Mr. President!" was the burden of the Wise Men's advice.

*In 1965 the leaders of the establishment were united in their
support of the comminment in Vietnam. Their view prevailed.
And at this time they supported the decision to escalate the
war.*

Episode II: The Barons' Revolt

In November 1967 President Johnson called in a larger and
more formal group of senior policy advisers, or Wise Old Men
(WOM, to some young officers) as they came to be called, inside the government. At that time the administration was in a
strongly optimistic mood. Ambassador Bunker and General
Westmoreland had been back to Washington and had spoken
about "light at the end of the tunnel" and even of beginning
to bring American troops home. Once more the Wise Men—
this time they included Acheson, Bundy (now president of
the Ford Foundation), Douglas Dillon, and Robert Murphy—
endorsed the president's policy. Again only George Ball
dissented.

Then came Tet.

It was on January 31, 1968 that the Vietcong struck in Saigon.
As early as February 7 General Westmoreland called for
studies of how many troops would be needed. No question
now of sending men home. By February 25 General Wheeler
was on his way back to Washington with a request for 206
thousand more troops. On March 1 Clark Clifford was sworn
in as secretary of defense.

Clifford had been a hawk all along. As chairman of the president's Foreign Intelligence Advisory Board he had access to
the most sensitive information, and in many private meetings
with the president he had supported the war and opposed
halting the bombing. A tour of Southeast Asia in the summer
of 1967 (with Maxwell Taylor) had put the first seeds of concern in his mind. After Tet, he hinted at some of this concern
at the Senate hearings on his confirmation in February, but
he only hinted.

The day after he was sworn in, Clifford ordered a comprehensive review of policy in the Pentagon, with the request for 206
thousand troops there, to "concentrate a man's mind won-
derfully." Clifford soon learned two things: that many of the
civilian officials in the Pentagon (establishment men almost
to a man) now had strong doubts about the wisdom of send-

ing more troops—and also of the bombing—and that the Joint Chiefs didn't seem to be giving him straight answers to his questions.

The Clifford task force's report did not bring his change of mind into the open. Sent to the White House on March 4, it accepted the immediate sending of some 20 thousand troops, and deferred the decision as to the rest. But, in fact, Clifford had changed his mind. And he set himself to change the president's.

It was Clifford, whether he foresaw the result or not, who suggested to the president at a Tuesday lunch in the White House in the middle of March that he might reconvene the Wise Men. On the evening of March 25 they foregathered at the State Department for briefings and dinner. The next day they were to go over to the White House to meet the president.

Dean Acheson was there along with Arthur Dean, George Ball, McGeorge Bundy, Douglas Dillon, Robert Murphy, and Cyrus Vance—all down from New York. The president's friend Abe Fortas, then a Supreme Court Justice, was there, and so were two legendary generals from World War II: Omar N. Bradley and Matthew B. Ridgway. Others who were not less important members of the establishment were there by virtue of the office they held in the administration: Dean Rusk, Clark Clifford, Richard Helms of the CIA, Walt Rostow, Nicholas Katzenbach, Henry Cabot Lodge, Paul Nitze, Averell Harriman, Arthur Goldberg, and the older Bundy brother, Bill. It was—for those who are moved by the romance of power—a sort of Round Table of the sedentary chivalry of the cold war; or, if you prefer, a board meeting of the most powerful enterprise on earth. It was also perhaps the last occasion on which so many leaders of the American establishment found themselves united.

The story has been told often enough. They read the briefing papers. They heard the briefings. And the next day, with McGeorge Bundy acting as their *rapporteur*, they stripped the president of their confidence, and perhaps of his. (Only Taylor and Fortas among those present are reported to have remained unshaken.)

It would be wrong to exaggerate the relative importance of the thumbs down from the Wise Men among the complex causes of President Johnson's decision not to run for reelection in 1968. The results of the New Hampshire primary and the prognosis for Wisconsin, the prospect of running against Robert Kennedy, the defection and the persuasion of Clark Clifford, his own bitterness and exhaustion, and his wife's awareness of them all—all these factors played their part, and there is no need here to express an opinion on how importantly the defection of the establishment loomed among all the omens of failure. The episode is relevant here for what it tells us not about the decision, but about the establishment. Deeply discouraged by the way military victory was receding like a mirage into the future, impressed by the passionate opposition to the war they encountered in their children, their law partners, their banking correspondents, and their contacts of every kind across the country, aghast at what might happen to the threatened dollar on the world's exchanges, faithful, finally, to its instinct for the center, the establishment made a characteristic decision not to put good money after bad.

In March 1968 the leaders of the establishment were united. They prevailed. But now they were against any further escalation of the war.

Episode III: Cambodia, or the Insiders on the Outside

After President Nixon's inauguration, the once pervasive influence of the foreign policy elite thawed and resolved itself into little more than the imposing, if enigmatic, figure of Dr. Henry Kissinger. True, high posts in the State Department went to men who meet my own tests for membership in the establishment: William P. Rogers, Elliot Richardson, and Richardson's successor as under secretary, John N. Irwin II (brother-in-law of Thomas J. Watson of IBM and Arthur Watson, Nixon's ambassador to Paris). All were corporation lawyers who had already served in important jobs under the Eisenhower administration. But it very soon became apparent that the State Department was being excluded as never before from the president's most important ventures in foreign policy: from all but nominal roles in the overtures to Russia and China, from the SALT negotiations, and even from Vietnam policy. For another, however great their talents, no one could say that Rogers, Richardson, and Irwin had been exactly prominent in the councils of the establishment before they took office, even compared to other Republicans. A handful of men who might have been said to adhere to the academic wing of the establishment went to work for Dr. Kissinger: the best known, Daniel Ellsberg (who was a consultant), and the most important in terms of his functions, Dr. Morton Halperin. Neither lasted very long, however. As for the president himself, while his long experience in foreign policy, not to mention his partnership in Nixon, Mudge, Rose, Guthrie, and Alexander, might seem to qualify him as a member of the establishment, there are few establishment people who have been eager to claim him as their own.*

By the spring of 1970, at any event, the establishment was thoroughly alienated from the Nixon administration, and *vice versa*. Soon after the inauguration, in March 1969, an establishment group met, classically, sometimes at the Council on Foreign Relations' premises at 68 and Park Avenue in New York, sometimes at the Cosmos Club on Embassy Row in Washington, and sometimes at the Harvard Center for International Affairs in Cambridge. The group included Robert Roosa, the banker and former under secretary of the Treasury, Cyrus Vance, Chester Cooper (formerly of the CIA and the White House staff), Robert Bowie of the Harvard Center for International Affairs, Paul Warnke, and Samuel Huntington of the Harvard government department. Together they hammered out a plan for peace in Vietnam. In May, several members of this group met with Henry Kissinger and Elliot Richardson to discuss their plan. "Elliot seemed interested," one of the group recalled sadly afterwards. "Henry obviously wasn't, and it's Henry that counts."

By May 1970, a year later, the administration had not only not brought the war to an end, it had actually widened it by invading Cambodia. A significant fraction of the establishment was not merely dissident: it was outraged. In their eagerness to reverse the offending policy, one group of these people— Cambridge academics who might be said to belong to the second echelon of the establishment—reached instinctively for the well-tried approach which had worked so well in the past. If you want something changed in Washington, what do

*Two of the few distinguished Americans who have ever resigned from the Council on Foreign Relations, incidentally, are both former employees of the Office of Price Administration: John Kenneth Galbraith and Richard Nixon.

you do? Why, you call a friend, and you get together a little group, very quietly of course, and you explain how wrong they are down there.

On May 7, 1970 thirteen Harvard professors, most of them with years of Washington experience both in appointive office and as consultants, flew down to see their contact, their former colleague, and—in most instances—their friend, Henry Kissinger. The group included Thomas Schelling, Richard Neustadt of the Kennedy Institute, an advocate of presidential power since the Truman administration, George Kistiakowsky, who had advised the Eisenhower administration on science policy, Francis Bator, who had been Walt Rostow's deputy in the White House, and Adam Yarmolinsky, McNamara's special assistant at the Pentagon.

Each member of the group had his turn at bat. Schelling began by making it plain to Kissinger that the group was visiting him not as old friends, but because they wanted to communicate through him to the president that the invasion of Cambodia was in their opinion "a disastrously bad foreign policy decision." Schelling maintains, in fact, that the purpose of the visit was not so much to influence Kissinger as to serve notice on him that they had come to a parting of the ways. "Essentially," he told me, "this was a group saying, 'We have so lost confidence that we are in effect saying good-bye. We are going to look to the Hill.' It was a renunciation." Others, apparently, did not see it in quite that light. "It was an impersonal visit," said one of them afterwards, with what anyone who knows Cambridge will recognize as the authentic Harvard arrogance, "to try to save the country."

The fact was that Henry Kissinger did not seem to feel that he needed his former colleagues' help in that enterprise. Indeed, there is some reason to believe that he resented it as an impertinence. The professors refused to speak off the record (truly a departure from establishment habit!), and Kissinger refused to speak on it. For an hour and a half, therefore, the delegation "presented views." But Kissinger hardly seemed interested, and when the professors fanned out and visited other officials later in the day, they were received almost contemptuously. It was humiliating, it was unthinkable, but Washington seemed to have been taken over by men who didn't understand how *important* these Harvard professors were.

As Francis Bator concluded, ". . . in the executive branch we've shot our bolt today. From now on, we'll just have to work with Congress."*

The very day that the Harvard group met with Henry Kissinger with such disconcerting and disappointing results, *The Washington Post* reported that the Senate Foreign Relations Committee was expected to send to the floor of the Senate for a vote in the near future an amendment sponsored by Senator Frank Church of Idaho and Senator John Sherman Cooper of Kentucky. The text, which was to be tacked on to a military sales bill that had already passed the House of Representatives, would have the effect of blocking U.S. military operations in Cambodia. On May 11 this amendment was duly voted by the committee.

Some of the nonacademic wing of the establishment had already quietly come to the conclusion that the professors reached so ruefully after their snub in Washington: it was no longer likely to prove profitable to attempt to work through the executive branch. That left the Congress. During the next three months in the summer of 1970 a stream of establishment people, including Katzenbach, Vance, and Kingman Brewster, president of Yale, took several opportunities to make public their support for the amendment and their growing conviction that the war must be ended. On May 15, for example, Averell Harriman told the Joint Economic Committee that "a timetable should be set for withdrawal of all U.S. troops," because, in his opinion, the war was militarily unwinnable. Two weeks later George Ball, in testimony to the House Foreign Affairs Committee, denounced "our Cambodian adventure." Some members of the establishment had broken with the habit of twenty-five years. They had gone public, and they had turned to the Congress. Two such substantial departures from tradition could only have been induced by the consciousness of impotence.

But though the Senate did pass the Cooper-Church amendment by 58-37 on July 1, after thirty-four days of debate and close to three hundred speeches, its preamble had by then been softened, and in any case on July 9 it was voted down by the House by a wide margin.

*There was an accurate account of this visit in the Harvard Crimson by Michael Kinsley, who accompanied the delegation to Washington. This was republished in the *Washington Monthly* in July 1970.

Stripped of its influence within the executive branch, the establishment reluctantly turned to Congress and went public to oppose the war; but it failed.

Episode IV: Home to Europe

Just one year after this reverse, the Elder Statesmen were back in the White House. But the circumstances were scarcely such as to suggest that their pristine power had been restored.

On May 13, 1971, the Mansfield Amendment, calling for a 50 percent cut in U.S. troop strength in Europe, was generally conceded to have an excellent chance of passing the Senate. White House head counters and Senate doves both calculated that Senator Mansfield probably had the votes to pass an amendment that would justly be taken as a high watermark in the country's swing, if not toward isolationism, at least away from that commitment to the defense of Europe that had been the bedrock of the establishment's foreign policy since the 1930 s.

That day President Nixon met for ninety minutes in the White House with a group whose names epitomized the establishment's commitment to Europe: Dean Acheson, then near the end of his life, George Ball, John J. McCloy, Henry Cabot Lodge, Nicholas Katzenbach, Cyrus Vance, and four former NATO commanders—Generals Lucius D. Clay, Alfred M. Gruenther, Lauris Norstad, and Lyman Lemnitzer. Dean Acheson, in particular, was in his most truculent mood. The amendment, he snorted, was "asinine"; he thought it "sheer nonsense."

Three days later, lest anyone should suppose that this endorsement was unrepresentative or narrowly based, the White House announced that twenty-four former high government officials supported the White House in its resistance to the Mansfield troop cuts. As well as some of those who had attended the White House meeting, they included Robert Lovett, Robert Murphy, Neil McElroy, Douglas Dillon, Thomas Gates, and Livingston Merchant. "It looked like a resurrection of the Old Guard," said Senator Mansfield unkindly. "It took me back twenty or twenty-five years."

But the Guard neither surrendered nor died. On May 20 the Mansfield Amendment was defeated with ease, 61-36.

Dean Acheson and Geòrge Ball did the lion's share of the lobbying on Capitol Hill. Others, like Cyrus Vance, contented themselves after the White House meeting with making phone calls to senators they knew. The effort, in any case, was successful. One reason, some of the protagonists believe, was that the Nixon administration, with foreign policy rather jealously clutched to Dr. Kissinger's bosom, had so neglected the views and indeed the egos of a number of senators, some of them Republicans, that they had become seriously disaffected. With men in this mood, a show of concern, a shrewd touch of ego massage, was effective.

But if the Old Guard won this particular Waterloo, it was largely because of help from a most unexpected and indeed disconcerting direction. It was rather as if Blucher had suddenly turned up at the end of the long afternoon's fighting and pitched in on the side of the French.

On May 14, the day after the Old Guard's meeting at the White House, Mr. Brezhnev abruptly announced an interest in the three-year-old American proposals for mutual and balanced force reduction. Secretary of State Rogers was quick to point out the moral to the Foreign Relations Committee: "If we do it unilaterally, we can kiss that initiative good-bye." And indeed, to all but the most determined opponents of the American presence in Europe, there did seem very little to be said for cutting American troops there for free, once the Russians had announced that they were ready to pay a price for cuts. As Chalmers Roberts commented dryly in *The Washington Post*, the situation had been "considerably transformed" by the Brezhnev initiative. There it was: the Old Guard had rallied to the call from Henry Kissinger, and it had helped to carry the day.

But, as one of them told the president, it could never be done again. And an ominous fraction of the once-united establishment had defected, even on the bedrock issue. The Mansfield Amendment, said Clark Clifford, was "a step in the right direction." It was no service to the alliance, said Arthur Goldberg, "for the United States now and for the indefinite future to continue to play the role of the dominant and dominating influence in the defense of Western Europe." Spoken like General de Gaulle.

Even more significant, as a straw in the wind, perhaps, was a column that appeared in *The Washington Post* under the joint by-line of Frank Mankiewicz and Tom Braden: Mankiewicz had been a centurion in the Kennedy legion and was to manage the Democratic presidential campaign in 1972, while Braden, an archetypal establishment figure in life style and background, was a former high CIA official. "These men," Braden and Mankiewicz wrote of Acheson and McCloy and the others who had rallied to President Nixon's side on the Mansfield Amendment, "created an American empire unparalleled in history . . . and they are through, as surely as they are old. For their countrymen no longer believe in the credo to which they devoted their lives. . . . The age of American imperialism is about to end."

By the spring of 1971, if the Old Guard of the establishment could still deliver an appreciable amount of persuasive muscle on its favorite issue—European defense—it could no longer be said that the establishment was united, even on that. The episode left an uncomfortable feeling, which some of the men involved were explicit about, that *where once the leaders of the establishment had been able to use the power of the presidency to turn their ideas into national policy, now the president was using them.*

Episode V: Rejection of an Heir Apparent

In May 1971, the same month as the Mansfield Amendment battle began, the Council on Foreign Relations in New York was able to offer its distinguished members what in happier times would have ranked without cavil as a gala attraction. McGeorge Bundy had consented to give three lectures on the lessons to be drawn from the American experience in Vietnam. The Council naturally treated the lectures as a major event. On the first night, Bundy was warmly introduced by the Council's chairman, David Rockefeller, of the Chase Manhattan Bank; on the second, by Hamilton Fish Armstrong, who was completing fifty years as the editor of *Foreign Affairs*; and on the third, by another journalist, Hedley Donovan, editor in chief of Time, Inc. And certainly, by all the standards the Council has been in the habit of applying, the speaker, the subject, and the former's qualifications for discussing the latter would all have entitled the lectures to a positively reverent hearing. Raised in the inner circle of the foreign policy establishment, Bundy's career had been grounded in all three of the places where a reputation among the makers of American foreign policy can be established: at Harvard, in the White House, and in Manhattan. At every stage of that career his personality exuded the two qualities—"brightness" and "effectiveness"—that are as much the passports in those worlds as "soundness" once was to the corridors of power in C. P. Snow's Whitehall. But for the war in Vietnam, in short, Bundy must have been regarded as the natural successor to the national presidency of the American establishment. Large audiences of the Council's members turned up to hear what he would say about American involvement in Southeast Asia, about a policy that had cost him, and them, so much.

Bundy began his first lecture with a handsome avowal that if any of his conclusions implied criticism of what had been done, "it should be aimed at myself." Certainly he was not hiding behind the institution of the presidency. On the other hand, he scarcely seemed to feel that any very searching criticism was called for.

He laid down two basic premises. One, certainly, was unexceptionable—though it can hardly be said that it had been scrupulously followed in the conduct of the war: that "all large efforts in foreign affairs" require support at home. The second was more controversial: that "it was right, in some form or other and by some means, to act to avoid a Communist victory in Vietnam in 1965." This was not, he supposed, a majority view today, "but it is mine."

Surprisingly, though he justified the actions of 1965, he came out for total, essentially unconditional withdrawal in 1971. In his third lecture, he proposed a six-point plan for ending the war, beginning by the setting of a public plan for the withdrawal of U.S. forces "from any combat role in Indochina," and endorsing the "Algerian solution" proposed by Professor Stanley Hoffmann of Harvard.* He would set only two conditions: the return of all prisoners and a guarantee that withdrawing forces would not be attacked. He advocated aid, but not reparations. "The nation is proud, and its purpose has been decent. It will recognize obligations of honor, but not of guilt."

*Stanley Hoffmann, "Vietnam: An Algerian Solution," Foreign Policy, Number 2, Spring 1971.

Bundy made only passing references to what he called "questions raised by the conduct of the war," such as search and destroy tactics, air attacks on populated areas, chemical warfare, herbicides, and the "generation" of refugees. The three subjects he picked for detailed discussion were: relations between the executive and the Congress, and in particular the Tonkin Gulf Resolution, relations between the president and the military, including the command and control system, and diplomacy, where he detected "wishful thinking."

On the Tonkin Gulf Resolution, he said, "the error was not in the resolution but in the fact that it was never reaffirmed or refined in later years."

Between civilian and military leaders, he said, there had been "bargaining and mutual wariness, rather than trust." He recommended that the president should "reach out to the professional military leadership."

Peace plans, he said, had tended to reflect an underestimate of Hanoi's intransigence. He gave no inkling of any thought that war plans might have reflected the same underestimate.

At a dinner after the third of Bundy's lectures, he was sharply taken to task by some members, who made it plain that they felt that if these were all the lessons he had learned from Vietnam, he had not learned enough.

Many of those who heard the lectures go a good deal further than that in private. "Disappointing," was one of the milder adjectives used. A very eminent member of the Council, a man who has held high office in Washington and who might well have held higher office if the Democrats had won the White House in 1972, put it like this: "He assumed, and he assumed that his audience assumed too, that the decision to go in was right. But in both those assumptions he was incorrect."

Another member, a New York banker who has also held office in Washington, was blunter. "I went to all three lectures," he told me. "I wanted to see what his mood about the past was. His mood was to ignore psychologically the fact that he had been grievously wrong. There was no real *mea culpa* about it. There was a long, convoluted series of arguments, which I thought were mostly bullshit. But then this is a New England Puritan, who deals in repression, not confession."

Although the Council discourages the reporting of its pro-
ceedings, lectures by a speaker of such eminence on a topic
of such importance would normally have been published.
Bundy himself considered publishing them. One of those
whose advice Bundy sought was an executive at *The New
York Times*, who advised flatly against publication. He was
conscious that his response might seem rude, but in truth his
motive was friendly, for he knew that the *Times* had the
Pentagon Papers in its possession. They were published, in
fact, only a couple of weeks later.

"Bundy has the luck of the devil," said another former colleague. "If he had published those lectures before the Pentagon Papers came out, they would have destroyed his reputation." He was specifically referring to the fact that in the lectures Bundy called for "continuous and candid" exposition of
policy; and he felt that Bundy's account of the Tonkin Gulf in
his first lecture could no longer, after the publication of the
Pentagon Papers, be called candid.

*By May 1971 the establishment was bitterly divided on the is-
sue of Vietnam*, with some still trying to justify what had
been done and others angrily tearing down the justifications.
The issue had not merely divided the establishment; *it had
corroded the bonds of seniority, authority, and respect that
used to hold it together.*

The Loss of Influence

The foreign policy elite is no longer sure that it exists, no
longer confident—that is, as it used to be—that it possesses
either the unity or the credibility to influence policy as it was
once able to. And there is something of a consensus that the
occasion, if not the fundamental cause, of this loss of influence was the war in Vietnam.

"The consensus of the elite was shattered by the war," says
James C. Thomson, a former White House Far Eastern specialist who is now the curator of the Nieman Foundation at
Harvard. "The war discredited the foreign policy elite," says
Paul Warnke, Washington lawyer and former Pentagon official. But then Warnke added: "I think you are bound to have a
fractionalization of views as the world becomes fractional-
ized." His former Pentagon colleague, Townsend Hoopes,
agrees: "The elite came into being because of finite circum-

stances. It has now come to an end because of different but
equally finite circumstances." When the threat of Communism appeared to be monolithic, in other words, the American
establishment was monolithic. In a multipolar world the discussion of foreign policy in the United States was bound to
become multipolar too. But it may well be futile to attempt to
distinguish whether the war or deeper underlying trends in
international relations caused the decline of the elite. For the
new multipolar conception of the world is itself partly a consequence of the war, and President Nixon's overtures to
Moscow and Peking were in part motivated by the need to
extricate the United States from it. Again, it can be argued
that not the war but the election of a Republican president in
1968 caused the downfall of the establishment. Only let the
Democrats win back the White House, this argument runs,
and we will see the establishment's men back in office,
bringing their train of assistant secretaries and special assistants and consultants and Wise Men with them. Even this
argument scarcely eliminates the war as a cause of the establishment's eclipse, however, since, as Professor Stanley
Hoffmann of Harvard puts it, "the way the war destroyed the
elite was by electing Nixon." And now that he has been
reelected, it is clear enough that the old foreign policy establishment will be out in the cold at least for four more years.

As an issue, Vietnam has receded from the central, dominant
position it has occupied in American foreign policy for close
to a decade. Other issues, too long neglected, some of them
indeed either partially caused, or at least intensified, by the
obsession with the war, crowd forward for attention. It is
time for new lines to be charted and new courses followed.

The accumulated experience of the individuals who made up
the old establishment guarantees that they will have a voice.
On certain issues, the influence of the old establishment in
something like its traditional, concerted form is likely to be
considerable. The New York banking community, for
example, in the persons of men like David Rockefeller and
Robert Roosa, will undoubtedly make its voice heard by the
administration in the process of developing the new foreign
economic policy, whomever that process is entrusted to.
Again, on disarmament, the advisory committee that President Nixon set up in 1969 to consider SALT is still theoreti-
cally in being. That was a thoroughbred establishment group,

with the inevitable John J. McCloy in the chair, and Dean Rusk, Cyrus Vance (who has since resigned), Douglas Dillon, and General Lauris Norstad among its members. On these and other matters the old establishment will make itself heard. The Council on Foreign Relations will no doubt continue to keep up its membership, and its head, Bayless Manning, shows no special haste to break sharply with its traditions. And the editor of *Foreign Affairs*, after all, is William P. Bundy.

Three Reasons for Change

Yet it seems probable that future historians will see the crisis of the Vietnam war as having marked an epoch, not only in the direction of American foreign policy but in its personnel. There are three powerful reasons why this should be so.

First, the war has set up a mortgage on the establishment's future power by alienating a large segment of those who might be expected to become its future recruits.

Second, it has fatally impugned the establishment's reputation for wisdom and the cachet that comes from a past record of uninterrupted success; and it is on these that the influence of any such elite ultimately depends.

Third, it has driven a wedge of division through the ranks of a group whose power in its heyday was the power that derives from a consensus that is based upon broadly shared assumptions.

The parallel between the Vietnam war and the Boer War has been drawn already by—among others—George Armstrong Kelly of Brandeis University.* But one aspect, in particular, of that parallel deserves reflection. In the long run, perhaps the most important single consequence of the Boer War for the British Empire, and it was mortal, was that it divided the British elite, bitterly and irreconcilably, on the question of the morality of the use of force to uphold what were perceived as national interests. But that consequence was delayed. Such immensely influential anti-imperialist books as George Orwell's *Shooting an Elephant* and E. M. Forster's *A Passage to India* have an intellectual ancestry that goes back to the "pro-Boers" of a generation earlier. So does the influence of

*See pp. 67-85.

the anti-imperialist elite within the Labor party, which did not even exist at the time of the Boer War. The American parallel is not, of course, exact. But it seems likely that among the more important consequences of the Vietnam war will be books, yet unwritten, by men who, if the war had not followed the course it did follow, would have taken their place without qualms in the foreign policy establishment. It seems equally likely that the McGeorge Bundys and Walt Rostows of the Class of '70 are not planning careers in national security affairs, nor studying the theory of counterinsurgency. Indeed, it is striking how often, in Cambridge or in Washington, one encounters young men, now working as radical journalists or even public interest lawyers, who tell one with a wry smile that when they entered Harvard ten years ago, their heroes were those men whom David Halberstam has called "the best and the brightest," and for whom such young men have now the opposite of admiration. As Professor Schelling of Harvard put it to me, a little wistfully, "there are a lot of people for whom foreign policy isn't fun anymore." These mute, inglorious Kaysens will not enjoy the satisfactions of "telling the whole world what to do."

Moreover, far fewer people are listening. Richard Steadman, a former civilian official in the Pentagon, summed up the effect of the war on the foreign policy elite like this: "I think the events of Tet in 1968 had a profound effect. I think the elite was profoundly shaken. The major thing that happened was that this group lost its certainty that what they thought was right. But this also involved a decision on the part of outsiders, especially the politicians and the press, about who's worth listening to, and the quality of their judgment. People will no longer consult the judgment of these men. People no longer care what guys who are on the Council on Foreign Relations think."

In certain respects, I believe that this is an overstatement of the case. There will continue to be, as I have suggested, a good deal of interest in the opinions of a large number of experienced and influential men who happen to be members of the Council on Foreign Relations, and in the opinions of the old foreign policy establishment generally.

But the decisive point is that those opinions will no longer be even broadly homogeneous. They will no longer spring, as they did spring before the Vietnam war, from a shared view of the world, and of the proper goals for American policy, to question the essentials of which would exclude one by definition as a member of the establishment.

Earlier, to illustrate the range of opinion now to be found among those who formerly belonged to the establishment, I borrowed the device of a continuum. But, in fact, there is a critical discontinuity in the middle of that continuum. It divides those who are ready to concede that the war was a disastrous mistake, the lessons of which must be learned, from those who cannot or will not accept this.

It is possible to argue that in time a new establishment will form from among those who are able to take as their starting point that the Vietnam war was a disaster. It is even possible that "Vietnam" may come to be a shibboleth for such a new establishment, rather as "Munich" was for the old. And ultimately, as the world changes, a Vietnam myth could breed false analogies and be as misleading as the Munich myth was. Other things being equal, however, a myth with an essential moral that it is much more difficult and dangerous to use force in support of foreign policy objectives than you might suppose, would seem less pernicious than one with the central moral that some people only understand force.

An establishment may always be with us. Foreign policy requires such specialized and recondite knowledge and remains in some respects so marginal to the concerns of a large majority of Americans that those in the academic or the business worlds who have made it their special study are bound to have some of the attributes of an elite. But, historically speaking, it is clear that *the* establishment that exercised such a remarkable influence over American foreign policy since World War II is dead, and that Vietnam, if not the murderer, was at least the occasion for its demise.

FOREIGN POLICY APPARATUS

CAN ONE MAN DO?
by I. M. Destler

The clandestine journey of Henry Kissinger to Peking was a tactical coup such as no other high American foreign policy maker has achieved for many years. It also offered a dramatic illustration of the Nixon-Kissinger style. The circle of men in on its preparation was very restricted. And it involved one of those large issues of strategic choice that both the president and his assistant for national security affairs consider to be suitable outlets for their talents. . . .

Yet despite frequent discussion of Kissinger as an individual, seldom do outside analysts take a serious, more general look at the strengths and limitations of the Nixon system of making foreign policy. It has given us an unusually effective presidential assistant. But is it enough for a president seeking to control the foreign affairs bureaucracy to have as his predominant instrument one talented White House adviser supported by a fifty-man professional staff?

The Shape of the System

When Kissinger came to Washington, he told a number of people of his determination to concentrate on matters of general strategy and to leave "operations" to the departments. Some dismissed this as the typical disclaimer of a new White House staff man. Yet much in Kissinger's writings suggests that his intention to devote himself to broad "policy" was real. He had repeatedly criticized our government's tendency to treat problems as "isolated cases" and "to identify foreign policy with the solution of immediate issues" rather than developing an interconnected strategy for coping with the world over a period of years.* And his emphasis was primarily on problems of decision *making*. He defined the problem basically as how to get the government to settle on

---

*Henry A. Kissinger: "The Policy-Maker and the Intellectual," in Jackson Subcommittee, *Organizing for National Security*, Vol. II, 1961, p. 257; "Domestic Structure and Foreign Policy," *Daedulus*, Spring 1966, p. 515.

"Can One Man Do?" is a shortened version of the essay published originally in *Foreign Policy*, Number 5, Winter 1971-72. It includes selections from "The Strategies of Presidents: Foreign Policy-Making under Kennedy, Johnson, and Nixon," in I.M. Destler, *Presidents, Bureaucrats, and Foreign Policy: The Politics of Organizational Reform* (copyright © 1971 by Princeton University Press), pp. 120-51, partly in revised and updated form. Reprinted by permission of Princeton University Press.

its major policy priorities and strategy and had been slow to recognize the difficulty of getting the bureaucracy to implement such a strategy once set.

Kissinger found a kindred spirit in a president whose campaign had denounced the Kennedy-Johnson de-emphasis on formal national security planning in favor of "catch-as-catch-can talkfests." And the system he put together for Nixon is designed above all to facilitate and illuminate major presidential foreign policy choices. Well over a hundred NSSMs (National Security Study Memoranda) have been issued by the White House to the various foreign affairs government agencies, calling for analysis of major issues and development of realistic alternative policy "options" on them. These studies are cleared through a network of general interdepartmental committees responsible to Kissinger, and the most important issues they raise are argued out before the president in the National Security Council. Nixon then makes a decision from among the options, usually "after further private deliberation."*

No one pretends that matters end there, that implementation of the decision follows automatically. The Nixon system provides for coordination of actual agency operations in several ways—in the work of Kissinger's "Operations Staff," in crisis coordination by the Kissinger-chaired Washington Special Actions Group (WSAG), in the secretary of state's formal role of overseeing "the execution of foreign policy," and in the operational coordination work of the interdepartmental Under Secretaries Committee headed by his deputy. Still, the system as designed and described clearly treats the carrying out of presidential aims as a secondary problem. Whereas Kennedy, in McGeorge Bundy's oft-quoted words, "deliberately rubbed out the distinction between planning and operation,"** Nixon has sought to restore it. Rejecting the Kennedy-Johnson assumption that the problem of presidential control over foreign policy is mainly one of intervening in operational issues to bring day-to-day bureaucratic actions into line with presidential wishes, Nixon has emphasized the

*Letter from Kissinger to Senator Henry Jackson, reprinted in Jackson Subcommittee, "The National Security Council: Comment by Henry A. Kissinger," March 1970, p. 2.

**Letter from Bundy to Senator Jackson, September 1961, reprinted in Jackson Subcommittee, *Organizing for National Security*, Vol. I, p. 1338.

priority of "policy" over "operations." As he expressed it in his first general foreign policy message to Congress: "In central areas of policy, we have arranged our procedure of policymaking so as to address the broader questions of long-term objectives first; we define our purposes, and then address the specific operational issues."*

The Nixon system is well designed for forcing consideration of such "broader questions." Unlike in the Eisenhower system it partially emulates, the national security assistant and his staff are responsible for the whole range of presidential foreign affairs business, whether NSC related or not. Thus the Nixon regime has a central policy official and group to run its "system" and force departments and agencies to take it seriously. The fact that Kissinger very quickly became Nixon's key foreign affairs official gave the new procedures about as much bureaucratic standing as any could ever hope for. . . .

Yet interviews with a number of officials involved suggest that the system has developed some serious problems. The number and comprehensiveness of the studies has been sufficient to create a serious bureaucratic logjam. And what departments present as "options" are often just advocacy in more sophisticated guise, like the Johnson-Nixon tendency to present our Vietnam choices (at least for public consumption) as: (1) blow up the world, (2) continue the present policy, or (3) scuttle and run. For these and other reasons, at least some of the studies may result in the worst of both worlds. They may be too important to disregard, given the commitment of the principal officials to (and investment of bureaucratic time in) the process; so Kissinger and his staff must devote considerable attention to them. Yet they may not be sufficiently useful to the president to serve as actual decision documents for him, thereby creating a malaise among the bureaucrats who prepare them.

More fundamental than the utility of this particular procedure, however, is the larger question of how effectively the president can control the bureaucracy through a limited number of specific decisions, however sophisticated the system is in facilitating them. Is the basic problem, as Nixon

*Richard M. Nixon, *United States Foreign Policy for the 1970's: A New Strategy for Peace* (Washington, D.C.: Government Printing Office, 1970), p. 12.

has characterized it, that of making possible "rational and deliberate" presidential choices which can then rather easily shape actions on "operational issues"?* Or is it more accurate to think of policy as his predecessors did, as evolving mainly from bureaucratic actions taken day by day, with a consequent need for the president to exercise continuing influence on them?

The Limits of Strategic Decisions

If Kissinger did not already know it, he learned quickly that the strategic thinker remains an exclamation point in the margins of foreign policy making if he does not join in bureaucratic battles to give general objectives operational meaning and effect. In December 1968 he may have talked of staying out of operations, but by July 1970 he was stressing how getting a decision made was not enough: ". . . the outsider believes a Presidential order is consistently followed out. Nonsense. I have to spend considerable time seeing that it is carried out and in the spirit the President intended."**

Thus the assistant to the president found personal involvement in operations critical to his influence and to the central role both he and the president wished him to play. On preparations for the Cambodia incursion, for example, there could be no practical separation between the "policy" judgment of what to do and the decisions about particular military operations, and the president inevitably wanted the same man to handle both for him. And because he has become the president's key man, Kissinger is under enormous operational pressure from below as well, since "getting to him" seems to many others to be *their* best hope for effective influence.

But the way the system concentrates power and presidential access in Kissinger's hands—which makes sense if the main problem is one of assuring a limited number of wise presidential decisions—becomes counterproductive if strategic decisions are not enough. For if one believes that day-to-day involvement in operations is essential to the shaping of

---

*Ibid., pp. 12-13.
**Quoted by Saul Pett in "Henry A. Kissinger: Loyal Retainer or Nixon's Svengali," *The Washington Post,* August 2, 1970.

policy, the problem of achieving presidential control
assumes far larger dimensions. Questions of "implementation" and "operational coordination" become vital. Those in
high positions cannot limit themselves to broad decisions;
they must engage in continuing bureaucratic combat. This
takes vastly greater amounts of time and energy. It limits the
number of issues one man can effectively influence, however
great his leverage. Consequently, it increases the number of
men a president requires to fight his battles if he is to make
the foreign affairs government his own. The question then
becomes whether building strength in the White House is
enough, even if Kissinger can dominate the issues on which
he can concentrate. The need would seem rather to go beyond this, to have other officials at key places in the foreign
affairs government who are responsive to the president's priorities and are armed with the leverage and the staff support
to influence policy in presidentially preferred directions.

And this is precisely what the Nixon system has failed to do.
It has not built centers of strength responsive to the president in other parts of the foreign affairs government. The co-
ordinating committee system designedly undercuts one such
potential center—the State Department's Seventh Floor*—by
having the regional Interdepartmental Groups (IGs) chaired
by assistant secretaries of state report directly to Kissinger.
For a while, Under Secretary Elliot Richardson's exception-
ally good relationship with Kissinger mitigated this problem,
and Kissinger's known confidence in him made him an effective agent in bringing presidential priorities to bear on a range
of departmental activities. But Richardson's successor has
no such relationship, and the Under Secretaries Committee
on which much of the formal operational coordination burden
is supposed to rest has had to refer all significant differences
to Nixon or Kissinger. Nor has the president done much to
make State's regional assistant secretaries responsive to him
either. . . . The IGs they chair have been minimally active,
serving not as vehicles for presidentially attuned leadership
but as formal coordinators of studies assigned by the White
House.

The situation at Defense is worse . . . [in part through] the
weakening of two key staff offices that had the role of chal-

*Where the offices of the secretary of state and his under secretaries are
located.

lenging service interests in the name of wider priorities. The Office of International Security Affairs (ISA) has become the home of a group of not very influential right-wing officials. The Systems Analysis office quickly lost its main source of strength—a secretary who would use its analyses as an important factor in his decisions.

The costs of such weakness to the president have apparently been considerable. Thus, by Arthur Schlesinger, Jr.'s account, it took Kennedy two years to get our diplomats to "indicate discreet sympathy" for Italy's opening to the left; Nixon's similar failure to make the State Department a presidential instrument meant an unavailing effort to get State to do more about Biafran relief. The weakness of ISA may not be entirely unrelated to the delays in implementing the directive ordering destruction of biological weapons stockpiles. And the lack of a strong alliance with the Office of the Secretary of Defense has undermined White House staff efforts to bring broad policy priorities to bear on the defense budget under the rubric of the Defense Programs Review Committee.*

Moreover, not only has the Nixon system failed to build strength beyond the White House. In the way it has operated, it has tended to limit the influence of men on the NSC staff itself.

The Attrition of the Staff

In February 1969 Washington was awed by the strength and depth of the Kissinger staff. By September it was talking about how many were leaving. Ten of the twenty-eight men on the February 6 staff list were absent from the list issued September 25, not counting one person who decided not to come on board at all. . . . May 1970 brought five more important resignations, three of them Cambodia related. By summer 1971 only about one-quarter of Kissinger's original twenty-eight staff professionals were still on board. And as impressive as the number of men who left was their quality.

*On Italy, see Arthur M. Schlesinger, Jr., *A Thousand Days* (Boston: Houghton Mifflin, 1965), pp. 876-81; on Biafra, see Elizabeth B. Drew in *Atlantic,* June 1970, pp. 4-30; on biological weapons, see Seymour M. Hersh, "U.S. Still Retains Weapons It Renounced," *The Washington Post,* September 20, 1970.

Just as attracting impressive staff men had been a major success, the inability to hold them was a major failure. The root problem was that though Kissinger's personal influence was virtually unassailable, his staff members found themselves operating from positions of substantially lesser strength. They were denied direct access to Nixon and the leverage that would bring. Moreover, many found it difficult to make contact with Kissinger, so preoccupied was he with fending off multiple pressures and meeting the president's considerable demands.

But the problem was not just contact. The most important senior staff people apparently could get to him the same day if they needed to, though they often had to wait until late evening. More serious was the matter of support, the degree to which staff members could act in Kissinger's name, the extent to which he wanted them to act and would back them up. Even if denied the power that comes from a direct presidential relationship, staff members could hope for substantial if lesser leverage if they were known to speak for Kissinger, or at least had relationships with him where he recognized the importance of giving them support.

It seems clear that in general they have not got this support. This grew to be recognized rather widely in the bureaucracy. It may not have undercut their effectiveness too much on matters (like National Security Studies) that would ultimately rise to the White House, but it has hurt them rather seriously in efforts to influence ongoing bureaucratic activities. Partly for this reason, a number of good men have left. And while others have replaced them, they have increasingly been career officials on detail rather than independently recruited men owing prime allegiance to the White House.

Can the National Security Assistant Manage Foreign Policy?

Thus what in certain respects is the main strength of the Nixon system—the unique leverage it gives to the prime policy official—turns out to be a source of major weakness as well. Kissinger is inundated with pressures from all directions to do things that no one else save the president has the influence to do. The pressure to serve Nixon effectively encourages Kissinger and his staff to handle things more and

more in house, thereby increasing the gap between the president and the bureaucracy that the system was supposed to
bridge. Yet even the staff finds itself on weak ground.

Obviously much of the problem is personalities. Kissinger's
inability to delegate authority is well known and widely
decried. So is Nixon's preference for handling issues through
a small number of people rather than reaching out to the
larger government. Many of the difficulties of the system reflect the fact that no one seems to be really trusted by Nixon
and Kissinger but Nixon and Kissinger.

But the problem goes beyond individual personalities and
styles. Kissinger's failure to support his staff—or to build in
the broader bureaucracy other centers of strength responsive
to him and the president—seems to reflect not just a
regrettable individual trait. A careful look suggests that he is
being asked to play two incompatible roles. His role as
personal staff adviser demands that he place top priority on
meeting the president's immediate, daily needs, handling the
president's own personal foreign affairs business. His overall
influence is inescapably tied to doing these things to the
president's satisfaction. But this means subordinating his
institutional role as kingpin of the NSC system and director
of the largest White House foreign policy staff in history. For
the latter requires not just service *ad hoc* on immediate presidential priorities but comprehensive management of a broad
range of issues, not just responsiveness upward but responsiveness downward, so that he can confer on those who must
wage many daily battles on behalf of him and the president
sufficient leverage to have a fighting chance of prevailing.

Why should the two roles conflict? One reason is time. Kissinger's personal service to the president leaves him markedly less time to support staff members or other bureaucratic
allies in their battles and to see that *their* needs for effectiveness are met. But the problem seems more fundamental. The
assistant to the president must protect his boss's flexibility;
to do this he must guard his own. But his subordinates need
authoritative guidance and the presumption of support.
Without this they cannot help the assistant make his
influence truly comprehensive. Ten years ago the Jackson
Subcommittee warned that the institutional responsibilities
of a foreign affairs "super-Cabinet" official could "mitigate

against the maintenance of his close, confidential, personal relationship with the president."* What we seem to have now is the converse—a man whose unavoidable decision to give priority to this personal relationship weakens his institutional role.

When considering the problem of building strength outside the White House, moreover, there is the question of whom Kissinger might "delegate" authority to even if he could. Strong, presidentially minded regional assistant secretaries of state would be immensely helpful to a president seeking to control the bureaucracy. Yet they do not work for Kissinger in form (except as chairmen of the IGs), and it is not difficult for a secretary of state sensitive about his own authority to find ways to limit their doing so in practice.

Two Types of Issues

The system, then, tends to divide issues into two types—those where Kissinger can be effectively engaged, and those where he cannot. The former may receive broad, high-quality analysis and be resolved in the way the president would wish. But the latter tend to drift and be governed by minimal, temporizing decisions or bureaucratic compromises, since no one has a sufficient power base to lead toward more serious action without threat of an embarrassing reversal. And because Kissinger must involve himself so deeply in the details of issues like Vietnam or China or the SALT talks, the list of issues neither he nor others can master for the president has grown quite large. The effort to control the defense budget through a Kissinger-chaired committee has proved but a paper solution to that large problem. Our policies toward major African and Latin American countries seem to have got very little presidential treatment. The system's failure to deal effectively with economic issues has been recognized in the establishment of a new Council on International Economic Policy which parallels the NSC. And though President Nixon was able to take vigorous economic policy action in August 1971—apparently due above all to strong advocacy by the new secretary of the treasury—no adviser from either the

*Jackson Subcommittee, "Super-Cabinet Officers and Super-Staffs," in *Organizing for National Security*, Vol. III, p. 19.

State Department or the NSC staff was intimately involved. This lack of any close participant (other than Nixon) with major general foreign policy responsibilities could prove quite costly to the success of the economic program and to our relations with Japan and Europe.

Such weaknesses would never have developed if issues like these could be controlled by a few presidential "decisions." But if a large part of foreign policy inevitably grows out of day-to-day actions taken and commitments made by officials outside the White House, a foreign affairs control system must build centers of strength responsive to the president around key officials in the larger bureaucracy or much of what the government does will fall outside of presidential influence. The assistant to the president for national security affairs is singularly ill-placed to concentrate on building such centers of strength. He is dominated by the immediate demands of the president. He lacks a general hierarchy of line subordinates to whom to delegate authority and confidence, even if this did not conflict with his role as personal adviser. He would therefore seem to be a poor man on whom to build an institutional system for the overall coordination and management of foreign policy.

But do we have any choice? If the difficulties of the Nixon system are tied to limitations inherent in the job of the assistant to the president for national security affairs, this suggests renewed attention to the possibility of building foreign affairs coordination around the only other serious candidate, the secretary of state. But would the secretary be able to do what the assistant cannot? Could he combine responsiveness to the president with responsiveness to key officials below him who are needed to master issues that the top men haven't the time to master themselves?

The secretary seems better placed to build up such subordinates. His job is less dominated by personal staff service to the president than is the assistant's. And unlike the assistant, he has important line officials to whom he can "delegate" authority—a deputy secretary, under secretaries, and assistant secretaries of state. The question is whether he could serve the needs of these subordinates and still remain the president's man, whether he could make the State Department into an instrument of the president and not the other way around. At minimum, he would need to conceive of his job not as "chief diplomat" but as leader and director of overall government foreign affairs activities. He would need to weigh all elements in a problem—not just "diplomatic" and "political" but also military and economic—and seek a resolution of that problem consistent with the president's broad responsibilities and priorities. To maintain such a role he would need a strong personal staff not identified with the traditional Department or Foreign Service. And his key subordinates would need to be men loyal primarily to him and the president rather than to the career service.

This is doubtless a large order. Yet it does not seem an impossible one if a president comes into office determined to bring it about. The alternative is to continue with a foreign affairs government where the president cannot extend his control beyond that small number of issues that are on the front burner in the White House kitchen.

KISSINGER'S APPARAT
by John Leacacos

Atop Washington's complex foreign affairs bureaucracy sits the National Security Council (NSC), which was given new status in 1969 when President Nixon moved to make it a kind of command and control center for his foreign policy. . . . Though the substance of its operations are necessarily secret, interviews with officials permit tentative evaluation of the strengths and weaknesses of the Kissinger NSC. There is broad agreement on the following seven points:

—The NSC has served President Nixon more or less as he desired, that is, in the ordered style of formal answers to detailed questionnaires. The volume of this paperwork has at times been staggering, but it has sharpened focus on the search for policy choices.

—The answers and the alternatives for action "coming up through the NSC" have produced few panaceas but have contributed greater coherence of outlook in foreign affairs management. NSC recommendations are more pragmatic than academic, reflecting Kissinger's view: "We don't make foreign policy by logical syllogism."

—Explicit insistence on the "limited" nature of U.S. power and the need for greater restraint and cautious deliberation about its exercise have been reinforced at the highest level by Nixon's habit of withdrawing to make final decisions in solitude and of frequently deciding on no action rather than accepting advice to initiate new action.

—By being close to the president and keeping his fingers on all aspects of the NSC process personally, Kissinger without question is the prime mover in the NSC system. The question arises whether the NSC would function as effectively without Kissinger and whether it can bequeath a heritage of accomplishment to be absorbed by the permanent machinery of government.

—The secretary of state operates within the NSC system and also utilizes it as a forum to establish whatever policy position is preferred by his State Department; but he sidesteps

"Kissinger's Apparat" is a shortened version of the essay published originally in *Foreign Policy*, Number 5, Winter 1971-72.

the NSC on occasion to carry his demurrer, dissent, or alternate position to the president privately.

—The secretary of defense is less personally involved in the NSC process, having apparent indifference to what he believes is unnecessary NSC paperwork, which he leaves to his deputy. . . . His International Security Affairs Bureau in the Pentagon performs poorly by Washington bureaucratic standards.

—The influence on foreign policy of the military, including the Joint Chiefs of Staff, who are usually represented in the NSC process, is at the lowest point in several years. This has been attributed to the anticlimactic winding-down atmosphere of the Vietnam war and to the fact that the Chiefs' once die-hard views and abstract argumentation on strategic nuclear superiority over the Soviet Union have been successfully emulsified into the Nixon-Kissinger basic principles for SALT negotiations with Russia. Kissinger has commented: "In my experience with the military, they are more likely to accept decisions they do not like than any other group."

From time to time, gears have clashed within the system. The State Department has complained bitterly of the Procrustean bed fashioned by the Kissinger staff. Meeting excessive White House demands, bureaucrats allege, robs State and Defense of manpower hours needed for day-to-day operations. After his first year, Kissinger conceded: "Making foreign policy is easy; what is difficult is its coordination and implementation."

White House NSC staffers, on the other hand, exuberant at their top-dog status, express a degree of condescension for the work of the traditional departments. In 1969 Kissinger staffers rated State-chaired studies and recommendations only "50 to 70 percent acceptable" and based on mediocre reporting that failed to sift wheat from chaff in the political cables constantly arriving from 117 U.S. embassies overseas. The Kissinger staff say that they have to hammer out the real choices on the hard issues, since a cynical and sometimes bored bureaucracy offers up too many "straw options." State's planners, for their part, criticize the NSC staff for overdoing the options game. As senior Foreign Service officers say, "After all, what needs to be done is usually fairly obvious common sense. The crux is *how* and *when* to do it."

Cogito Ergo IG

The NSC system today is not the tidy blueprint of January 1969. The older it has got, the more informal and overlapping its procedures have become. The amounts of analysis manufactured sometimes threaten to outrun the capacity of the decision makers to absorb. Crucial issues have been maneuvered to committees chaired by Kissinger, thence directly to the president. The frequency of full NSC meetings has diminished. . . .

Normally, an NSC study is jointly prepared through the IGs (Interdepartmental Groups) by all concerned agencies (State, Defense, CIA, and so on). There are six IGs: for Europe, the Far East, the Middle East, Africa, Latin America, and politico-military affairs, all headed by assistant secretaries of state . . . .

Vietnam policy has been under close White House NSC supervision. Subsidiary NSC units at State, Defense, and CIA serve as operational checkpoints for coordination and update and verify information required for decision via the NSC Vietnam Special Studies Group. The quality of that group's analysis is rated high by Kissinger—on a par with the exhaustive SALT inquiries. . . . Kissinger keeps a close eye on SALT via the NSC Verification Panel, Washington's "action center" for the talks with the Soviets. . . .

What the Nixon administration sees as its five principal areas of foreign affairs initiative—Vietnam, the Middle East, arms control, Berlin, China—have all been under more or less tight NSC White House grip, that is, direct Nixon-Kissinger overview. The NSC took special satisfaction in the August 1971 four-power Berlin accord because *there*, it felt, it had prevented the bureaucracy from rushing into a premature agreement. Progress on SALT and dramatic changes in China policy are also cited as achievements of the new NSC system, although Vietnam remains a more ambiguous test case and most Middle East peace moves have come directly from the State Department, not the NSC.

WSAG To The Rescue

Between the interdepartmental groups at the base and himself and his personal staff at the apex of the NSC pyramid, Kissinger has created several special units for unique tasks.

One is the Under Secretaries Committee, chaired by the under secretary of state and originally designed as the chief implementing body to carry out many (but not all) presidential NSC directives. Its actual importance (never very great) continues to lapse.

Another unit is the Senior Review Group, now at an under secretary level and chaired by Kissinger, which usually gives final approval to the NSC study memoranda after making sure that "all realistic alternatives are presented." Kissinger also chairs the Defense Programs Review Committee, the purpose of which is to keep the annual defense budget in line with foreign policy objectives. A further group, again chaired by Kissinger, through not formally part of the NSC structure, is the "forty committee," which supervises covert intelligence operations—though CIA and green beret commando missions in Laos and Cambodia have been transferred to a separate NSC committee, the Washington Special Actions Group.

This last-named unit, the WSAG, is the top-level operations center for sudden crises and emergencies. It watches developing situations that could gravely affect U.S. interests, such as the apparent imminence of hostilities in 1969 between the Russians and Chinese on the Ussuri River. WSAG kept tabs on Soviet submarines in Cuba in 1969, the Jordan crisis in 1970, and the East Pakistan revolt in 1971 and acted as the watchdog during the Cambodian sweep and the Laos incursion. It was created in April 1969 after Nixon's surprise and embarrassment when the North Koreans shot down an American EC-121 aircraft and the normal bureaucratic mechanisms "muffed" the incident through overcaution. WSAG's chairman is Kissinger, naturally.

Regarding WSAG's work on the Jordan crisis, Kissinger recalled: "We deliberately kept options open to do enough to discourage irresponsibility, but not so much as to give a sense of irreversibility to what was going on; to restrain outside forces (Syrian) that had intervened, but not to the point where we'd trigger a whole set of other forces (Israeli), and to make sure that Soviet power would not be used." The WSAG command-and-control function in this and other crises appeared to work more smoothly than did White House controls on Vietnam in the Johnson administration. A classic pre-WSAG snafu occurred in 1966-67, when air power advocates made detailed arrangements for the rendezvous of thirteen aircraft carriers, practically all those in service, to immobilize the port of Haiphong before North Vietnam's air defenses could be organized—only to be turned down at the last minute by President Johnson.

Temporary White House NSC groups have been formed from time to time for special projects such as postmortems over Cambodia (pre-invasion intelligence had failed to pinpoint North Vietnamese supply capabilities) and Chile (the narrow election win of socialist President Allende was a bit of a surprise, and its implications for future U.S. policy were at first unclear).

The WSAG and the Verification Panel have emerged as the president's innermost councils of war, the closest Nixon approximation to John F. Kennedy's "ExCom," which handled the Cuban missile crisis in 1962. . . . The WSAG likes to work with as few aides as possible. As one of its members says, this eliminates kibitzers and guards against leaks.

Thirty Key Officials

In all this elaborate series of NSC channels and committees only some thirty key officials are estimated to be involved in making critical decisions. Another three hundred, at maximum, including officials of State, Defense, and CIA, have a partial role in contributing to the decision-making process and in carrying out presidential directives.

Despite his perfectionist impatience with the State Department, Kissinger realizes that his unique personal role tends to weaken the institutional role of the permanent bureaucracy. He has frequently said that he would consider it a signal achievement if his NSC system goaded the State Department into "better and better" performance. The more effective State became, the less the White House staff would have to do.

In mid-1971 State began to take up the Kissinger challenge. At Secretary Rogers' urging, a new system of evaluating, country by country, programs, costs, and resources, especially those controlled overseas by other agencies, is being installed within State. The goal is to give State more weight bureaucratically vis-à-vis other agencies in the implementation of foreign policy, thus compensating in part for the ineffectiveness of the moribund NSC Under Secretaries Committee. The long-term objective is to "institutionalize" within State the procedural patterns of the Nixon NSC, thus assuring that they survive beyond the Nixon presidency. . . . But if State is to get more of the action in this administration, it will have to revise the trade-shop slogan of its professionals, who say that "policy is made in the cables," that is, that the actual pattern of U.S. foreign policy in the field is literally made by the spot instructions drafted in Washington. The White House NSC's more intellectualized approach is that policy is made in Washington *after* all the incoming cables from the field have been sifted, weighed, and related to an *a priori* grand strategy. Kissinger aides finally got a handle on significant outgoing cables when new LDX (Limited Distribution Xerox) communications equipment was installed in the White House basement. This gave the NSC presidential assistants enhanced technological means to enforce White House "clearance" of all important outgoing cables.

Much of Kissinger's time is spent writing memoranda to the president, compressing the summaries of lengthy NSC studies to six pages or less. Beyond these formal tasks he has spent countless hours with the president discussing specific problems and also responding to Nixon's contrapuntal remarks and queries concerning philosophy, history, student restlessness, foreign personalities, public opinion. Presumably Kissinger finds in Nixon a sympathetic audience for observations like this one, which he made after Cambodia in May 1970:

The unrest on the campus has very deep . . . maybe even metaphysical, causes, in that it is the result of the seeming purposelessness of the modern bureaucratic state, of the sense of impotence that is produced in the individual in relation to decisions that far transcend him, and that he does not know how to influence—the result of thirty years of debunking by my colleagues and myself in which now the academic community has managed to take the clock apart and doesn't know how to put it together again.

To young staff members, who have sometimes argued with him about the generation gap, Kissinger has asserted that what today's youth need are fathers, that they do not need brothers.

From Vigor to Rigor

Behind the Nixon-Kissinger table of organization lies a philosophy that is not easily articulated in public but seems nonetheless real. What began in mid-1969 to be called the "Nixon Doctrine" is intended, for all its ambiguity, to symbolize a fundamental shift of foreign policy. The doctrine looks to the beginnings of a more multipolar, less bipolar balance of world power, greater emphasis on military reserves at home rather than troops abroad, and a phasing out of U.S. experiments in unilateral "social engineering" in developing nations. It is a conscious attempt to liquidate some of the vestiges (such as Vietnam) of an outworn global containment policy, but to do so in a way that does not leave gaping power vacuums in the wake of U.S. "limited disengagement" and also does not provoke a domestic backslide into isolationism.

From the start Kissinger has sought to make the operating bureaucracy tie specific objectives to these broader purposes. There had, he felt, been far too much instant diplomacy in the past, too much crisis reaction and concentration on tactical rather than long-term strategic interests. A new bureaucratic methodology based on probing questions followed by searching and systematic analysis of every major U.S. policy was designed to provide Washington officialdom with "a new intellectual grid." To the catchword of the Kennedy administration—"vigor"—Kissinger added "rigor." The desired end product of a massive reanalysis of foreign policy within the NSC was to be a series of logical options, alternatives, or choices consistent with long-range U.S. goals.

In 1969, in the first weeks of the Nixon administration, Kissinger installed the framework of the new NSC system, arguing that it would help stimulate "conceptualized foreign policy germination." But the structured NSC system made for an orderliness that the bureaucracy could also translate as routine, prompting Kissinger to say later: "Process itself is a boring subject. You can make awfully stupid decisions with a brilliant process. The basic question the president has asked me to produce from the bureaucracy is: where are we going, and how are we to get there? It is the question he keeps constantly before us."

Kissinger felt that the McGeorge Bundy and Walt Rostow NSC systems of 1961-69 were too loose, had too many prima donnas, and lacked sufficient "checks and balances" to prevent factual error or premature judgments based on false assumptions. Hence, Kissinger's passion for elaborate filters, safety valves, controls. At a background briefing he once said rather sadly:

Anybody who has seen high officials in Washington will recognize that one of the nightmarish aspects about it is that, contrary to what I knew in academic life where, when one is identified with a problem, one could work on it as long as necessary, [here] one is forced to develop a hierarchy of priorities. . . . There are many issues that senior officials may know are coming. They may even know how they will deal with these issues—if they only had the time to get around to them. So one of the arts of policy-making is to order your issues in such a way that the most urgent ones get solved before some that appear less urgent hit you. . . . The greater number of issues that a country takes on, the more it taxes the psychological resilience of its leadership group. It is not possible to act wisely at every moment of time in every part of the world. It isn't possible for domestic opinion to understand long-range policy in every part of the world at every moment of time.

The National Security Study Memoranda

It is increasingly clear that the Kissinger method has succeeded in shifting a number of American foreign policy assumptions. This has occurred not through any revolution-by-*Diktat* but instead through a subtler process of evolution-by-memorandum. It is in part by forcing his staff and the larger bureaucracy to answer searching questions in detailed written memoranda, and by refusing to "accept" those memos if they are not sufficiently "rigorous," that Kissinger has churned out the beginnings of new policies toward China, arms control, and European security. His cumbersome method is at its simplest a way of making the bureaucracy think harder.

The process began in January 1969, when he asked for a study that would answer twenty-six questions on Vietnam. Ten more study assignments were given out in the next ten days. The subjects were: the Middle East, U.S. military posture, foreign aid, Japan, NATO, international monetary policy, "review of the international situation," East-West relations, Nigeria, and contingency planning.

In his first hundred days, Kissinger assigned fifty-five such study memoranda, or "term papers" as they are sometimes called. . . . Most of the studies and many of the early efforts were returned to their bureaucratic authors for further work on further questions before winning Kissinger's approval. Some studies, complete with annexes and tables, were a foot high. These contributed to the overkill of planning by not being read by the principal NSC officials because they were simply too long to digest. But shorter studies, prepared in a careful format to outline proposed choices, costs, and consequences did succeed in widening the horizons of policymakers. NSC aides felt the sharpness of Kissinger's displeasure whenever they let a major policy consideration "fall between the cracks.". . .

Among the most vital of all the studies are those relating to nuclear weapons, done in preparation for the Strategic Arms Limitation Talks (SALT) with the Soviet Union. . . . They are Kissinger's pride. He has asserted that the SALT studies, centered in the Verification Panel, have been the most thorough and meticulous analyses ever made of the politics of nuclear strategy. He also asserts that they have virtually eliminated the narrow adversary approach to arms limitation hitherto practiced within the U.S. government, an approach that used to provoke bitter intramural controversies leading to stultified international negotiations. Half the time used to be spent negotiating among ourselves, Kissinger says, one-quarter with our allies, and one-quarter with the Russians.

Four principles of U.S. military posture identified in the early NSC studies as guidelines for SALT were: (1) the need to retain a second-strike capability; (2) the need for stable forces in a crisis, that is, forces sufficiently safeguarded so as to be invulnerable to a sudden attack; (3) the requirement that the Russians not be allowed large leverage in the parity of inflicted damage (after all, there are more industrial and urban concentrations to destroy in the United States than in Russia); and (4) the need for adequate defenses against threats from third countries that have actual nuclear weapons (France, China) or nuclear potential (Japan, India, Egypt, Israel, Cuba, among others). The Kissinger-directed review examined the capabilities of every known weapon system and combination of systems and the attendant risks and gains that would follow from their limitation. This analysis pre-

pared the way for Soviet and American negotiators to seek
concurrent accords on defensive and offensive arms. . . .

The Richardson Factor

One stalwart of the Kissinger NSC system, whose absence
has been sorely missed, is Elliot Richardson, who resigned
on June 23, 1970 as under secretary of state to become secretary of health, education, and welfare [and later moved on
to the departments of Defense and Justice]. A laconic
Bostonian, Richardson impressed Kissinger (and nearly
everybody else) with his incisive knowledge of how to make
the bureaucracy move and combined this with an air of
slightly gelid insouciance. Washington wags used to
compare Richardson to Sherlock Holmes' brother, Mycroft,
that veritable one-man NSC staff of Edwardian Britain, whose
Foreign Office assignment was to determine "how each
factor would affect the other." Kissinger and Richardson
lunched together every Tuesday. . . . As a fellow Harvard
alumnus, Richardson had no difficulty understanding what
Kissinger meant when he said that knowledge depends upon
the ability to abstract generalizations from individual events
and that the higher the level of authority, the greater the
degree of abstraction necessary.

Kissinger and Richardson then . . . would together decide
what NSC study memoranda to order and would also frame
an average of ten to fifteen questions they wanted each study
to answer. "You cannot get the right answers," says Kissinger, "unless you've asked the right questions." Richardson
also managed to alter Kissinger's rather low opinion of the
Foreign Service, just as at the beginning of the Nixon administration Secretary Rogers had some effect in muting the
president's own heavy bias against the State Department.
Richardson is missed at State not only for his decisiveness
and common sense but also for his ability to exploit the talents of the career Foreign Service, whose morale has stayed
generally low because its personnel have felt underutilized
and distrusted by the Nixon administration.

Two Weak Spots

The Achilles' heel of the NSC system has been international
economics; its albatross has been foreign intelligence. As

Kissinger is the first to admit, his reputation in diplomacy and nuclear strategy does not extend to economics, a field largely beyond his knowledge or competence. Thus the NSC has had only marginal, if not minimal, impact on economic policy.

Early efforts in 1969 to secure the staff services of a national authority in the foreign economic field lapsed under the pressure of more immediate problems. During that first year about 70 percent of the bureaucracy's contributions to NSC economic studies came from the Treasury Department and only 30 percent from State. No senior interdepartmental group for economics was organized. Receiving little attention from Kissinger, the NSC's own economic specialists carried no bureaucratic clout. . . .

The NSC's second weak spot, intelligence, is probably Kissinger's greatest personal disappointment. He had once said that the test of statesmanship was the ability to anticipate and evaluate threats before they occurred. His passion for objectivity and commitment to rigorous analysis appear in this case to have fallen afoul of the disorganized chaos of the multiple intelligence agencies in the U.S. government.

One major exception to this general failure stands out. The single field in which an "agreed factual basis" for policy formulation has been more or less achieved has been SALT. Kissinger claims, "The Verification Panel has made 98 percent of intelligence disagreements disappear." The reason: policymakers and intelligence analysts sit on the same panel and directly argue out their differences over facts and policies. On most other questions the rigid distinction between "operators" and "analysts" is maintained; it is established doctrine in the intelligence community that these two types of officials be kept separate. But Kissinger has been plainly unhappy with what he calls "the theologians of intelligence," officials more interested in advancing their particular agency interests than with seeking rigorously rational answers to difficult, government-wide questions.

Six Types of Ambiguity in the Modern CIA

Kissinger uses the euphemism "intelligence ambiguities" rather than "failures" to blunt the public thrust of his private unhappiness. Details of at least six such "ambiguities" are widely known, and one assumes there are additional cases that have not yet surfaced in public. Washington received no advance warning of the September 1969 revolutionary coup in Libya. Similarly no notice was given of the coup against Prince Sihanouk in Cambodia in March 1970, mainly because, at the insistence of Senate Majority Leader Mike Mansfield, no CIA agents had been stationed in the country. Because of disputes over the evidence, no definitive evaluation was made all through 1969 of the importance of Sihanoukville to the North Vietnamese supply buildup in the "sanctuary" provinces opposite the main population zones of South Vietnam. (The Defense Intelligence Agency [DIA], it eventually turned out, had been more correct than the CIA.) Another failure, apparently one of poor coordination within the U.S. government, was the inability to act on advance knowledge that the North Vietnamese might quickly marshal 35 thousand troops against the 17 thousand South Vietnamese forces in the Laotian incursion of February 1971. In the blighted Defense Department operation of November 1970 to rescue U.S. prisoners of war at Sontay in North Vietnam, intelligence officials failed to report the obvious conclusion, on the basis of available evidence, that the prisoners were probably no longer there. The internal logic of the admittedly incomplete information on hand—credibility, verifiability, perishability—pointed clearly to that conclusion, particularly after agents on the ground failed to get close enough to Sontay in time for confirmation. Finally, there was the failure of timely aerial reconnaissance just before the August 7, 1970 Israeli-Egyptian cease-fire along the Suez Canal took effect.

In addition, NSC staffers criticize the looseness of mental discipline ("sponginess" in Kissinger's phrase) that seems to infect nearly all intelligence bodies. IG and NSC officials working on National Security Study Memoranda have often been unable to "pry loose" from CIA basic intelligence evaluations of the subject under study; too frequently intelligence estimates have had a cautious, "cover all bets" quality not very useful to policymakers; and coordination between NSC studies and CIA's own internal studies has been less than complete. The quality of intelligence assessments varies widely, and the NSC has been unable to develop any agreed yardstick to "evaluate the evaluators" and root out hidden assumptions. Hence, intelligence estimators remain essentially their own judge and jury. Their biases, according to NSC officials, include a narrow concern for the special interests and "missions" of their particular agencies, over-emphasis on foreign capabilities as opposed to intentions, and "cold war" blinders that may exaggerate both the importance of a given foreign event to the U.S. and the involvement or advantage gained by Communists. The policymakers say they want intelligence "on tap, not on top" and sometimes show considerable impatience with the "speculative opinions" of intelligence briefers. But they have not found a method to insure against future "ambiguities" and to provide the better structure and controls now lacking.

These criticisms fall impartially on the Defense Intelligence Agency (too big, not professional enough, service oriented) and the Central Intelligence Agency (self-serving bias on SALT judgments). In addition, the NSC is concerned about the confusion generated by mission-motivated estimates among military G-2 intelligence sections in large subordinate theater commands overseas. In their eagerness to accomplish a mission G-2 staffs may be more prone to wishful thinking than others without similar stakes, and they tend to slip away from effective control from the top. At the same time there are generals who use their stars to short-circuit or unbalance G-2 procedures. There is a habitual oversell of Air Force capabilities, which complicates equitable consideration of intelligence targets. There is, finally, a disposition among some generals to weigh all intelligence in the light of an ultimate nuclear war against the Soviet Union. This produces an unbalanced outlook, making most intelligence seem either inconsequential or overpoweringly important; it contributes to a syndrome of nuclear preoccupation that has overshadowed foreign policy for a generation. . . .

A final missing element in the intelligence process is caused by the long-standing unwritten prohibition against including in intelligence evaluations any explicit consideration of U.S. policy interests or resources. Knowledge of the policy options available to the U.S. could well affect the assessment of many foreign situations. The ironclad exclusion of these policy possibilities from intelligence evaluations prevents the factor of the American presence in a foreign area, whether active or passive, being given weight as one important element in the equation. Similarly, foreign and adversary perceptions of U.S. interests and of what the United States might do or fail to do in a given situation are frequently left out of intelligence evaluations for the NSC. These omissions work against the grain of the Kissinger method: the sorting out of every implication of an issue by close adherence to the screen of U.S. purpose, which shakes out the pattern of priorities.

The Options Game

How realistic are the famous "options"? Judging by the results thus far, Nixon has been better served by his more formalized national security advisory system than either Lyndon Johnson or John F. Kennedy were served by their informal systems, even though it was Robert McNamara, as defense secretary to the two predecessor presidents, who first made the options concept fashionable. The idea was simple enough: serve up the president a bundle of alternatives. But one sometimes wonders, while prowling the White House basement, whether often-repeated phrases like "keeping the options open" and "the president's spread of options" don't have more a liturgical than intellectual significance. The options mystique has even inspired some critics to accuse Kissinger of cynically circumventing the bureaucracy by hogtying it to meaningless NSC studies while he and his staff focus on the essential issues. The charge would have more plausibility if Kissinger were indeed the Nietzschean superman his critics assume—and commanded a sufficient number of junior supermen to perform the whole job in the White House.

The path from Kissinger wish to NSC consummation has been by no means easy. President Nixon, recalling the recommendations of the Eisenhower administration NSC, felt they had been too homogenized. In the Johnson regime, the NSC did not act as a functioning process binding agencies together; by contrast with the Nixon system, the Johnson NSC was practically nonexistent. And Johnson staffers only infrequently and informally presented the president with options. After all, it was felt, "There were only one or two sensible things to do."

So Kissinger upon entering the White House basement found little rough-and-ready argumentation among bureaucrats over alternative policy courses. He inherited, instead, the bureaucracy's time-tested habit of elaborate, negotiated "consensus" among subordinate officials and agencies (with an occasional dissenting view included as a footnote) *prior* to their submission of advice to the president. He shook this system up by passing out new kinds of study assignments. Harvard professor that he is, he made the bureaucrats write theses and proved to be a tough grader. He rated many of the early NSC studies no better than "C"—barely passing. He also came to recognize that the options game could frequently be a disguised form of special advocacy: two or three obviously untenable "straw options" served up alongside only one clearly realistic choice.

What is less clear is whether the NSC options game shades analysis toward competition within the bureaucracy for discovery of the most striking plausibility that can appeal to the holders of political power. By stimulating foreign affairs officials to engage in an adversary process, does one perhaps change the whole focus of the system toward scoring bureaucratic points on opponents rather than defining national objectives and deciding how best to attain them?

And there may be a final dilemma, evident in the unhappiness of the Nixon NSC with the intelligence it is getting. Intelligence evaluators, by the very nature of their function, restrict options; their role is to determine likely, "reliable" outcomes, probable and feasible patterns of events. The role of the president's men, on the other hand, is to avoid being squeezed into one course and to maintain and expand the options.

The product of all the memos and meetings, questionnaires and options is the refined raw material of presidential decision making, the identification of what opportunities and escape hatches are open to the nation's leadership. To date, Nixon's foreign policy record has indicated the seizure of opportunities, and so the NSC process that made those opportunities apparent must be judged a success.

WHY BUREAUCRATS PLAY GAMES
by Morton H. Halperin

. . . When American government officials consider a proposed change in American foreign policy, they often see and
emphasize quite different things and reach different conclusions. A proposal to withdraw American troops from Europe,
for example, is to the Army a threat to its budget and size, to
the Office of Management and Budget examiners a way to
save money, to the Treasury a balance-of-payments gain, to
the State Department Bureau of European Affairs a threat to
good relations with NATO, to the president's congressional
adviser an opportunity to remove a major irritant in the president's relations with Capitol Hill.

What determines what an official sees? What accounts for
his stand? The examples provide some clues.

Participants in the national security policy process in the
American government believe that they should and do take
stands that advance the national security of the United
States. Their problem is to determine what is in fact in the
national security interest. Officials seek clues and guidelines
from a variety of sources. Some hold to a set of beliefs about
the world which provide strong clues; for example, the Soviet
Union is expansionist and must be stopped by American military power. Others look to authorities within the government
or beyond it for guidance. Many bureaucrats define what is
necessary for the nation's security by a set of more specific
intermediate interests. For some, these may be personal:
"Since, in general, I know how to protect the nation's security
interests, whatever increases my influence is in the national
interest." For others, the intermediate interests relate to
domestic political interests: "Since a sound economy is a
prerequisite to national security, I must oppose policies that
threaten the economy"; or, "Since only my party knows how
to defend the security interests of the United States, I must
support policies that keep my party in power."

For many participants, the intermediate objectives that provide strong clues for what is in the nation's security interest
are the interests of the organization to which they belong.

"Why Bureaucrats Play Games" is a shortened version of the essay published originally in *Foreign Policy*, Number 2, Spring 1971.

Career officials come naturally to believe that the health of their organization is vital to the nation's security. So also do individuals who are appointed by the president to senior posts in Washington foreign policy bureaucracies. This tendency varies depending on the individual, the strength of his prior conviction, his image of his role, and the nature of the organization he heads. On many issues a secretary of the Air Force will be strongly guided by the organizational interests of his service. A secretary of state, on the other hand, is likely to be less influenced by the organizational interests of his department and the Foreign Service, since these provide less clear-cut clues and in many cases conflicting guidelines to the nation's security interest. Some senior officials, moreover, will seek clues less from their organizations' interests than from the interests of the president, as they define them.

Despite the different interests of the participants and the different faces of an issue that they see, officials still frequently agree about what should be done. This may occur when there is strong presidential leadership or when there is a national security argument that most participants view as decisive. In many cases, however, officials reach consensus by designing an ambiguous policy that avoids substantial costs to the different interests of the participants, including the interests of the organizations involved. The compromise avoids making choices on priorities and leaves organizations free to continue operating as they have in the past and to control their own operations. Once a decision is made, the organizations themselves shape the way in which it is implemented.

Organizational interests, then, are for many participants a dominant factor in determining the face of the issue that they see and the stand that they take in pursuit of the nation's security interests. In large part they constitute U.S. foreign policy. Before there is any hope of mastering them, their mysteries—and their mystique—must be explored. What are these organizational interests? From what do they derive?

Organizational Interests

All organizations seek *influence*; many also have a *mission* to perform, either overseas or at home; and some organizations need to maintain expensive *capabilities* in order to perform their missions effectively.

Influence: Organizations with missions seek influence to promote the missions. Those that also have large operational capabilities—like the armed forces—seek influence on decisions in part to maintain the capability necessary to perform their mission. Some organizations, such as the Office of International Security Affairs in the Office of the Secretary of Defense and the Policy Planning Staff in the State Department, have neither large capabilities nor stable, organizationally defined missions. Hence, their only organizational interest is in enhancing influence for its own sake and because individuals in such organizations share with those in other organizations the belief that they can best judge the nation's security interests.

Stands on issues are affected by the desire to maintain influence. This could lead to support for certain policies that will require greater reliance on the organization. It can also lead officials to avoid opposing a particular policy in the belief that to do so would reduce their influence on other issues.

Missions: Most organizations are charged with specific missions. Some of these can be accomplished entirely at home (such as maintaining good relations with the Congress); others require actions abroad (such as deterring a Soviet attack on the United States).

Bureaucrats will examine any policy proposal from the point of view of whether or not it will increase the effectiveness with which the mission of their particular organization will be carried out. For example, in examining a proposal for a new security commitment, the Office of Management and Budget and the Comptroller's Office in the Pentagon will ask themselves how it will affect their ability to keep down the defense budget, Treasury will ask how it will affect its ability to maintain the U.S. balance of payments in equilibrium, while the military will be concerned with its ability to meet existing commitments. State Department officials may be concerned with the impact of the security arrangement on political relations with that country and its neighbors.

Capabilities: The missions of some organizations in the national security field lead them to maintain substantial and expensive capabilities that may be employed abroad. The armed services, in particular, are responsible for creating very expensive military forces. Organizations with expensive

capabilities will see the face of an issue that affects their
ability to maintain what according to their view is the necessary capability.

Organizations with large capabilities will be particularly concerned about budget decisions and about the budgeting implications of policy decisions. Organizations with missions
but low-cost capabilities will be primarily concerned with
policy decisions and their implications for missions. This is
an important difference between the armed services and the
State Department.

Organizations with missions strive to maintain or to improve
their (1) autonomy, (2) organizational morale, (3) organizational "essence," and (4) roles and missions. Organizations
with high-cost capabilities are also concerned with maintaining or increasing their (5) budgets.

1. Autonomy

Members of an organization believe that they are in a better
position than others to determine what capabilities they
should have and how they can best fulfill their missions.
They attach very high priority to controlling their own
resources. They want to be in a position to spend the money
allocated to them in the way that they choose, to station their
manpower as they choose, and to implement policy in their
own way. Organizations resist efforts by senior officials to
get control of their activities by arguing that effective
functioning of the organization requires freedom to determine its own procedures. The priority attached to autonomy
is shown by the experiences of two recent secretaries of defense. Robert S. McNamara caused great consternation in
the Pentagon in 1961 by instituting new decision procedures
that reduced the autonomy of the services, despite the fact
that he increased defense spending by six billion dollars and
did not seek to alter the missions of the services. Secretary of
Defense Melvin Laird, by contrast, improved the Pentagon
morale in 1969 by increasing service autonomy on budget
matters while reducing the Defense budget by more than four
billion dollars. The quest for autonomy leads organizations
to resist policies that will require them to yield their autonomy to senior officials or to work closely with another organization. The belief that autonomy is necessary in the performance of missions results in organizations informing senior

officials that particular options are feasible only if full responsibility for carrying them out is delegated to the operating organization. During the 1958 Quemoy crisis, for example, the military repeatedly pressed for freedom to use nuclear weapons on their own authority. They informed the president that they could guarantee to defend this offshore island against a Chinese Communist attack only if granted this autonomy.*

2. Organizational Morale

An organization functions effectively only if its personnel are highly motivated. They must believe that what they are doing makes a difference and is in support of the national interest, that the organization's efforts are appreciated and its role in the scheme of things is not diminishing and preferably is increasing, that the organization controls its own resources, and that there is room for advancement in the organization.

Because they have learned the vital importance of morale for the effective functioning of an organization, bureaucrats give close attention to the likely effects of any change of policy or patterns of action on the morale of the organization and will resist changes that they feel will have a severe effect on morale. Officials may resist changes that even they believe would improve their organization's effectiveness in carrying out its missions if they also believe that such actions would severely affect the morale of the organization. In particular, they will be concerned about the effects on the promotion patterns of the organization. Short-run accomplishments of goals and even increases in budgets will be subordinated to the long-run health of the organization. Bureaucrats know that ignoring morale can have disastrous consequences. . . .

3. The Organization's "Essence"

Career officials generally have a clear notion of what the essence of their organization is and should be, both in terms of capabilities and of missions. In some organizations the same view of the essence will be shared by all of those in the same promotion and career structure; in other cases there will be differences of view. This can be seen in the following brief discussion of the organizational essence of some of the major U.S. national security organizations:

*Dwight D. Eisenhower, *Waging Peace* (New York: Doubleday, 1965), p. 299.

Air Force officers agree that the essence of their program is the development of a capability for combat flying, particularly involving the delivery of nuclear weapons. Officers whose orientation is toward the Strategic Air Command (SAC) emphasize the mission of strategic bombing; those in the Tactical Air Command (TAC) emphasize interdiction of enemy supply lines. Providing close combat support is not seen by most Air Force officers as part of the essence of their mission, nor is the development of a capability to transport Army troops and equipment.

Army officers seek to develop a capability to engage in ground combat operations employing traditional Army divisions deployed according to traditional Army doctrine. Some Army officers emphasize tank operations; others stress air mobility. Air defense, advisory missions for foreign governments, and "elite" specialized forces such as the green berets are not regarded as being part of the essence of the Army.

Navy officers agree only on the general proposition that the Navy's business is to man combat naval ships and that their mission is to maintain control of the seas. In fact, the Navy is split into three traditional groups and a fourth whose weight may be growing. Navy flyers (brown shoe) emphasize carrier-based air; others (black shoe) stress the surface Navy; the submariners focus on attack submarines. The fourth group looks to missile-firing submarines and puts emphasis on the mission of strategic deterrence (advocated in the 1940s and '50s by the flyers). No influential group sees the transport of men and materiel as part of the Navy's essence, and most senior naval officers have tended to view the Polaris missile-firing submarines as a service to the nation extraneous to the Navy's "essential" tasks.

Foreign Service officers see their essential functions as representation and negotiation and political reporting. Managing programs and embassies and even analyzing policy alternatives are not part of the essence of the State Department's functions.

Career *CIA* officials appear to be split between those who emphasize analysis, on one hand, and those who view the agency's essence as its unique role of covert intelligence gathering and operations.

The stand of bureaucrats on a policy issue is influenced by its impact on the ability of their organization to pursue its essential programs and missions. They resist most strongly efforts to take away these functions or to share them with other organizations. They also resist proposals to reduce funds for these programs or missions. Autonomy is most precious as it affects the essence of the organization.

Conversely, bureaucrats feel less strongly about "marginal" functions, particularly those that require cooperation with other organizations or are viewed as support for them (for example, naval and air transport for the Army). Left alone, they will devote fewer resources to such programs and missions, and ambitious career officials will ignore them. For example, during the 1950s neither the Navy nor the Air Force built air- or sea- lift capability. The best Army officers, to take another example, seek to avoid advisory assignments in Vietnam, seeking instead to lead troops in combat and to serve on a combat staff.

If pressed by senior officials, bureaucrats will take on new programs or missions if they believe that they can earn support that can be used on more crucial issues and if persuaded that the new activities will not divert funds from the essence of the organization. They resist or seek to give up functions that they believe will use up more resources than they bring in, or that will require the recruitment of new personnel, with new skills and interests, who may dilute or seek to change the organization's essence. For example, the Army after World War II urged the creation of a separate Air Force in the belief that if this was not done, flyers would come to dominate the Army. Similarly, State has resisted efforts to assign to it the operational responsibility for aid, propaganda, and intelligence functions.

Organizations seek new functions only if they believe that their failure to get responsibility for them would jeopardize their sole responsibility in critical areas. Thus the Navy and Air Force insist on performing the troop transport role and the Air Force rejects Army efforts to perform the close air support role. If the Army transported its own troops by sea, they might well build ships that enabled Army troops to come ashore firing—the Marine function. By performing this mission, the Navy is able, for example, to insist that the proposed Fast Deployment Logistic (FDL) ships be carefully constructed so that they cannot be used for amphibious operations, denying an option that in some crises a president might wish to have. The Air Force, to cite another example, fought for the medium-range missile program after it failed to kill that program, because it feared that the Army would use the missiles as a foot-in-the-door on the strategic deterrence mission.

4. Roles and Missions

Few sharp dividing lines exist between the responsibilities for programs and missions of various parts of the U.S. foreign affairs bureaucracy. Some missions may be performed simultaneously by two organizations. Both the Air Force Minuteman force and the Navy Polaris force contribute to deterrence of a Soviet nuclear attack on the United States. Both the State Department and the Central Intelligence Agency evaluate the likely reaction of foreign governments to particular courses of action.

A program that at one time is shared may later be assigned to a single organization or be phased out. For example, at one time the Air Force and the Army shared responsibility for the development of medium-range missiles (MRBMs); the function was later assigned to the Air Force and eliminated.

Some missions, once the exclusive province of one bureaucratic entity, may at a later date be transferred to another—either an already existing organization or a new organization. For example, intelligence functions once performed by the military and the State Department were transferred to the CIA in 1947.

Organizations are specially sensitive to this issue because of a number of disputes about roles and missions extending back to the postwar period. . . . The three classic disputes that divided the services in the 1940s and continue to divide them now are: the struggle between the Navy and Air Force over naval aviation, that between the Army and Air Force over combat support, and that between the Army and Marines over Marine participation in ground combat operations. The Air Force has sought authority for all combat operations. The Navy fights hard to protect its role in air operations over the sea and has sought parity with the Air Force in tactical and strategic bombing, which it attained in Vietnam. The Army seeks control over close combat support air operations. The Army-Marine rivalry involves the Army effort to limit the Marines to amphibious operations and the Marine desire to participate in all ground combat.

Two other disputes have pitted the CIA against older established organizations. The CIA would like to have control over all *covert operations.* The military would also like control of all such missions, or at least those that involve combat operations. The military apparently pointed to the Bay of Pigs fiasco as proof that they and not the CIA should manage combat operations. The CIA and the Air Force have fought from the start over which organization should control U-2 operations.

State and the CIA have never agreed where the Agency's responsibility for "intelligence" *evaluation* ends and State's responsibility for political reporting begins. Nor has there been agreement on the line between CIA's functions and the military intelligence functions of the armed services and their responsibility for evaluating allied and U.S. military forces and operations.

New technology produces disputes over nuclear weapons and space operations. Sensing that most of the money for aviation would be allocated to nuclear delivery, naval aviators sought to have the Navy share the nuclear deterrence mission with the Air Force, leading to the once famous but now forgotten "revolt of the admirals." With the development of missiles the Navy gained a role in strategic deterrence, as the Army did for a brief period when it had a medium-range missile under development. In a somewhat similar manner, first the Army and Air Force fought for a major role in space, with the Navy showing some interest. The Air Force, after winning, saw much of its function transferred to NASA, although it continues to seek a role in space.

Disputes over roles and missions affect the stands taken by organizations and the information they report to senior officials. For example, according to a former Air Force intelligence officer, both the Air Force and Navy exaggerated the effectiveness of their own bombing of North Vietnam. Both recognized that the postwar dispute over the Navy's bombing

role would be affected by evaluation of their bombing operations in Vietnam. Each, believing (or fearing) that the other
service would exaggerate, was forced to emphasize the positive in order to protect its position.*

In implementing missions that they know to be coveted by
another organization, organizations may bend over backward
to avoid the charge that they demonstrated by their behavior
that the mission should be shifted. . . . In periods of crisis,
bureaucrats calculate how alternative policies and patterns of
action will affect future definitions of roles and missions.
They do not put forward options that might lead to changes
in roles and missions to their detriment. They may argue that
such options are, in fact, infeasible. Bureaucrats may also
feel obliged to distort information reported to senior officials
in order to guard against the danger that it will in the future
affect roles and missions. Disputes over roles and missions
also affect policy stands and the way policy decisions are
implemented.

Bureaucrats have learned over time that changes in roles and
missions frequently occur during crisis situations. Thus an
organization concerned about its mission and desiring either
to expand it or prevent others from expanding at its cost may
be particularly alert to both challenges and opportunities
during a crisis. Because this phenomenon is widely understood, organizations cannot trust other organizations not to
take advantage of a crisis situation, and must be on guard.
Frequently, after a crisis, an organization whose functions
were expanded during the crisis will try to argue that it has
now established a precedent and should continue to perform
the new function. . . .

5. Budgets

Bureaucrats examine any proposed change in policy or patterns of action for its effect on the budget of their organization. They prefer larger to smaller budgets and support policy
changes that they believe will lead to larger budgets.

There is, however, a substantial asymmetry between the
Department of Defense and the Department of State in regard
to the impact of policy issues on budget issues. The State

*Morris J. Blackman, "The Stupidity of Intelligence," in Charles Peters, ed.,
Inside the System (New York: Praeger, 1970).

Department budget is relatively small, and very few of the foreign policy matters with which the State Department deals have any direct effect on its budget. For the military services, most policy issues are likely to have important budgetary implications. For example, the question of the United States military forces in Europe does not have any implications for the State Department budget, while it could have very important consequences for the budget of the United States Army and the Defense Department as a whole.

An organization will be concerned with whether a proposed change in policy that generates a new function will in fact lead to a budget increase, or whether the new function may be added to its responsibilities without any corresponding increase in budget. The estimate of whether a new function will lead to an increased budget will depend in part upon the nature of the budget-making process. For example, during the 1950s the budgets for the military services were largely determined by allocating fixed percentages of an overall budgetary ceiling established by the president. Thus, in general, new responsibilities had to be financed out of existing budgetary levels. By contrast, during the 1960s there was at least no explicit budgetary ceiling. The budget was determined by the secretary of defense on the basis of functional categories and responsibilities. Thus the services believed that new functions tended to mean increased budget levels.

The question of whether a new function will lead to new funds and hence should be desired, or to a reallocation of old funds, which perhaps needs to be resisted, will also depend in part on whether the new function is seen as closely related to existing functions or substantially new ones. For example, the Army was interested in acquiring responsibility for the deployment of MRBMs in the 1950s, in part because this would give the Army a strategic nuclear role. The Army hoped that this would justify its getting an increased share of the overall defense budget, since the existing allocation was based on the Army's having no strategic function. On the other hand, the Air Force recognized that MRBMs would simply be considered another strategic weapon and that it would be forced to finance their development and deployment out of existing budget funds. Thus, in terms of its budgetary interests, the Army sought the MRBM role, while the Air Force was reluctant to take it on. (Concern with protecting its "essence," however, meant that if there was to be an MRBM program, the Air Force was determined to have it.)

Organizations are concerned not only about their absolute share of the budget, but also about their relative share of a relevant larger budget. This proposition applies particularly to each of the military services, although it may also apply to parts of the AID organization. In part, this objective seems to be based simply on the sense of competition between the services. It also apparently derives, however, from the fear that once established levels change in an adverse direction, they may continue to change, leading to substantial reductions in the activities of a particular service, which could have substantial effects on morale.

This objective frequently leads the services to resist proposals that may lead to increases in their own budget if they fear that it may lead to a less than proportionate increase in their budget as compared to other parts of the defense establishment. It also leads the services to prefer the certainty of a particular share of the budget to an unknown situation in which budgets may increase but shares may change. For example, in 1957 the Gaither Committee appointed by President Eisenhower recommended substantial increases in the budgets of all three services, arguing the need for secure second-strike retaliatory forces and for larger limited-war capabilities. However, none of the services supported these proposals, in part because they were uncertain what the implications would be for shares of the budget and preferred a known process with known division of the budget to a new process that, while it might mean increased budgets for all, might involve changes in the shares of the budget.*

What Every President Should Know

Organizations have interests. Career officials in these organizations believe that protecting these interests is vital to the security of the United States. They therefore take stands on issues that advance these interests and maneuver to protect these interests against other organizations and senior officials, including the president.

*Morton H. Halperin, "The Gaither Committee and the Policy Process," *World Politics,* April 1961.

This process affects policy decisions and action in a number of ways and limits the power of the president and his senior associates. Every president needs to know how bureaucratic interests interact, in order to be the master rather than the prisoner of his organizations, and also in order to mold the rational interests of the bureaucracies into the national interest as he sees it. The beginning of wisdom for any chief executive is to understand that organizational interests and maneuvers affect policy in at least four main areas.

1. *Information*: Organizations focusing on acquiring the information necessary to protect their interests tend to supply to others information designed to protect these interests and to lead senior officials to do what the organizations believe needs to be done. This means that the selection of information is different from what the president would like to have—and many think he is getting.

2. *Presentation of options*: Organizations construct a menu of options to meet any situation based on their notion of what the essence of their mission is. Options that involve cooperation between organizations and that would require an organization to alter its structure or perform extraneous missions are unlikely to be advanced.

3. *Freedom to choose options:* Organizations seek to prevent the president from choosing an option that runs contrary to their interests. They do so by asserting that the option is infeasible or by demanding full freedom for implementation if the option is chosen. They may leak the proposed option to the press or to congressional allies.

4. *Implementation:* In implementing presidential decisions, organizations feel free to vary their behavior from that required by a faithful adherence to the letter and spirit of the president's action. When organization interests conflict with directed behavior, organizations may obey the letter rather than the spirit, they may delay, or they may simply disobey.

In seeking to mitigate the consequences of this behavior, senior officials and the president must begin by accepting the inevitability of organizational interests and maneuvers to support them. Neither appeals to patriotism nor changes in personnel will lead career officials and many of their bosses to lose their belief in the importance of the health of their organization and the need to protect it.

Awareness of organizational interests would lead senior officials to recognize that those with whom they deal see different faces of an issue and, because they have different interests, reach different stands. Abstract national security arguments usually do not change these stands. Being aware of maneuvers in support of organizational interests, senior officials learn to be skeptical of information that tends to support these interests and of analyses of options presented by organizations. They can then look to other sources for options or information. Beyond that, they can seek organizational changes to mitigate the consequences of organizational interests for high priority objectives, and they can seek to design programs, missions, and policies to reduce their incompatibility with organizational interests.

Organizational changes can involve creating new organizations, altering the internal structure of an existing organization, or changing the rules of the game by which decisions are made. NASA is an instance of the first option, the green berets of the second, and the McNamara program budgeting system of the third. Such moves are time consuming and their consequences frequently difficult to predict.

Designing policies to reduce organizational opposition requires a clear understanding of the relevant interests and an ability to fashion an option that accomplishes its purpose while minimizing organizational costs. For example, proposals to withdraw forces from overseas are likely to meet less opposition if they do not appear to threaten service interests in autonomy (they might delegate to the services the choice of the mix of forces to be withdrawn) or force levels and budgets (they might decouple force level and budget decisions from force dispositions).

Presidents need vigorous organizations manned by highly motivated officials who believe in what they are doing. Such men cannot be expected to have the same interests as the president, to see the same face of an issue, or to take the same stand. These facts limit a president's options and make it impossible for him to do some things he would like to do. If, however, the president and his senior associates are clear about their own priorities, select options with care, and understand that the name of the bureaucratic game is "organizational interests," they can lead rather than follow the bureaucracies. They may even be able to put them to constructive use.

ARE BUREAUCRACIES IMPORTANT?
by Stephen D. Krasner

Who and what shapes foreign policy? In recent years analyses have increasingly emphasized not rational calculations of
the national interest or the political goals of national leaders,
but rather bureaucratic procedures and bureaucratic politics.
Starting with Richard Neustadt's *Presidential Power*, a judicious study of leadership published in 1960, this approach
has come to portray the American president as trapped by a
permanent government that is more enemy than ally. Bureaucratic theorists imply that it is exceedingly difficult if not
impossible for political leaders to control the organizational
web that surrounds them. Important decisions result from
numerous smaller actions taken by individuals at different
levels in the bureaucracy who have partially incompatible
national, bureaucratic, political, and personal objectives.
They are not necessarily a reflection of the aims and values of
high officials. . . .

The bureaucratic interpretation of foreign policy has become
the conventional wisdom. My argument here is that this
vision is misleading, dangerous, and compelling: misleading
because it obscures the power of the president, dangerous
because it undermines the assumptions of democratic politics by relieving high officials of responsibility, and compelling because it offers leaders an excuse for their failures and
scholars an opportunity for innumerable reinterpretations
and publications.

The contention that the chief executive is trammeled by the
permanent government has disturbing implications for any
effort to impute responsibility to public officials. A democratic political philosophy assumes that responsibility for the
acts of governments can be attributed to elected officials.
The charges of these men are embodied in legal statutes. The
electorate punishes an erring official by rejecting him at the
polls. Punishment is senseless unless high officials are responsible for the acts of government. Elections have some
impact only if government, that most complex of modern organizations, can be controlled. If the bureaucratic machine
escapes manipulation and direction even by the highest officials, then punishment is illogical. Elections are a farce not

"Are Bureaucracies Important?" is a shortened version of the essay published originally in *Foreign Policy*, Number 7, Summer 1972.

because the people suffer from false consciousness but because public officials are impotent, enmeshed in a bureaucracy so large that the actions of government are not responsive to their will. What sense to vote a man out of office when his successor, regardless of his values, will be trapped in the same web of only incrementally mutable standard operating procedures?

The Rational Actor Model

Conventional analyses that focus on the values and objectives of foreign policy, what Graham Allison, in *Essence of Decision: Explaining the Cuban Missile Crisis,* calls the Rational Actor Model, are perfectly coincident with the ethical assumptions of democratic politics. The state is viewed as a rational unified actor. The behavior of states is the outcome of a rational decision-making process. This process has three steps. The options for a given situation are spelled out. The consequences of each option are projected. A choice is made that maximizes the values held by decision makers. The analyst knows what the state did. His objective is to explain why, by imputing to decision makers a set of values that are maximized by observed behavior. These values are his explanation of foreign policy.

The citizen, like the analyst, attributes error to either inappropriate values or lack of foresight. Ideally, the electorate judges the officeholder by governmental performance, which is assumed to reflect the objectives and perspicacity of political leaders. Poor policy is made by leaders who fail to foresee accurately the consequences of their decisions or who attempt to maximize values not held by the electorate. Political appeals, couched in terms of aims and values, are an appropriate guide for voters. For both the analyst who adheres to the Rational Actor Model, and the citizen who decides elections, values are assumed to be the primary determinant of government behavior.

The bureaucratic politics paradigm points to quite different determinants of policy. Political leaders can only with great difficulty overcome the inertia and self-serving interests of the permanent government. What counts is managerial skill. . . . Administrative feasibility, not substance, becomes the central concern.

The paradoxical conclusion—that bureaucratic analysis with its emphasis on policy guidance implies political nonresponsibility—has most clearly been brought out by discussions of American policy in Vietnam. . . . For adherents of the bureaucratic paradigm, Vietnam was a failure of the "machine," a war, in Arthur Schlesinger, Jr.'s words, "which no President. . . desired or intended."* The machine dictated a policy that it could not successfully terminate. The machine, not the cold war ideology and hubris of Kennedy and Johnson, determined American behavior in Vietnam. Vietnam could hardly be a tragedy; for tragedies are made by choice and character, not fate. A knowing electorate would express sympathy, not levy blame. Machines cannot be held responsible for what they do, nor can the men caught in the workings.

The strength of the bureaucratic web has been attributed to two sources: organizational necessity and bureaucratic interest. The costs of coordination and search procedures are so high that complex organizations *must* settle for satisfactory rather than optimal solutions. Bureaucracies have interests defined in terms of budget allocation, autonomy, morale, and scope, which they defend in a game of political bargaining and compromise within the executive branch.

The imperatives of organizational behavior limit flexibility. . . . A division of labor among and within organizations reduces the job of each particular division to manageable proportions. Once this division is made, the complexity confronting an organization or one of its parts is further reduced through the establishment of standard operating procedures. To deal with each problem as if it were *sui generis* would be impossible given limited resources and information processing capacity, and it would make intraorganizational coordination extremely difficult. Bureaucracies are, then, unavoidably rigid; but without the rigidity imposed by division of labor and standard operating procedures, they could hardly begin to function at all.

However, this rigidity inevitably introduces distortions. All of the options to a given problem will not be presented with equal lucidity and conviction unless by some happenstance the organization has worked out its scenarios for that partic-

*Quoted in Daniel Ellsberg, "The Quagmire Myth and the Stalemate Machine," *Public Policy*, Spring 1971, p. 218.

ular problem in advance. It is more likely that the organization will have addressed itself to something *like* the problem with which it is confronted. It has a set of options for such a hypothetical problem, and these options will be presented to deal with the actual issue at hand. Similarly, organizations cannot execute all policy suggestions with equal facility. The development of new standard operating procedures takes time. The procedures that would most faithfully execute a new policy are not likely to have been worked out. The clash between the rigidity of standard operating procedures, which are absolutely necessary to achieve coordination among and within large organizations, and the flexibility needed to spell out the options and their consequences for a new problem and to execute new policies is inevitable. It cannot be avoided even with the best of intentions of bureaucratic chiefs anxious to execute faithfully the desires of their leaders.

The Costs of Coordination

The limitations imposed by the need to simplify and coordinate indicate that the great increase in governmental power accompanying industrialization has not been achieved without some costs in terms of control. Bureaucratic organizations and the material and symbolic resources that they direct have enormously increased the ability of the American president to influence the international environment. But the president operates within the limits set by organizational procedures.

A recognition of the limits imposed by bureaucratic necessities is a useful qualification of the assumption that states always maximize their interest. This does not, however, imply that the analyst should abandon a focus on values or assumptions of rationality. Standard operating procedures are rational given the costs of search procedures and the need for coordination. The behavior of states is still determined by values, although foreign policy may reflect satisfactory rather than optimal outcomes. . . .

Bureaucratic analysts do not, however, place the burden of their argument on standard operating procedures, but on bureaucratic politics. The objectives of officials are dictated by their bureaucratic position. Each bureau has its own interests. The interests that bureaucratic analysts emphasize are not clientalistic ties between government departments and societal groups, or special relations with congressional committees. They are, rather, needs dictated by organizational survival and growth—budget allocations, internal morale, and autonomy. Conflicting objectives advocated by different bureau chiefs are reconciled by a political process. Policy results from compromises and bargaining. It does not necessarily reflect the values of the president, let alone of lesser actors. . . .

Bureaucratic analysis is . . . inadequate in its description of how policy is made. Its axiomatic assumption is that politics is a game with the preferences of players given and independent. This is not true. The president chooses most of the important players and sets the rules. He selects the men who head the large bureaucracies. These individuals must share his values. Certainly they identify with his beliefs to a greater extent than would a randomly chosen group of candidates. They also feel some personal fealty to the president, who has elevated them from positions of corporate or legal significance to ones of historic significance. While the bureau chiefs are undoubtedly torn by conflicting pressures arising either from their need to protect their own bureaucracies or from personal conviction, they must remain the president's men. At some point disagreement results in dismissal. . . .

The president has an important impact on bureaucratic interests. Internal morale is partially determined by presidential behavior. The obscurity in which Secretary of State Rogers languished during the China trip affected both State Department morale and recruitment prospects. Through the budget the president has a direct impact on that most vital of bureaucratic interests. While a bureau may use its societal clients and congressional allies to secure desired allocations, it is surely easier with the president's support than without it. The president can delimit or redefine the scope of an organization's activities by transferring tasks or establishing new agencies. Through public statements he can affect attitudes toward members of a particular bureaucracy and their functions.

The President as "King"

The success a bureau enjoys in furthering its interests depends on maintaining the support and affection of the president. The implicit assumption of the bureaucratic politics approach that departmental and presidential behavior are independent and comparably important is false. . . . In general, bureaucratic analysts ignore the critical effect that the president has in choosing his advisers, establishing their access to decision making, and influencing bureaucratic interests.

All of this is not to deny that bureaucratic interests may sometimes be decisive in the formulation of foreign policy. Some policy options are never presented to the president. Others he deals with only cursorily, not going beyond options presented by the bureaucracy. This will only be the case if presidential interest and attention are absent. The failure of a chief executive to specify policy does not mean that the government takes no action. Individual bureaucracies may initiate policies that suit their own needs and objectives. The actions of different organizations may work at cross purposes. The behavior of the state, that is, of some of its official organizations, in the international system appears confused or even contradictory. This is a situation that develops, however, not because of the independent power of government organizations but because of failures by decision makers to assert control.

The ability of bureaucracies to independently establish policies is a function of presidential attention. Presidential attention is a function of presidential values. The chief executive involves himself in those areas that he determines to be important. When the president does devote time and attention to an issue, he can compel the bureaucracy to present him with alternatives. He may do this, as Nixon apparently has, by establishing an organization under his special assistant for national security affairs, whose only bureaucratic interest is maintaining the president's confidence. The president may also rely upon several bureaucracies to secure proposals. The president may even resort to his own knowledge and sense of history to find options that his bureaucracy fails to present. Even when presidential attention is totally absent, bureaus are sensitive to his values. Policies that violate pres-

idential objectives may bring presidential wrath. . . . Within
the structure that the president has partially created himself,
he can, if he chooses, further manipulate both the options
presented to him and the organizational tools for implementing them.

Neither organizational necessity nor bureaucratic interests
are the fundamental determinants of policy. The limits
imposed by standard operating procedures as well as the
direction of policy are a function of the values of decision
makers. The president creates much of the bureaucratic environment that surrounds him through his selection of bureau
chiefs, determination of "action channels," and statutory
powers. . . .

Conclusion

A glimpse at almost any one of the major problems confronting American society indicates that a reformulation and clar-
ification of objectives, not better control and direction of the
bureaucracy, is critical. Conceptions of man and society long
accepted are being undermined. The environmentalists present a fundamental challenge to the assumption that man
can control and stand above nature, an assumption rooted
both in the successes of technology and industrialization and
Judeo-Christian assertions of man's exceptionalism. The nation's failure to formulate a consistent crime policy reflects in
part an inability to decide whether criminals are freely willing
rational men subject to determinations of guilt or innocence,
or the victims of socio-economic conditions or psychological
circumstances over which they have no control. The economy
manages to defy accepted economic precepts by sustaining
relatively high inflation and unemployment at the same time.
Public officials and economists question the wisdom of economic growth. Conflicts exist over what the objectives of the
nation should be and what its capacities are. On a whole
range of social issues the society is torn between attributing
problems to individual inadequacies and social injustice.

None of these issues can be decided just by improving managerial techniques. Before the niceties of bureaucratic implementation are investigated, it is necessary to know what
objectives are being sought. Objectives are ultimately a reflection of values, of beliefs concerning what man and society ought to be. The failure of the American government to

take decisive action in a number of critical areas reflects not so much the inertia of a large bureaucratic machine as a confusion over values which afflicts the society in general and its leaders in particular. It is, in such circumstances, too comforting to attribute failure to organizational inertia, although nothing could be more convenient for political leaders who, having either not formulated any policy or advocated bad policies, can blame their failures on the governmental structure. Both psychologically and politically, leaders may find it advantageous to have others think of them as ineffectual rather than evil. But the facts are otherwise—particularly in foreign policy. There the choices—and the responsibility—rest squarely with the president.

CONTRIBUTORS

I. M. DESTLER has taught at Princeton University and at the University of Nigeria and has held several foreign policy-related staff positions in the executive branch and on Capitol Hill. He is now on the foreign policy studies staff of the Brookings Institution.

JOHN KENNETH GALBRAITH is professor of economics at Harvard. He was U.S. ambassador to India from 1961 to 1963; he is the author of numerous books, including *The Triumph*, *The Affluent Society*, *A Theory of Price Control*, *Economics*, *Peace, and Laughter*, *The New Industrial State*, and *Economics and the Public Purpose*.

LESLIE H. GELB is a senior fellow at the Brookings Institution and is currently at work on a history of the U.S. involvement in Vietnam. During 1967-68 he served as director for policy planning and arms control in the Defense Department and in 1968-69 was acting deputy assistant secretary for international security affairs.

MORTON H. HALPERIN is a senior fellow at the Brookings Institution and was deputy assistant secretary of defense for international security affairs, 1967-69. He has also served on the National Security Council staff. His latest book is *Defense Strategies for the 1970's,* and he will publish *Bureaucratic Politics and Foreign Policy* in 1974.

PIERRE HASSNER is research associate at the Centre d'Etude des Relations Internationales, Paris, and is professor of politics at the Bologna Center of The Johns Hopkins University. He has long been a commentator on U.S. affairs.

GODFREY HODGSON was the Washington correspondent for the *London Observer* (1962-65), and editor of the *London Sunday Times* Insight team, which produced the book *An American Melodrama*. Subsequently a fellow of the Woodrow Wilson International Center for Scholars, Mr. Hodgson is currently in England, where he is working on a history of America in the 1960s.

STANLEY HOFFMANN is professor of government at Harvard University. Mr. Hoffmann is working on a book of essays on postwar France and will soon publish *The Burden and the Balance*. He is also author of *In Search of France: The Economy, Society, and Political System in the Twentieth Century, The Relevance of International Relations, and Conditions of World Order.*

GEORGE ARMSTRONG KELLY is professor of politics at Brandeis University. He is the author of *Idealism, Politics, and History* and co-author of *Struggles in the State*.

GEORGE F. KENNAN, the former ambassador to the Soviet Union and Yugoslavia, is now at the Institute of Advanced Studies in Princeton. His *Memoirs II: 1950-1963* was published in 1972.

STEPHEN D. KRASNER, an assistant professor in the department of government at Harvard, is the author of several articles on political aspects of international commodity trade.

JOHN P. LEACACOS has retired as Washington bureau chief of the *Cleveland Plain Dealer,* a position he assumed in 1958 after 15 years as the *Plain Dealer's* roving foreign correspondent in Europe and the Middle East. He is author of *Fires in the In-Basket: ABC's of the State Department.*

CHALMERS M. ROBERTS is retired from *The Washington Post*, after many years as diplomatic correspondent. He is the author of *Nuclear Years: The Arms Race and Arms Control, 1945-1970*.

ROBERT W. TUCKER holds a joint position as professor of political science at The John Hopkins University and at the university's School of Advanced International Studies in Washington, D.C., where he is also director of the Washington Center of Foreign Policy Research. Among his previously published books are *Nation or Empire? The Debate over American Foreign Policy*, *The Radical Left and American Foreign Policy*, and *A New Isolationism: Threat or Promise?*

WILLIAM WATTS is president of Potomac Associates. He has served in the U.S. Foreign Service, with posts in Moscow and Seoul, and in the Office of Mainland China Affairs in the Department of State. He has been a program officer of the Office of Policy and Planning at the Ford Foundation, director of the New York State Office for Urban Innovation, and, most recently, staff secretary of the National Security Council under Dr. Henry A. Kissinger. With Lloyd A. Free, he wrote *State of the Nation*.

20-400

DATE DUE

50725